MW00424141

COMPLETE WRITINGS ON AMERICA

Complete Writings on America

Edmund Burke

With an Introduction by
Bruce P. Frohnen

CLUNY MEDIA

Cluny Media edition, 2016

This is a reprint of the Everyman's Library edition (No. 340) of *Burke's Speeches and Letters on American Affairs*, first published by E.P. Dutton in 1908.

This Cluny edition includes minor editorial revisions to the original text which may include deletion of obsolete references.
For information regarding editorial revisions, please write to info@clunymedia.com or to John Clarke, Cluny Media, Department of Editing and Production
4619 Slayden Rd. NE, Tacoma, WA, 98422

ISBN: 9781944418069

Cover design by Clarke & Clarke
Cover image: Thomas Cole, *Study for "Catskill Creek,"* c. 1844/1845
Image used courtesy of National Gallery of Art, Washington

Contents

Appendix

Index

Introduction

This volume includes every substantive speech and writing on America by the eighteenth-century philosopher and statesman, Edmund Burke. The Irish-born Burke served as a Member of the British Parliament throughout the American colonial crisis, even acting for a number of years as agent or representative of the colony of New York. He was a prominent, spirited, and wise defender of Americans' inherited rights as rooted in a proper, limited understanding of British imperial power and its likely effects on the British Constitution itself.

Burke shared the American view that it was Parliamentary taxation and related policies that agitated Americans, eventually to the point of revolution. The American Revolution, as explained by Burke, was of a very particular kind. Burke understood the Americans to be demanding, not radical change, but rather a return to the British policies and American rights of significant self-government that had become customary over the preceding decades. The American

Revolution was no attempt to tear society asunder in pursuit of an abstract vision of perfection. As Burke understood and explained that revolution, Americans were seeking merely to preserve their accustomed constitutions and ways of life. From this perspective, the American Revolution was beneficial to both sides, in the end, as it also helped protect the British Constitution against those who sought to centralize power in the name of abstract rights of political sovereignty.

Burke was a well-known orator who enjoyed a decades-long public career, whose speeches were republished many times in America during the nineteenth century, and whose works on political and philosophical issues continue to be highly influential today. He often is credited with founding modern conservatism, especially through his most famous, late work, *Reflections on the Revolution in France*. Somewhat ironically that book, written after the French Revolution began but before the beheading of the French King and commencement of the bloody Reign of Terror, was seen by many at the time as a betrayal of the principles Burke had espoused earlier in his career.

In addition to his defense of America, Burke had opposed British laws punishing Irish Catholics for retaining their faith and the imposition on the Indian people of the British East India Company's reign of violence and corruption. Some saw these as enlightened (today we would say "progressive") positions undermined by Burke's violent opposition to the French Revolutionary regime. Burke denied the charge of inconsistency along with the political labels. He pointed out that he always had sought to defend the British Constitution—with its customs, traditions, institutions, and laws upholding limited government—against attempts, arising from whatever source, to establish unchecked power. He saw the French Revolution as the product of an armed doctrine of atheism seeking to destroy the influence of religion, history, and natural human sympathies in pursuit of the utopian fantasy of rule by abstract reason. Such a pursuit, he argued, denied the social and religious nature of the person; it denied that there is a natural law guiding persons and societies toward lives of decency, order, and happiness within the fundamental associations (or "little platoons") of local life. It was this life that Burke saw as natural to man. Such a life always would be difficult to establish and maintain amidst the tragic circumstances of war, economic dislocation, and political and philosophical pride to which all societies are prone. Once established, whether in Great Britain, America, Ireland, or India, a life of decency generated "prescriptive rights" or reasonable expectations of continuity and stability. It was these rights, of custom and tradition, rather than mere abstractions stemming from philosophical theories, that all governments and colonial powers had a duty to respect.

Burke was born in 1729 to a Catholic mother and a lawyer father who was a member of the Church of Ireland, a branch of the established Anglican Church of England. Burke was schooled in part by Quakers and spent much of his childhood with Catholic relatives. He studied first at Trinity College, Dublin, then at London's Middle Temple, the training ground for lawyers seeking to practice within the British Empire. Soon tiring of the narrow education and professional life afforded to the lawyer, Burke travelled briefly and then resettled in London, where he soon became something of a literary figure. He published *A Vindication of Natural Society* anonymously in 1756. This

book brilliantly affected the style of Lord Bolingbroke, a
famous figure at the time whose work questioned the truth
and beneficial influence of revealed religion. Burke satirized Bolingbroke by showing how his logic would apply
with equal force to all the institutions of civilized life. In
this way he also satirized the popular myth of a "state of
nature" as the locus of human virtue. In 1757 Burke published *A Philosophical Enquiry into the Origin of Our Ideas of
the Sublime and the Beautiful.* The latter volume established
him as a figure of note in intellectual circles. In that same
year he took on the role of editor and principal author
of *The Annual Register*, a review of literature and politics
he would helm for most of the remainder of his life and
which would become an important organ of the Whig
political party he would serve. Around this time he also
joined the circle of the famous essayist, Samuel Johnson,
which included the Anglo-Irish playwright and poet Oli-
ver Goldsmith, among other notables.

In 1762 Burke became private secretary to William Ge-
rard Hamilton who was Chief Secretary for Ireland. The
relationship lasted three years, a time punctuated by some
acrimony, ascribed variously to personal conflicts and dis-
agreements concerning the harsh treatment of Irish Catholics by the British government. In 1765 Burke took a position
as private secretary to Charles, Marquess of Rockingham,
then serving as Prime Minister in the British Parliament. At
this time the American colonies were in a state of agitation
on account of newly enacted taxes imposed by the crown.
Rockingham secured repeal of the taxes, though he also
saw enacted a Declaratory Act restating Parliament's abstract right to re-impose them if it saw fit. The Rockingham
government soon fell on account of internal dissensions,

but Burke would continue to serve Rockingham until his mentor's untimely death in 1782.

For three decades Burke would champion the principles of the Rockingham faction within the Whig Party. Great Britain's Whigs often are portrayed as a precursor to modern liberal political parties. But the Whigs actually were a very loose coalition held together by common interests and a determination to defend the powers of Parliament in its conflicts with the monarch. The Rockingham faction in particular was opposed to any radical change in Great Britain's mixed constitution of king, nobles, and commons. Instead, the Rockingham Whigs sought to preserve traditions and practices rooted in the Glorious Revolution of 1688, when Parliament had finally established legal limits to the monarch's prerogative powers.

Burke himself contributed greatly to the emergence of coherent political parties. In his early pamphlet, *Thoughts on the Cause of the Present Discontents*, he defined a party as "a body of men united for promoting by their joint endeavours the national interest upon some particular principle in which they are all agreed." The Rockingham Whigs in particular were united in defense of a conception of the British constitution as a proper balance of forces and dedicated to the preservation of customary institutions, beliefs, and practices in large measure through adherence to tradition and respect for inherited, prescriptive rights.

The liberal or progressive characterization of the Whig party rests on two political commitments or programs. First is the Whigs' strong opposition to royal attempts at political aggrandizement. Second is a reforming zeal that progressively took hold of Whig Party members and constituents, particularly over the course of the nineteenth century. Burke shared the first commitment and participated vigorously in programs and reforms aimed at limiting royal power. He rejected the second commitment and set about opposing the resultant program, arguably transforming British politics by awakening the opposing Tory Party from its then-dominant stance of mere support for established powers. Particularly near the end of his career, Burke showed the need for principled opposition to radical change and support for a balanced, mixed constitution that valued rural as well as urban, agricultural as well as industrial interests and communities within the structures of limited government and established tradition.

Commentators generally describe Burke's public life as centered on four principal imperial crises, dealing with Ireland, America, India, and France. It is important to note, however, that Burke's career was forged in the crucible of conflict with King George III, who sought to re-establish royal control over political administration. In his earliest days in Parliament Burke gained a reputation as a reformer for his attempts to reign in corruption and the King's use of minor offices as means of controlling votes in Parliament. It was in defense of Parliamentary independence that Burke opposed radical changes in Parliamentary representation, fearing the King's ability to influence elections through his prestige and ability to spend vast sums to defeat his opponents at the polls. Most of Burke's Parliamentary career was spent representing "pocket boroughs." These were geographical areas in which elections were controlled by a particular nobleman or prominent family. Pocket boroughs were quite common at the time and it was considered a great honor that Burke actually was chosen to represent a wider constituency in the great commercial city of Bristol.

Burke's popularity in Bristol suffered, however, because of his opposition to laws discriminating against Irish commerce. He returned to representing a pocket borough and continued his support of Parliamentary independence rooted in tradition rather than simple numbers cast at the polls.

As to Ireland, Burke paid a high price for his persistent defense of the rights and interests of Irish Catholics in particular. By marrying a Catholic, Burke gave further ammunition to those who portrayed him as a secret "papist." It is highly doubtful that Burke was Catholic in any formal sense. Rather, he held to a reading of the natural law, well known among Catholics but hardly unknown among Anglicans of his time, according to which "All human laws are, properly speaking, only declaratory; they may alter the mode and application, but have no power over the substance of original justice." These words are taken from Burke's early (but only posthumously published) *Tracts on the Popery Laws*. They were written in opposition to the anti-Catholic laws imposed on Ireland by the British. The popery laws denied Catholics the ability to engage in most professions and even stripped them of their property under a variety of circumstances (conversion from Protestantism to Catholicism being the most obvious). Burke criticized such laws, not merely as violations of abstract claims of radical individual rights, but as offenses against common humanity and the natural, proper tendency of all peoples to forge and hold to their own traditions and ways of life.

Later in his Parliamentary career Burke took up his defense of the rights of the people of India. Particularly in his prosecution in Parliament of Warren Hastings, who served as Governor-General of India from 1773 to 1785, Burke sought to end the abuse of power by the East India

Company. Burke blamed Hastings' administration for massive destruction and impoverishment, as well as the undermining of the entire Indian civilization. Here Burke was forced to argue against "geographical morality," by which he meant the view put forward by the East India Company that the norms of good government suited to Great Britain were inappropriate to rule in India. Burke was a great defender of local traditions, but showed that he was no mere utilitarian by rejecting the East India Company's reliance on expediency as a rule of government. It was one thing to defend the variety of human institutions and societies, quite another to excuse corruption and violence as "appropriate" to certain circumstances or peoples. Never questioning the importance and superiority of Christian civilization and faith, Burke insisted on the duty of governors everywhere to respect the traditions of those they rule, ameliorating abuses without seeking to "refound" society on the ashes of what they themselves destroy.

The final imperial crisis of Burke's career concerned the Revolution in France. This Revolution showed the limits of Burke's respect for local variety. For it was in this Revolution that tradition and law itself were subjected to the demands of ideologues who trumpeted the abstract Rights of Man while murdering their king and slaughtering supposed enemies among nobles, priests, and common people. These ideologues stirred up mobs to tear down churches, then set up a "goddess of reason," and set out to conquer their neighbors in the name of "Liberty, Equality, Fraternity." Burke found the murderous results of the French Revolutionaries' violent passions and their violent attachment to abstract principles to be no surprise. In his mind the element lacking in their plans of good government was simple good character. As he put it in the *Reflections*, "It is ordained in the eternal constitution of things, that men of intemperate minds cannot be free. Their passions forge their fetters." In rejecting religion, tradition, and law, the French Revolutionaries became something less than fully human and unleashed, not reason, but the basest passions.

Burke's stance on the French Revolution cost him many friends among members of the Whig Party. Though his work also gained him admirers—including King George III—his old age was spent in pain and isolation. A final blow to Burke's hopes came with his son's untimely death. With his son died Burke's hopes of founding a great family and soon after, in 1797, he followed to his own grave, fearful for his people as they faced the end of the age of chivalry and the dawn of an age "of sophisters, economists, and calculators."

This volume reprints Burke's writings from a more hopeful time. During the American crisis Burke was reaching his stride as an orator and statesman. Having recently assumed his Parliamentary duties, he had immediately established through his defense of the Americans a reputation for deep thought, command of detail, and oratorical skill. The imperial crisis in America lasted well over a decade and took up much of Burke's and the Rockingham Whigs' time and effort. Yet their goal was compromise and stability rather than any grand scheme of conquest or aggrandizement. As the reader will see in the materials reprinted here Burke sought, for the sake of Great Britain as well as America, to prevent overreach on the part of Parliament and to spur reconciliation so that the Empire might return to its spirit of comity and its unwritten constitution of limited self-rule within relatively loose structures of law and custom.

The first selection, Burke's *Speech on Conciliation with the Colonies*, is without doubt the most important of his writings on the American crisis. It is his most comprehensive discussion of the origins and dangers of that conflict for both America and Great Britain. In it Burke also lays out the approach to politics that is central to his own career, and essential to any form of politics opposing the kind of rationalistic ideology he later identified with the French Revolution. In place of Parliament's abstract claims to sovereign rights, Burke proposed a politics of attachment rooted in familiarity and cooperation. "My hold of the colonies is in the close affection which grows from common names, from kindred blood, from similar privileges, and equal protection. These are ties which, though light as air, are as strong as links of iron. Let the colonies always keep the idea of their civil rights associated with your government—they will cling and grapple to you, and no force under heaven will be of power to tear them from their allegiance."

Delivered before Burke's *Speech on Conciliation*, the *Speech on American Taxation* is a more detailed treatment of financial and constitutional issues. Here Burke critiques the ruling Ministry's plans for taxation of the American colonies. Exploding claims of practical necessity, he sets forth a primary argument used by the colonists themselves: that Great Britain already taxed the colonies through her restrictive trade policies, rendering any additional direct taxation of commodities and activities within the colonies themselves excessive as well as intrusive on their customary rights. Here we find one of Burke's greatest criticisms of abstract claims of political right, in which he warns Parliament, "if intemperately, unwisely, fatally, you sophisticate and poison the very source of government by urging subtle deductions, and consequences odious to those you govern, from the unlimited and illimitable nature of supreme sovereignty, you will teach them by these means to call that sovereignty itself in question.... If that sovereignty and their freedom cannot be reconciled, which will they take? They will cast your sovereignty in your face. No body of men will be argued into slavery."

Also included are Burke's speeches to the Electors of Bristol, those men of commerce who called him to be their Parliamentary representative. In these relatively brief speeches Burke gives, first, a concise and powerful rehearsal of central issues regarding America and, second, an important restatement of the theory of representation that would motivate him throughout his career. This latter theory of representation would prove important in America, where rule by consent from the beginning was an essential element of political legitimacy. To the perpetual question whether representatives should serve as mere mouthpieces for their constituents, acting on specific directions, or risk offending them by exercising independent judgment, Burke's answer was unequivocal: "Your representative owes you, not his industry only, but his judgment; and he betrays, instead of serving you, if he sacrifices it to your opinion."

Also included here are shorter selections, including letters and addresses from Burke to the Marquess of Rockingham, King George III, and an exchange with America's own Benjamin Franklin. They give the reader access to a deeper understanding of the background and context of the American crisis. Taken together, these writings provide insight into both the issues at stake in the American Revolution and their relationship to British imperial and constitutional debates, all explicated by a great statesman concerned to preserve the liberties and ways of life of two increasingly separate, important peoples.

The Text

The materials presented here, including editorial notes, are taken from the Everyman's edition of 1908 edited by Hugh Law. Retaining that text and notes, we have chosen, in addition to adding a new introduction, to place Burke's most famous and important speech on America, his *Speech on Conciliation with the Colonies*, at the front of the book. While changing the order of presentation for pedagogical reasons, we retain the full contents of that volume to provide readers with a full account of Burke's thoughts and actions in regard to this critical crisis in American history and, more generally, the development of constitutionalism.

Bruce P. Frohnen
Fostoria, Ohio
February, 2016

SPEECHES

On Conciliation with the Colonies (March 22, 1775)

I hope, Sir, that, notwithstanding the austerity of the Chair, your good nature will incline you to some degree of indulgence towards human frailty. You will not think it unnatural that those who have an object depending, which strongly engages their hopes and fears, should be somewhat inclined to superstition. As I came into the House full of anxiety about the event of my motion, I found, to my infinite surprise, that the grand penal bill[1] by which we had passed sentence on the trade and sustenance of America, is to be returned to us from the other House. I do confess, I could not help looking on this event as a fortunate omen. I look upon it as a sort of providential favor, by which we are put once more in possession of our deliberative capacity upon a business so very questionable in its nature, so very uncertain in its issue. By the return of this bill, which seemed to have taken its flight forever, we are at this very instant nearly as free to choose a plan for our American government as we were on the first day of the session. If,

Sir, we incline to the side of conciliation, we are not at all
embarrassed (unless we please to make ourselves so) by
any incongruous mixture of coercion and restraint. We
are therefore called upon, as it were by a superior warning
voice, again to attend to America; to attend to the whole
of it together, and to review the subject with an unusual
degree of care and, calmness.

Surely it is an awful subject, or there is none so on this
side of the grave. When I first had the honor of a seat in
this House, the affairs of that continent pressed themselves
upon us as the most important and most delicate object
of Parliamentary attention. My little share in this great
deliberation oppressed me. I found myself a partaker in a
very high trust, and having no sort of reason to rely on the
strength of my natural abilities for the proper execution of
that trust, I was obliged to take more than common pains to
instruct myself in everything which relates to our colonies.
I was not less under the necessity of forming some fixed
ideas concerning the general policy of the British empire.
Something of this sort seemed to be indispensable in order,
amidst so vast a fluctuation of passions and opinions, to
concenter my thoughts, to ballast my conduct, to preserve
me from being blown about by every wind of fashionable
doctrine. I really did not think it safe, or manly, to have
fresh principles to seek upon every fresh mail which should
arrive from America.

1.   The Act to restrain the trade and commerce of the provinces of
Massachusetts Bay and New Hampshire, and colonies of Connecticut and Rhode Island, and Providence Plantation, in North America, to Great Britain, Ireland, and the British Islands in the West
Indies; and to prohibit such provinces and colonies from carrying
on any fishery on the banks of Newfoundland, and other places
therein mentioned, under certain conditions and limitations.

At that period I had the fortune to find myself in perfect concurrence with a large majority in this House. Bowing under that high authority, and penetrated with the sharpness and strength of that early impression, I have continued ever since, without the least deviation, in my original sentiments. Whether this be owing to an obstinate perseverance in error or to a religious adherence to what appears to me truth and reason, it is in your equity to judge.

Sir, Parliament having an enlarged view of objects, made during this interval more frequent changes in their sentiments and their conduct than could be justified in a particular person upon the contracted scale of private information. But though I do not hazard anything approaching to censure on the motives of former Parliaments to all those alterations, one fact is undoubted—that under them the state of America has been kept in continual agitation, Everything administered as remedy to the public complaint, if it did not produce, was at least followed by a heightening of the distemper; until, by a variety of experiments, that important country has been brought into her present situation—a situation which I will not miscall, which I dare not name, which I scarcely know how to comprehend in the terms of any description.

In this posture, Sir, things stood at the beginning of the session. About that tune, a worthy member [Mr. Rose Fuller] of great Parliamentary experience, who in the year 1766 filled the chair of the American committee with much ability, took me aside, and, lamenting the present aspect of our politics, told me things were come to such a pass that our former methods of proceeding in the House would be no longer tolerated. That the public tribunal (never too indulgent to a long and unsuccessful opposition)

would now scrutinize our conduct with unusual severity.
That the very vicissitudes and shiftings of ministerial measures, instead of convicting their authors of inconstancy
and want of system, would be taken as an occasion of
charging us with a predetermined discontent which nothing could satisfy; while we accused every measure of vigor
as cruel and every proposal of leniency as weak and irreso-
lute. The public, he said, would not have patience to see us
play the game out with our adversaries: we must produce
our hand. It would be expected, that those who for many
years had been active in such affairs should show that they
had formed some clear and decided idea of the principles
of colony government, and were capable of drawing out
something like a platform of the ground which might be
laid for future and permanent tranquility.

I felt the truth of what my honorable friend represented, but I felt my situation too. His application might
have been made with far greater propriety to many other gentlemen. No man was indeed ever better disposed,
or worse qualified, for such an undertaking than myself.
Though I gave so far in to his opinion that I immediately
threw my thoughts into a sort of Parliamentary form, I
was by no means equally ready to produce them. It generally argues some degree of natural impotence of mind, or
some want of knowledge of the world, to hazard plans of
government except from a seat of authority. Propositions
are made, not only ineffectually, but somewhat disrepu-
tably, when the minds of men are not properly disposed
for their reception; and for my part I am not ambitious of
ridicule, not absolutely a candidate for disgrace.

Besides, Sir, to speak the plain truth, I have in general no
very exalted opinion of the virtue of paper government, nor

of any politics in which the plan is to be wholly separated from the execution. But when I saw that anger and violence prevailed every day more and more, and that things were hastening towards an incurable alienation of our colonies, I confess my caution gave way. I felt this as one of those few moments in which decorum yields to a higher duty. Public calamity is a mighty leveler; and there are occasions when any, even the slightest, chance of doing good, must he laid hold on even by the most inconsiderable person.

To restore order and repose to an empire so great and so distracted as ours is, merely in the attempt, an undertaking that would ennoble the flights of the highest genius and obtain pardon for the efforts of the meanest understanding. Struggling a good while with these thoughts, by degrees I felt myself more firm. I derived at length some confidence from what in other circumstances usually produces timidity. I grew less anxious, even from the idea of my own insignificance. For, judging of what you are by what you ought to be, I persuaded myself that you would not reject a reasonable proposition because it had nothing but its reason to recommend it. On the other hand, being totally destitute of all shadow of influence, natural or adventitious, I was very sure that, if my proposition were futile or dangerous, if it were weakly conceived or improperly timed, there was nothing exterior to it of power to awe, dazzle, or delude you. You will see it just as it is, and you will treat it just as it deserves. The proposition is peace. Not peace through the medium of war; not peace to be hunted through the labyrinth of intricate and endless negotiations; not peace to arise out of universal discord fomented from principle in all parts of the empire; not peace to depend on the juridical determination of perplexing questions or the precise marking the shadowy boundaries of a complex government. It is simple peace, sought in its natural course and in its ordinary haunts—it is peace sought in the spirit of peace, and laid in principles purely pacific. I propose, by removing the ground of the difference, and by restoring the *former unsuspecting confidence of the colonies in the mother-country*, to give permanent satisfaction to your people; and (far from a scheme of ruling by discord) to reconcile them to each other in the same act, and by the bond of the very same interest which reconciles them to British government.

My idea is nothing more. Refined policy ever has been the parent of confusion, and ever will be so as long as the world endures. Plain good intention, which is as easily discovered at the first view as fraud is surely detected at last, is, let me say, of no mean force in the government of mankind. Genuine simplicity of heart is a healing and cementing principle. My plan, therefore, being formed upon the most simple grounds imaginable, may disappoint some people when they hear it. It has nothing to recommend to it the pruriency of curious ears. There is nothing at all new and captivating in it. It has nothing of the splendor of the project which has been lately laid upon your table by the noble lord in the blue riband.[2] It does not propose to fill

---

2.   On 27th February, 1775, Lord North introduced, and subsequently carried, a bill undertaking not to tax any colony which should contribute such an amount to the imperial revenue as should be approved by Parliament. This was supplementary to the retaliatory measures above referred to. It was recommended to the colonists by Lord Dartmouth in very conciliatory terms. The colonial assemblies were left an absolute discretion as to ways and means, no specific sum was mentioned, and only a discretionary approval was reserved to Parliament. These proposals may be compared with those attributed to Grenville (p. 120, note). They had been refused then and were not likely to be acceptable now.

your lobby with squabbling colony agents, who will require the interposition of your mace at every instant to keep the peace among them. It does not institute a magnificent auction of finance, where captivated provinces come to general ransom by bidding against each other, until you knock down the hammer and determine a proportion of payments beyond all the powers of algebra to equalize and settle.

The plan which I shall presume to suggest derives, however, one great advantage from the proposition and registry of that noble lord's project. The idea of conciliation is admissible. First, the House, in accepting the resolution moved by the noble lord, has admitted, notwithstanding the menacing front of our address, notwithstanding our heavy bill of pains and penalties—that we do not think ourselves precluded from all ideas of free grace and bounty.

The House has gone further, it has declared conciliation admissible, *previous* to any submission on the part of America. It has even shot a good deal beyond that mark, and has admitted that the complaints of our former mode of exerting the right of taxation were not wholly unfounded. That right thus exerted is allowed to have had something reprehensible in it, something unwise or something grievous, since in the midst of our heat and resentment we, of ourselves, have proposed a capital alteration; and, in order to get rid of what seemed so very exceptionable, have instituted a mode that is altogether new, one that is, indeed, wholly alien from all the ancient methods and forms of Parliament.

The *principle* of this proceeding is large enough for my purpose. The means proposed by the noble lord for carrying his ideas into execution, I think, indeed, are very indifferently suited to the end; and this I shall endeavor to show

you before I sit down. But, for the present, I take my ground
on the admitted principle. I mean to give peace. Peace implies reconciliation, and, where there has been a material
dispute, reconciliation does in a manner always imply concession on the one part or on the other. In this state of things
I make no difficulty in affirming that the proposal ought to
originate from us. Great and acknowledged force is not impaired, either in effect or in opinion, by an unwillingness to
exert itself. The superior power may offer peace with honor
and with safety. Such an offer from such a power will be
attributed to magnanimity. But the concessions of the weak
are the concessions of fear. When such a one is disarmed he
is wholly at the mercy of his superior, and he loses forever
that time and those chances which, as they happen to; all
men, are the strength and resources of all inferior power.

The capital leading questions on which you must this day
decide are these two—first, whether you ought to concede;
and secondly, what your concession ought to be. On the
first of these questions we have gained (as I have just taken
the liberty of observing to you) some ground. But I am sensible that a good deal more is still to be done. Indeed, Sir,
to enable us to determine both on the one and the other
of these great questions with a firm and precise judgment,
I think it may be necessary to consider distinctly the true
nature and the peculiar circumstances of the object which
we have before us. Because after all our struggle, whether
we will or not, we must govern America according to that
nature and to those circumstances, and not according to
our own imaginations, nor according to abstract ideas of
right—by no means according to mere general theories of
government, the resort to which appears to me, in our present situation, no better than arrant trifling. I shall therefore

endeavor, with your leave, to lay before you some of the most material of these circumstances in as full and as clear a manner as I am able to state them.

The first thing that we have to consider with regard to the nature of the object is the number of people in the colonies. I have taken for some years a good deal of pains on that point. I can by no calculation justify myself in placing the number below two millions of inhabitants of our own European blood and color, besides at least 500,000 others, who form no inconsiderable part of the strength and opulence of the whole. This, Sir, is, I believe, about the true number. There is no occasion to exaggerate where plain truth is of so much weight and importance. But whether I put the present numbers too high or too low is a matter of little moment. Such is the strength with which population shoots in that part of the world that, state the numbers as high as we will, while the dispute continues, the exaggeration ends. While we are discussing any given magnitude, they are grown to it. While we spend our time in deliberating on the mode of governing two millions, we shall find we have millions more to manage. Your children do not grow faster from infancy to manhood than they spread from families to communities, and from villages to nations.

I put this consideration of the present and the growing numbers in the front of our deliberation, because, Sir, this consideration will make it evident to a blunter discernment than yours that no partial, narrow, contracted, pinched, occasional system will be at all suitable to such an object. It will show you, that it is not to be considered as one of those *minima* which are out of the eye and consideration of the law; not a paltry excrescence of the state, not a mean dependent, who may he neglected with little damage and provoked with little danger. It will prove that some degree of care and caution is required in the handling such an object; it will show that you ought not, in reason, to trifle with, so large a mass of the interests and feelings of the human race. You could at no time do so without guilt, and be assured you will not be able to do it long with impunity.

But the population of this country, the great and grow-ing population, though a very important consideration, will lose much of its weight if not combined with other circumstances. The commerce of your colonies is out of all proportion beyond the numbers of the people. This ground of their commerce indeed has been trod some days ago, and with great ability, by a distinguished person [Mr. Glover], at your bar. This gentleman, after thirty-five years—it is so long since he first appeared at the same place to plead for the commerce of Great Britain—has come again before you to plead the same cause, without any other effect of time than that to the fire of imagina-tion and extent of erudition which even then marked him as one of the first literary characters of his age, he has added a consummate knowledge in the commercial inter-est of his country, formed by a long course of enlightened and discriminating experience.

Sir, I should be inexcusable in coming after such a per-son with any detail, if a great part of the members who now fill the House had not the misfortune to be absent when he appeared at your bar. Besides, Sir, I propose to take the matter at periods of time somewhat different from his. There is, if I mistake not, a point of view from whence if you will look at this subject it is impossible that it should not make an impression upon you. I have in my hand two accounts: one a comparative state of the export trade of

England to its colonies, as it stood in the year 1704 and as it stood in the year 1772; the other a state of the export trade of this country to its colonies alone, as it stood in 1772, compared with the whole trade of England to all parts of the world (the colonies included) in the year 1704. They are from good vouchers, the latter period from the accounts on your table, the earlier from an original manuscript of Davenant, who first established the inspector-general's office, which has been ever since his time so abundant a source of Parliamentary information.

The export trade to the colonies consists of three great branches. The African, which, terminating almost wholly in the colonies, must be put to the account of their commerce; the West Indian, and the North American. All these are so interwoven that the attempt to separate them would tear to pieces the contexture of the whole, and, if not entirely destroy, would very much depreciate the value of all the parts. I therefore consider these three denominations to be, what in effect they are, one trade.

The trade to the colonies, taken on the export side, at. the beginning of this century, that is in the year 1704, stood thus. Exports to North America and the West Indies: £483,265. To Africa: £86,665. Total: £569,930.

In the year 1772, which I take as a middle year between the highest and lowest of those lately laid on your table, the account was as follows: To North America and the West Indies: £4,791,734. To Africa: £866,398. To which, if you add the export trade from Scotland, which had in 1704 no existence: £364,000. Total: £6,022,132.

From five hundred and odd thousand it has grown to six millions. It has increased no less than twelvefold. This is the state of the colony trade as compared with itself at

these two periods within this century—and this is matter
for meditation. But this is not all. Examine my second account. See how the export trade to the colonies alone in
1772 stood in the other point of view—that is, as compared
to the whole trade of England in 1704.

The whole export trade of England, including that to
the colonies, in 1704: £6,509,000. Export to the colonies
alone, in 1772: £6,024,000. Difference: £485,000

The trade with America alone is now within less than
£500,000 of being equal to what this great commercial nation, England, carried on at the beginning of this century
with the whole world! If I had taken the largest year of
those on your table it would rather have exceeded. But it
will be said, is not this American trade an unnatural pro-
tuberance that has drawn the juices from the rest of the
body? The reverse. It is the very food that has nourished
every other part into its present magnitude. Our general
trade has been greatly augmented, and augmented more or
less in almost every part to which it ever extended; but with
this material difference, that of the six millions which in
the beginning of the century constituted the whole mass of
our export commerce, the colony trade was but one-twelfth
part; it is now (as a part of sixteen millions) considerably
more than a third of the whole. This is the relative proportion of the importance of the colonies at these two periods;
and all reasoning concerning our mode of treating them
must have this proportion as its basis, or it is a reasoning
weak, rotten, and sophistical.

Mr. Speaker, I cannot prevail on myself to hurry over
this great consideration. It is good for us to be here. We
stand where we have an immense view of what is, and
what is past. Clouds, indeed, and darkness rest upon the

future. Let us, however, before we descend from this noble eminence, reflect that this growth of our national prosperity has happened within the short period of the life of man. It has happened within sixty-eight years. There are those alive whose memory might touch the two extremities. For instance, my Lord Bathurst[3] might remember all the stages of the progress. He was in 1704 of an age at least to be made to comprehend such things. He was then old enough *acta parentum jam legere, ei quae sit poterit cognoscere virtus.*[4] Suppose, Sir, that the angel of this auspicious youth, foreseeing the many virtues which made him one of the most amiable as he is one of the most fortunate men of his age, had opened to him in vision that when, in the fourth generation, the third prince of the House of Brunswick had sat twelve years on the throne of that nation which (by the happy issue of moderate and healing councils) was to be made Great Britain, he should see his son, Lord Chancellor of England, turn back the current of hereditary dignity to its fountain and raise him to a higher rank of peerage, while he enriched the family with a new one—if amidst these bright and happy scenes of domestic honor and prosperity, that angel should have drawn up the curtain and unfolded the rising glories of his country, and while he was gazing with admiration on the then commercial grandeur of England, the genius should point out to him a little speck, scarce visible in the mass of the national interest, a small seminal principle rather than a formed body, and should tell him, "Young man, there is America, which at this day serves for little more than to

---

3. Born 1684, and a member of Parliament 1705.

4. Virgil, *Eclogues*, IV, 26. "To study the doings of his forefathers, and to learn what virtue is."

amuse you with stories of savage men and uncouth manners, yet shall, before you taste of death, show itself equal to the whole of that commerce which now attracts the envy of the world. Whatever England has been growing to by a progressive increase of improvement, brought in by varieties of people, by succession of civilizing conquests and civilizing settlements in a series of seventeen hundred years, you shall see as much added to her by America in the course of a single life!" If this state of his country had been foretold to him, would it not require all the sanguine credulity of youth, and all the fervid glow of enthusiasm, to make him believe it? Fortunate man, he has lived to see it! Fortunate indeed if he lives to see nothing that shall vary the prospect and cloud the setting of his day!

Excuse me, Sir, if turning from such thoughts I resume this comparative view once more. You have seen it on a large scale, look at it on a small one. I will point out to your attention a particular instance of it in the single province of Pennsylvania. In the year 1704, that province called for £11,459 in value of your commodities, native and foreign. This was the whole. What did it demand in 1772? Why nearly fifty times as much; for in that year the export to Pennsylvania was £507,909, nearly equal to the export to all the colonies together in the first period.

I choose, Sir, to enter into these minute and particular details, because generalities, which in all other cases are apt to heighten and raise the subject, have here a tendency to sink it. When we speak of the commerce with our colonies fiction lags after truth, invention is unfruitful, and imagination cold and barren.

So far, Sir, as to the importance of the object in view of its commerce, as concerned in the exports from England. If

I were to detail the imports, I could show how many enjoyments they procure which deceive the burden of life, how many materials which invigorate, the springs of national industry, and extend and animate every part of our foreign and domestic commerce. This would be a curious subject indeed—but I must prescribe bounds to myself in a matter so vast and various.

I pass therefore to the colonies in another point of view, their agriculture. This they have prosecuted with such a spirit that, besides feeding plentifully their own growing multitude, their annual export of grain, comprehending rice, has some years ago exceeded a million in value. Of their last harvest, I am persuaded they will export much more. At the beginning of the century some of these colonies imported corn from the mother country. For some time past, the Old World has been fed from the New. The scarcity which you have felt would have been a desolating famine if this child of your old age, with a true filial piety, with a Roman charity, had not put the full breast of its youthful exuberance to the mouth of its exhausted parent.

As to the wealth which the colonies have drawn from the sea by their fisheries, you had all that matter fully opened at your bar. You surely thought these acquisitions of value, for they seemed even to excite your envy; and yet the spirit by which that enterprising employment has been exercised ought rather, in my opinion, to have raised your esteem and admiration. And pray, Sir, what in the world is equal to it? Pass by the other parts, and look at the manner in which the people of New England have of late carried on the whale fishery. While we follow them among the tumbling mountains of ice, and behold them penetrating into the deepest frozen recesses of Hudson's Bay and Davis's

Straits, while we are looking for them beneath the arctic circle, we hear that they have pierced into the opposite region of polar cold, that they are at the antipodes, and engaged under the frozen serpent of the south. Falkland Island, which seemed too remote and romantic an object for the grasp of national ambition, is but a stage and resting place in the progress of their victorious industry. Nor is the equinoctial heat more discouraging to them than the accumulated winter of both the poles. We know that while some of them draw the line and strike the harpoon on the coast of Africa, others run the longitude and pursue their gigantic game along the coast of Brazil. No sea but what is vexed by their fisheries. No climate that is not witness to their toils. Neither the perseverance of Holland, nor the activity of France, nor the dexterous and firm sagacity of English enterprise ever carried this most perilous mode of hard industry to the extent to which it has been pushed by this recent people—a people who are still, as it were, but in the gristle, and not yet hardened into the bone of manhood. When I contemplate these things, when I know that the colonies in general owe little or nothing to any care of ours, and that they are not squeezed into this happy form by the constraints of watchful and suspicious government, but that, through a wise and salutary neglect, a generous nature has been suffered to take her own way to perfection; when I reflect upon these effects, when I see how profitable they have been to us, I feel all the pride of power sink, and all presumption in the wisdom of human contrivances melt and die away within me. My rigor relents. I pardon something to the spirit of liberty.

I am sensible, Sir, that all which I have asserted in my detail is admitted in the gross, but that quite a different conclusion is drawn from it. America, gentlemen say, is a noble object. It is an object well worth fighting for. Certainly it is, if fighting a people be the best way of gaining them. Gentlemen in this respect will he led to their choice of means by their complexions and their habits. Those who understand the military art will of course have some predilection for it. Those who wield the thunder of the state may have more confidence in the efficacy of arms. But I confess, possibly for want of this knowledge, my opinion is much more in favor of prudent management than of force, considering force not as an odious, but a feeble instrument for preserving a people so numerous, so active, so growing, so spirited as this in a profitable and subordinate connection with us.

First, Sir, permit me to observe that the use of force alone is but *temporary*. It may subdue for a moment, but it does not remove the necessity of subduing again; and a nation is not governed which is perpetually to be conquered.

My next objection is its *uncertainty*. Terror is not always the effect of force, and an armament is not a victory. If you do not succeed, you are without resource; for, conciliation failing, force remains, but, force failing, no further hope of reconciliation is left. Power and authority are sometimes bought by kindness, but they can never be begged as alms by an impoverished and defeated violence.

A further objection to force is, that you *impair the object* by your very endeavors to preserve it. The thing you fought for is not the thing which you recover, but depreciated, sunk, wasted, and consumed in the contest. Nothing less will content me than *whole America*. I do not choose to consume its strength along with our own, because in all parts it is the British strength that I consume. I do not choose to be caught by a foreign enemy at the end of this exhausting conflict, and still less in the midst of it. I may escape, but I can make no assurance against such an event. Let me add, that I do not choose wholly to break the American spirit, because it is the spirit that has made the country.

Lastly, we have no sort of *experience* in favor of force as an instrument in the rule of our colonies. Their growth and their utility has been owing to methods altogether different. Our ancient indulgence has been said to be pursued to a fault. It may be so. But we know, if feeling is evidence, that our fault was more tolerable than our attempt to mend it, and our sin far more salutary than our penitence.

These, Sir, are my reasons for not entertaining that high opinion of untried force by which many gentlemen, for whose sentiments in other particulars I have great respect, seem to be so greatly captivated. But there is still behind a third consideration this object, which serves to determine my opinion on the sort of policy which ought to be pursued in the management of America, even more than its population and its commerce—I mean its *temper and character*.

In this character of the Americans, a love of freedom is the predominating feature which marks and distinguishes the whole; and as an ardent is always a jealous affection, your colonies become suspicious, restive, and intractable whenever they see the least attempt to wrest from them by force or shuffle from them by chicane what they think the only advantage worth living for. This fierce spirit of liberty is stronger in the English colonies probably than in any other people of the earth; and this from a great variety of powerful causes, which, to understand the true temper of their minds and the direction which this spirit takes, it will not be amiss to lay open somewhat more largely.

First, the people of the colonies are descendants of Englishmen.[5] England, Sir, is a nation which still I hope respects, and formerly adored, her freedom. The colonists emigrated from you when this part of your character was most predominant, and they took this bias and direction the moment they parted from your hands. They are therefore not only devoted to liberty, but to liberty according to English ideas and on English principles. Abstract liberty, like other mere abstractions, is not to be found. Liberty inheres in some sensible object; and every nation has formed to itself some favorite point, which by way of eminence becomes the criterion of their happiness. It happened, you know, Sir, that the great contests for freedom in this country were from the earliest times chiefly upon the questions of taxing. Most of the contests in the ancient commonwealths turned primarily on the right of election of magistrates, or on the balance among the several orders of the state. The question of money was not with them so immediate. But in England it was otherwise. On this point of taxes the ablest pens and most eloquent tongues have been exercised; the greatest spirits have acted and suffered. In order to give the fullest satisfaction concerning the importance of this point it was not only necessary for those who in argument defended the excellence of the English constitution to insist

---

5. The colonies, of course, were the direct outcome of political and religious struggles in the seventeenth century. Massachusetts was founded by refugee Puritans, 1629. A body of Independents had already landed at New Plymouth from the *Mayflower* in 1620. Rhode Island was founded in 1630 by William Rogers on the principle of complete religious liberty, and the same idea underlay the foundations of Pennsylvania in 1681. Virginia, however, the earliest of the colonies (1586–1610), was always Episcopalian and royalist, and furnished asylum for many cavaliers after the fall of Charles I.

on this privilege of granting money as a dry point of fact, and to prove that the right had been acknowledged in ancient parchments and blind usages to reside in a certain body called a House of Commons. They went much further; they attempted to prove, and they succeeded, that in theory it ought to be so, from the particular nature of a House of Commons, as an immediate representative of the people, whether the old records had delivered this oracle or not. They took infinite pains to inculcate, as a fundamental principle, that in all monarchies the people must in effect themselves, mediately or immediately, possess the power of granting their own money, or no shadow of liberty could subsist. The colonies draw from you, as with their life-blood, these ideas and principles. Their love of liberty, as with you, fixed and attached on this specific point of taxing. Liberty might be safe or might be endangered in twenty other particulars, without their being much pleased or alarmed. Here they felt its pulse, and as they found that beat they thought themselves sick or sound. I do not say whether they were right or wrong in applying your general arguments to their own case. It is not easy indeed to make a monopoly of theorems and corollaries. The fact is, that they did thus apply those general arguments; and your mode of governing them, whether through leniency or indolence, through wisdom or mistake, confirmed them in the imagination that they, as well as you, had an interest in these common principles. They were further confirmed in this pleasing error by the form of their provincial legislative assemblies. Their governments are popular in a high degree, some are merely popular, in all the popular representative is the most weighty, and this share of the people in their ordinary government never fails to inspire them with lofty sentiments and with a strong aversion from whatever tends to deprive them of their chief importance.

If anything were wanting to this necessary operation of the form of government, religion would have given it a complete effect. Religion, always a principle of energy, in this new people is no way worn out or impaired, and their mode of professing it is also one main cause of this free spirit. The people are Protestants, and of that kind which is the most adverse to all implicit submission of mind and opinion. This is a persuasion not only favorable to liberty, but built upon it. I do not think, Sir, that the reason of this averseness in the dissenting churches, from all that looks like absolute government, is so much to be sought in their religious tenets as in their history. Everyone knows that the Roman Catholic religion is at least coeval with most of the governments where it prevails, that it has generally gone hand in hand with them, and received great favor and every kind of support from authority. The Church of England, too, was formed from her cradle under the nursing care of regular government. But the dissenting interests have sprung up in direct opposition to all the ordinary powers of the world, and could justify that opposition only on a strong claim to natural liberty. Their very existence depended on the powerful and unremitted assertion of that claim. All Protestantism, even the most cold and passive, is a sort of dissent. But the religion most prevalent in our northern colonies is a refinement on the principle of resistance; it is the dissidence of dissent and the Protestantism of the Protestant religion. This religion, under a variety of denominations agreeing in nothing but in the communion of the spirit of liberty, is predominant in most of the northern provinces, where the Church of England, notwithstanding its legal rights, is in reality no more than a sort of private sect, not composing most probably the tenth of the people. The colonists left England when this spirit was high, and in the emigrants was the highest of all; and even that stream of foreigners, which has been constantly flowing into these colonies, has, for the greatest part, been composed of dissenters from the establishments of their several countries, and have brought with them a temper and character far from alien to that of the people with whom they mixed.

Sir, I can perceive by their manner that some gentlemen object to the latitude of this description; because in the southern colonies the Church of England forms a large body and has a regular establishment. It is certainly true. There is, however, a circumstance attending these colonies which, in my opinion, fully counterbalances this difference, and makes the spirit of liberty still more high and haughty than in those to the northward. It is, that in Virginia and the Carolinas they have a vast multitude of slaves. Where this is the case in any part of the world, those who are free are by far the most proud and jealous of their freedom. Freedom is to them not only an enjoyment, but a kind of rank and privilege. Not seeing there that freedom, as in countries where it is a common blessing and as broad and general as the air, may be united with much abject toil, with great misery, with all the exterior of servitude, liberty looks among them like something that is more noble and liberal. I do not mean, Sir, to commend the superior morality of this sentiment, which has at least as much pride as virtue in it; but I cannot alter the nature of man. The fact is so; and these people of the southern colonies are much more strongly, and with a higher and more stubborn spirit, attached to liberty than those to the northward. Such were

all the ancient commonwealths, such were our Gothic ancestors, such in our days were the Poles, and such will be all
masters of slaves who are not slaves themselves. In such a
people, the haughtiness of domination combines with the
spirit of freedom, fortifies it, and renders it invincible.

Permit me, Sir, to add another circumstance in our colonies, which contributes no mean part towards the growth
and effect of this intractable spirit. I mean their education.
In no country perhaps in the world is the law so general
a study. The profession itself is numerous and powerful,
and in most provinces it takes the lead. The greater number of the deputies sent to the congress were lawyers. But
all who read, and most do read, endeavor to obtain some
smattering in that science. I have been told by an eminent
bookseller that in no branch of his business, after tracts of
popular devotion, were so many books as those on the law
exported to the plantations. The colonists have now fallen
into the way of printing them for their own use. I hear that
they have sold nearly as many of Blackstone's Commen-
taries in America as in England. General Gage marks out
this disposition very particularly in a letter on your table.
He states that all the people in his government are lawyers,
or smatterers in law, and that in Boston they have been
enabled, by successful chicane, wholly to evade many parts
of one of your capital penal constitutions. The smartness
of debate will say, that this knowledge ought to teach them
more clearly the rights of legislature, their obligations to
obedience, and the penalties of rebellion. All this is mighty
well. But my honorable and learned friend [the Attorney
General] on the floor, who condescends to mark what I say
for animadversion, will disdain that ground. He has heard,
as well as I, that when great honors and great emoluments

do not win over this knowledge to the service of the state,
it is a formidable adversary to government. If the spirit be
not tamed and broken by these happy methods, it is stubborn and litigious. *Abeunt studia in mores.*[6] This study renders
men acute, inquisitive, dexterous, prompt in attack, ready
in defense, full of resources. In other countries, the people, more simple and of a less mercurial cast, judge of an
ill principle in government only by an actual grievance;
here they anticipate the evil and judge of the pressure of
the grievance by the badness of the principle. They augur
misgovernment at a distance, and snuff the approach of
tyranny in every tainted breeze.

The last cause of this disobedient spirit in the colonies is
hardly less powerful than the rest, as it is not merely moral,
but laid deep in the natural constitution of things. Three
thousand miles of ocean lie between you and them. No con-
trivance can prevent the effect of this distance in weakening
government. Seas roll, and months pass, between the order
and the execution, and the want of a speedy explanation of
a single point is enough to defeat a whole system. You have,
indeed, winged ministers of vengeance, who carry your bolts
in their pounces to the remotest verge of the sea. But there
a power steps in that limits the arrogance of raging passions
and furious elements, and says, "So far shalt thou go, and no
farther." Who are you, that should fret and rage and bite the
chains of nature? Nothing worse happens to you than does
to all nations who have extensive empire; and it happens in
all the forms into which empire can be thrown. In large bodies, the circulation of power must be less vigorous at the extremities. Nature has said it. The Turk cannot govern Egypt,
and Arabia, and Kurdistan, as he governs Thrace; nor has

---

6.   Ovid, *Heroid*, Ep. XV, 83. "Pursuits influence character."

he the same dominion in Crimea and Algiers which he has at Brusa and Smyrna. Despotism itself is obliged to truck and huckster. The Sultan gets such obedience as he can. He governs with a loose rein that he may govern at all; and the whole of the force and vigor of his authority in his center is derived from a prudent relaxation in all his borders. Spain, in her provinces, is, perhaps, not so well obeyed as you are in yours. She complies too, she submits, she watches times. This is the immutable condition, the eternal law, of extensive and detached empire.

Then, Sir, from these six capital sources: of descent, of form of government, of religion in the northern provinces, of manners in the southern, of education, of the remoteness of situation from the first mover of government—from all these causes a fierce spirit of liberty has grown up. It has grown with the growth of the people in your colonies, and increased with the increase of their wealth; a spirit that unhappily meeting with an exercise of power in England which, however lawful, is not reconcilable to any ideas of liberty, much less with theirs, has kindled this flame that is ready to consume us.

I do not mean to commend either the spirit in this excess or the moral causes which produce it. Perhaps a more smooth and accommodating spirit of freedom in them would be more acceptable to us. Perhaps ideas of liberty might be desired more reconcilable with an arbitrary and boundless authority. Perhaps we might wish the colonists to be persuaded that their liberty is more secure when held in trust for them by us (as their guardians during a perpetual minority) than with any part of it in their own hands. The question is not whether their spirit deserves praise or blame but what, in the name of God, shall we do with it? You have before you the object, such as it is, with all its glories, with all its imperfections on its head. You see the magnitude, the importance, the temper, the habits, the disorders. By all these considerations we are strongly urged to determine something concerning it. We are called upon to fix some rule and line for our future conduct which may give a little stability to our politics and prevent the return of such unhappy deliberations as the present. Every such return will bring the matter before us in a still more intractable form. For, what astonishing and incredible things have we not seen already! What monsters have not been generated from this unnatural contention! While every principle of authority and resistance has been pushed, upon both sides, as far as it would go, there is nothing so solid and certain, either in reasoning or in practice, that has not been shaken. Until very lately, all authority in America seemed to be nothing but an emanation from yours.[7] Even the popular part of the colony constitution derived all its activity, and its first vital movement, from the pleasure of the crown. We thought, Sir, that the utmost which the discontented colonists could do was to disturb authority; we never dreamt they could of

---

7. As we have seen, the chief difficulty of England was the impossibility of getting the colonists to act together. See the conduct of Massachusetts in the Indian War of 1763, alluded to above (p. 26, note). During the same war a scheme of Franklin's for union fell through, because the colonists thought it endangered their independence. The contest with England did what the contest with France had failed to do. In 1767 Massachusetts issued a circular to all the colonial assemblies urging them to combine in resisting the measures of Lord Townshend. During 1772 and 1773 committees of correspondence were appointed in most of the assemblies and actively engaged in preparing for common action. The result of their labors was the first continental congress which met at Philadelphia in 1774, all the colonies being represented except Georgia.

themselves supply it, knowing in general what an operose business it is to establish a government absolutely new. But having, for our purposes in this contention, resolved that none but an obedient assembly should sit, the humors of the people there, finding all passage through the legal channel stopped, with great violence broke out another way. Some provinces have tried their experiment, as we have tried ours—and theirs has succeeded. They have formed a government, sufficient for its purposes, without the bustle of a revolution or the troublesome formality of an election. Evident necessity and tacit consent have done the business in an instant. So well they have done it, that Lord Dunmore (the account is among the fragments on your table) tells you that the new institution is infinitely better obeyed than the ancient government ever was in its most fortunate periods. Obedience is what makes government and not the names by which it is called; not the name of governor, as formerly, or committee, as at present. This new government has originated directly from the people, and was not transmitted through any of the ordinary artificial media of a positive constitution. It was not a manufacture ready formed and transmitted to them in that condition from England. The evil arising from hence is this: that the colonists, having once found the possibility of enjoying the advantages of order in the midst of a struggle for liberty, such struggles will not henceforward seem so terrible to the settled and sober part of mankind as they had appeared before the trial.

Pursuing the same plan of punishing by the denial of the exercise of government to still greater lengths, we wholly abrogated the ancient government of Massachusetts. We were confident that the first feeling, if not the very prospect of anarchy, would instantly enforce a complete submission. The experiment was tried. A new, strange, unexpected face of things appeared. Anarchy is found tolerable. A vast province has now subsisted, and subsisted in a considerable degree of health and vigor, for near a twelvemonth, without governor, without public council, without judges, without executive magistrates. How long it will continue in this state, or what may arise out of this unheard-of situation, how can the wisest of us conjecture? Our late experience has taught us that many of those fundamental principles, formerly believed infallible, are either not of the importance they were imagined to be, or that we have not at all adverted to some other far more important and far more powerful principles which entirely overrule those we had considered as omnipotent. I am much against any further experiments, which tend to put to the proof any more of these allowed opinions, which contribute so much to the public tranquility. In effect, we suffer as much at home by this loosening of all ties, and this concussion of all established opinions, as we do abroad. For, in order to prove that the Americans have no right to their liberties, we are every day endeavoring to subvert the maxims which preserve the whole spirit of our own. To prove that the Americans ought not to be free, we are obliged to depreciate the value of freedom itself; and we never seem to gain a paltry advantage over them in debate without attacking some of those principles, or deriding some of those feelings, for which our ancestors have shed their blood.

But, Sir, in wishing to put an end to pernicious experiments, I do not mean, to preclude the fullest inquiry. Far from it. Far from deciding on a sudden or partial view, I would patiently go round and round the subject and survey it minutely in every possible aspect. Sir, if I were capable of engaging you to an equal attention, I would state that, as far as I am capable of discerning, there are but three ways of proceeding relative to this stubborn spirit which prevails in your colonies and disturbs your government. These are: to change that spirit, as inconvenient, by removing the causes; to prosecute it as criminal; or, to comply with it as necessary. I would not be guilty of an imperfect enumeration; I can think of but these three. Another has indeed been started, that of giving up the colonies; but it met so slight a reception that I do not think myself obliged to dwell a great while upon it. It is nothing but a little sally of anger, like the frowardness of peevish children, who, when they cannot get all they would have, are resolved to take nothing.

The first of these plans, to change the spirit as inconvenient, by removing the causes, I think is the most like a systematic proceeding. It is radical in its principle, but it is attended with great difficulties, some of them little short, as I conceive, of impossibilities. This will appear by examining into the plans which have been proposed.

As the growing population in the colonies is evidently one cause of their resistance, it was last session mentioned in both Houses, by men of weight, and received not without applause, that in order to check this evil it would be proper for the crown to make no further grants of land. But to this scheme there are two objections. The first, that there is already so much unsettled land in private hands as to afford room for an immense future population, although the crown not only withheld its grants, but annihilated its soil. If this be the case, then the only effect of this avarice of desolation, this hoarding of a royal wilderness, would be to raise the value of the possessions in the hands of the great private monopolists, without any adequate check to the growing and alarming mischief of population.

But if you stopped your grants, what would be the consequence? The people would occupy without grants. They have already so occupied in many places. You cannot station garrisons in every part of these deserts. If you drive the people from one place, they will carry on their annual tillage, and remove with their flocks and herds to another. Many of the people in the back settlements are already little attached to particular situations. Already they have topped the Appalachian [Alleghany] mountains. From thence they behold before them an immense plain, one vast, rich, level meadow—a square of five hundred miles. Over this they would wander without a possibility of restraint; they would change their manners with the habits of their life, would soon forget a government by which they were disowned, would become hordes of English Tartars, and, pouring down upon your unfortified frontiers a fierce and irresistible cavalry, become masters of your governors and your counsellors, your collectors and comptrollers, and of all the slaves that adhered to them. Such would, and in no long time must be, the effect of attempting to forbid as a crime, and to suppress as an evil, the command and blessing of Providence, "Increase and multiply." Such would be the happy result of an endeavor to keep as a lair of wild beasts that earth which God, by an express charter, has given to the children of men. Far different and surely much wiser has been our policy hitherto. Hitherto we have invited our people, by every kind of bounty, to fixed establishments. We have invited the husbandman to look to authority for his title. We have taught him piously to believe in the mysterious virtue of wax and parchment. We have thrown each tract of land, as it was peopled, into districts, that the ruling power should never be wholly out of sight. We have settled all we could, and we have carefully attended every settlement with government. Adhering, Sir, as I do, to this policy, as well as for the reasons I have just given, I think this new project of hedging-in population to be neither prudent nor practicable.

To impoverish the colonies in general, and in particular to arrest the noble course of their marine enterprises, would be a more easy task. I freely confess it. We have shown a disposition to a system of this kind—a disposition even to continue the restraint after the offense; looking on ourselves as rivals to our colonies, and persuaded that of course we must gain all that they shall lose. Much mischief we may certainly do. The power inadequate to all other things is often more than sufficient for this, I do not look on the direct and immediate power of the colonies to resist our violence as very formidable. In this, however, I may be mistaken. But when I consider that we have colonies for no purpose but to be serviceable to us, it seems to my poor understanding a little preposterous to make them unserviceable in order to keep them obedient. It is, in truth, nothing more than the old and, as I thought, exploded problem of tyranny, which proposes to beggar its subjects into submission. But remember, when you have completed your system of impoverishment, that nature still proceeds in her ordinary course; that discontent will increase with misery; and that there are critical moments in the fortune of all states, when they who are too weak to contribute to your prosperity may be strong enough to complete your ruin. *Spoliatis arma supersunt.*

The temper and character which prevail in our colonies are, I am afraid, unalterable by any human art. We cannot, I fear, falsify the pedigree of this fierce people, and persuade them that they are not sprung from a nation in whose veins the blood of freedom circulates. The language

in which they would hear you tell them this tale would detect the imposition—your speech would betray you. An Englishman is the least fit person on earth to argue another
Englishman into slavery.

I think it is nearly as little in our power to change their
republican religion as their free descent, or to substitute the
Roman Catholic as a penalty, or the Church of England
as an improvement. The mode of inquisition and dra-
gooning is going out of fashion in the Old World, and I
should not confide much to their efficacy in the New. The
education of the Americans is also on the same unalterable
bottom with their religion. You cannot persuade them to
bum their books of curious science, to banish their lawyers
from their courts of laws, or to quench the lights of their
assemblies by refusing to choose those persons who are best
read in their privileges. It would be no less impracticable
to think of wholly annihilating the popular assemblies in
which these lawyers sit. The army, by which we must govern in their place, would be far more chargeable to us, not
quite so effectual, and, perhaps, in the end full as difficult
to be kept in obedience.

With regard to the high aristocratic spirit of Virginia
and the southern colonies, it has been proposed, I know,
to reduce it by declaring a general enfranchisement of
their slaves. This project has had its advocates and pan-
egyrists; yet I never could argue myself into any opinion
of it. Slaves are often much attached to their masters. A
general wild offer of liberty would not always be accepted. History furnishes few instances of it. It is sometimes as
hard to persuade slaves to be free as it is to compel freemen to be slaves; and in this auspicious scheme we should
have both these pleasing tasks on our hands at once. But

when we talk of enfranchisement, do we not perceive that the American master may enfranchise too, and arm servile hands in defense of freedom? A measure to which other people have had recourse more than once, and not without success, in a desperate situation of their affairs.

Slaves as these unfortunate black people are, and dull as all men are from slavery, must they not a little suspect the offer of freedom from that very nation which has sold them to their present masters? From that nation, one of whose causes of quarrel with those masters is their refusal to deal any more in that inhuman traffic? An offer of freedom from England would come rather oddly, shipped to them in an African vessel, which is refused an entry into the ports of Virginia or Carolina, with a cargo of three hundred Angola negroes. It would be curious to see the Guinea captain attempting at the same instant to publish his proclamation of liberty, and to advertise his sale of slaves.

But let us suppose all these moral difficulties got over. The ocean remains. You cannot pump this dry; and as long as it continues in its present bed, so long all the causes which weaken authority by distance will continue. "Ye gods, annihilate but space and time and make two lovers happy!"[8] was a pious and passionate prayer; but just as reasonable as many of the serious wishes of very grave and solemn politicians.

If then, Sir, it seems almost desperate to think of any alterative course for changing the moral causes (and not quite easy to remove the natural) which produce prejudices irreconcilable to the late exercise of our authority, but that the spirit infallibly will continue, and, continuing, will produce such effects as now embarrass us, the second mode

---

8.   From the *Art of Sinking in Poetry*.

under consideration is, to prosecute that spirit in its overt acts as *criminal*.

At this proposition I must pause a moment. The thing seems a great deal too big for my ideas of jurisprudence. It should seem to my way of conceiving such matters that there is a very wide difference in reason and policy between the mode of proceeding on the irregular conduct of scattered individuals, or even of bands of men, who disturb order within the state and the civil dissensions which may, from time to time, on great questions, agitate the several communities which compose a great empire. It looks to me to be narrow and pedantic to apply the ordinary ideas of criminal justice to this great public contest. I do not know the method of drawing up and indictment against a whole people. I cannot insult and ridicule the feelings of millions of my fellow-creatures as Sir Edward Coke insulted one excellent individual [Sir Walter Raleigh] at the bar. I hope I am not ripe to pass sentence on the gravest public bodies, entrusted with magistracies of great authority and dignity and charged with the safety of their fellow-citizens, upon the very same title that I am. I really think that for wise men this is not judicious; for sober men, not decent; for minds tinctured with humanity, not mild and merciful.

Perhaps, Sir, I am mistaken in my idea of an empire as distinguished from a single state or kingdom. But my idea of it is this: that an empire is the aggregate of many states under one common head, whether this head be a monarch or a presiding republic. It does, in such constitutions, frequently happen (and nothing but the dismal, cold, dead uniformity of servitude can prevent its happening) that the subordinate parts have many local privileges and immunities. Between these privileges and the supreme common authority the line may be extremely nice. Of course disputes, often, too, very bitter disputes, and much ill blood, will arise. But though every privilege is an exemption (in the case) from the ordinary exercise of the supreme authority, it is no denial of it. The claim of a privilege seems rather, *ex vi termini*, to imply a superior power. For to talk of the privileges of a state, or of a person, who has no superior, is hardly any better than speaking nonsense. Now, in such unfortunate quarrels among the component parts of a great political union of communities, I can scarcely conceive anything more completely imprudent than for the head of the empire to insist that, if any privilege is pleaded against his will or his acts, his whole authority is denied—instantly to proclaim rebellion, to beat to arms, and to put the offending provinces under the ban. Will not this, Sir, very soon teach the provinces to make no distinctions on their part? Will it not teach them that the government, against which a claim of liberty is tantamount to high treason, is a government to which submission is equivalent to slavery? It may not always be quite convenient to impress dependent communities with such an idea.

We are, indeed, in all disputes with the colonies, by the necessity of things, the judge. It is true, Sir. But I confess that the character of judge in my own cause is a thing that frightens me. Instead of filling me with pride, I am exceedingly humbled by it. I cannot proceed with a stern, assured, judicial confidence, until I find myself in something more like a judicial character. I must have these hesitations as long as I am compelled to recollect that, in my little reading upon such contests as these, the sense of mankind has, at least, as often decided against the superior as the subordinate power. Sir, let me add too, that the opinion of my having some abstract right in my favor would not put me much at my ease in passing sentence, unless I could be sure that there were no rights which, in their exercise under certain circumstances, were not the most odious of all wrongs and the most vexatious of all injustice. Sir, these considerations have great weight with me, when I find things so circumstanced that I see the same party at once a civil litigant against me in point of right and a culprit before me; while I sit as a criminal judge on acts of his whose moral quality is to be decided upon the merits of that very litigation. Men are every now and then put, by the complexity of human affairs, into strange situations; but justice is the same, let the judge be in what situation he will.

There is, Sir, also a circumstance which convinces me that this mode of criminal proceeding is not (at least in the present stage of our contest) altogether expedient; which is nothing less than the conduct of those very persons who have seemed to adopt that mode by lately declaring a rebellion in Massachusetts Bay, as they had formerly addressed to have traitors brought hither, under an Act of Henry the Eighth, for trial. For though rebellion is declared, it is not proceeded against as such, nor have any steps been taken towards the apprehension or conviction of any individual offender, either on our late or our former address; but modes of public coercion have been adopted, and such as have much more resemblance to a sort of qualified hostility towards an independent power than the punishment of rebellious subjects. All this seems rather inconsistent, but it shows how difficult it is to apply the juridical ideas to our present case.

In this situation, let us seriously and coolly ponder. What is it we have got by all our menaces, which have been many and ferocious? What advantage have we derived from the penal laws we have passed, and which for the time have been severe and numerous? What advances have we made towards our object by the sending of a force which, by land and sea, is no contemptible strength? Has the disorder abated? Nothing less. When I see things in this situation, after such confident hopes, bold promises, and active exertions, I cannot, for my life, avoid a suspicion that the plan itself is not correctly right.

If then the removal of the causes of this spirit of American liberty be, for the greater part, or rather entirely, impracticable; if the ideas of criminal process be inapplicable, or, if applicable, are in the highest degree inexpedient— what way yet remains? No way is open, but the third and last—to comply with the American spirit as necessary, or, if you please, to submit to it as a necessary evil.

If we adopt this mode, if we mean to conciliate and concede, let us see of what nature the concession ought to be: to ascertain the nature of our concession, we must look at their complaint. The colonies complain that they have not the characteristic mark and seal of British freedom. They complain that they are taxed in a Parliament in which they are not represented. If you mean to satisfy them at all, you must satisfy them with regard to this complaint. If you mean to please any people, you must give them the boon which they ask; not what you may think better for them, but of a kind totally different. Such an act may be a wise regulation, but it is no concession: whereas our present theme is the mode of giving satisfaction.

Sir, I think you must perceive that I am resolved this day to have nothing at all to do with the question of the right of taxation. Some gentlemen startle—but it is true; I put it totally out of the question. It is less than nothing in my consideration. I do not indeed wonder, nor will you. Sir, that gentlemen of profound learning are fond of displaying it on this profound subject. But my consideration is narrow, confined, and wholly limited to the policy of the question. I do not examine whether the giving away a man's money be a power excepted and reserved out of the general trust of government; and how far all mankind, in all forms of polity, are entitled to an exercise of that right by the charter of nature. Or whether, on the contrary, a right of taxation is necessarily involved in the general principle of legislation and inseparable from the ordinary supreme power. These are deep questions, where great names militate against each other, where reason is perplexed, and an appeal to authorities only thickens the confusion. For high and reverend authorities lift up their heads on both sides, and there is no sure footing in the middle. This point is *the great Serbonian bog betwixt Damiata and Mount Casius old, where armies whole have sunk.*[9] I do not intend to be overwhelmed in that bog, though in such respectable company. The question with me is, not whether you have a right to render your people miserable, but whether it is not your interest to make them happy. It is not what a lawyer tells me I *may* do, but what humanity, reason, and justice tell me I ought to do. Is a politic act the worse for being a generous one? Is no concession proper but that which is made from your want of right to keep what you grant? Or does it lessen the grace or dignity of relaxing in the exercise of an odious claim because you have your evidence-room full of titles, and your magazines stuffed with arms to enforce them? What signify all those titles and all those arms? Of what avail are they, when the reason of the thing tells me that the assertion of my title is the loss of my suit, and that I could do nothing but wound myself by the use of my own weapons?

9.   *Paradise Lost,* II, 592.

Such is steadfastly my opinion of the absolute necessity of keeping up the concord of this empire by a unity of spirit, though in a diversity of operations, that, if I
were sure the colonists had at their leaving this country
sealed a regular compact of servitude, that they had solemnly abjured all the rights of citizens, that they had made a
vow to renounce all ideas of liberty for them and their posterity to all generations, yet I should hold myself obliged
to conform to the temper I found universally prevalent in
my own day, and to govern two millions of men, impatient
of servitude, on the principles of freedom. I am not determining a point of law; I am restoring tranquility—and
the general character and situation of a people must determine what sort of government is fitted for them. That point
nothing else can or ought to determine.

My idea, therefore, without considering whether
we yield as matter of right or grant as matter of favor, is
to admit the people of our colonies into an interest in the constitution;
and, by recording that admission in the journals of Parliament, to give them as strong an assurance as the nature of
the thing will admit that we mean for ever to adhere to that
solemn declaration of systematic indulgence.

Some years ago the repeal of a revenue Act, upon its
understood principle, might have served to show that we intended an unconditional abatement of the exercise of taxing
power. Such a measure was then sufficient to remove all suspicion and to give perfect content. But unfortunate events
since that time may make something further necessary; and
not more necessary for the satisfaction of the colonies than
for the dignity and consistency of our own future proceedings.

I have taken a very incorrect measure of the disposition
of the House if this proposal in itself would be received with

dislike, I think, Sir, we have few American financiers. But our
misfortune is we are too acute, we are too exquisite in our
conjectures of the future, for men oppressed with such great
and present evils. The more moderate among the opposers
of Parliamentary concession freely confess that they hope no
good from taxation; but they apprehend the colonists have
further views, and if this point were conceded, they would instantly attack the trade laws. These gentlemen are convinced
that this was the intention from the beginning, and the quarrel of the Americans with taxation was no more than a cloak
and cover to this design. Such has been the language of a
gentleman [Mr. Rice] of real moderation, and of a natural
temper well-adjusted to fair and equal government. I am,
however, Sir, not a little surprised at this kind of discourse
whenever I hear it; and I am the more surprised on account
of the arguments which I constantly find in company with
it, and which are often urged from the same mouths and on
the same day.

For instance, when we allege that it is against reason to
tax a people under so many, restraints in trade as the Americans, the noble lord [Lord North] in the blue riband shall
tell you that the restraints on trade are futile and useless;
of no advantage to us and of no burden to those on whom
they are imposed; that the trade to America is not secured
by the Acts of Navigation, but by the natural and irresistible advantage of a commercial preference.

Such is the merit of the trade laws in this posture of the
debate. But when strong internal circumstances are urged
against the taxes, when the scheme is dissected, when experience and the nature of things are brought to prove, and do
prove, the utter impossibility of obtaining an effective revenue from the colonies—when these things are pressed, or

rather press themselves, so as to drive the advocates of colony taxes to a clear admission of the futility of the scheme, then, Sir, the sleeping trade laws revive from their trance, and this useless taxation is to be kept sacred, not for its own sake, but as a counterguard and security of the laws of trade.

Then, Sir, you keep up revenue laws which are mischievous, in order to preserve trade laws that are useless. Such is the wisdom of our plan in both its members. They are separately given, up as of no value; and yet one is always to be defended for the sake of the other. But I cannot agree with the noble lord, nor with the pamphlet from whence he seems to have borrowed these ideas, concerning the inutility of the trade laws. For, without idolizing them, I am sure they are still in many ways of great use to us; and in former times they have been of the greatest. They do confine, and they do greatly narrow, the market for the Americans. But my perfect conviction of this does not help me in the least to discern how the revenue laws form any security whatsoever to the commercial regulations, or that these commercial regulations are the true ground of the quarrel, or that the giving way, in any one instance of authority, is to lose all that may remain unconceded.

One fact is clear and indisputable. The public and avowed origin of this quarrel was on taxation. This quarrel has indeed brought on new disputes on new questions, but certainly the least bitter, and the fewest of all, on the trade laws. To judge which of the two be the real, radical cause of quarrel we have to see whether the commercial dispute did, in order of time, precede the dispute on taxation? There is not a shadow of evidence for it. Next, to enable us to judge whether at this moment a dislike to the trade laws be the real cause of quarrel, it is absolutely necessary to put the taxes out of the question by a repeal. See how the Americans act in this position, and then you will be able to discern correctly what is the true object of the controversy, or whether any controversy at all will remain. Unless you consent to remove this cause of difference it is impossible, with decency, to assert that the dispute is not upon what it is avowed to be. And I would, Sir, recommend to your serious consideration whether it be prudent to form a rule for punishing people not on their own acts, but on your conjectures? Surely it is preposterous at the very best. It is not justifying your anger by their misconduct, but it is converting your ill-will into their delinquency.

But the colonies will go further.[10] Alas! Alas! When will this speculating against fact and reason end? What will quiet these panic fears which we entertain of the hostile effect of a conciliatory conduct? Is it true that no case can exist in which it is proper for the sovereign to accede to the desires of his discontented subjects? Is there anything peculiar in this case to make a rule for itself? Is all authority of course lost when it is not pushed to the extreme? Is it a certain maxim that the fewer causes of dissatisfaction are left by

---

10. As a matter of historical accuracy Burke's argument was probably wrong. By 1775 the Americans had come to dispute the whole system of external as well as internal taxation. We have seen that Townshend set up a Board of Commissioners of Customs. In 1771 orders were given that the salaries of those officials were not to be taxed, and the governor of Massachusetts refused his assent to a money bill containing no clause to this effect. In their protest the Assembly said; "We know of no commissioners of his Majesty's customs, nor of any revenue his Majesty has a right to establish in North America; we know and we feel a tribute levied and extorted from those who, if they have property, have an absolute right to the disposal of it." This amounts to an absolute denial of the right of England to tax trade in any form.

Government the more the subject will be inclined to resist and rebel?

All these objections being in fact no more than suspicions, conjectures, divinations, formed in defiance of fact and experience, they did not, Sir, discourage me from entertaining the idea of a conciliatory concession, founded on the principles which I have just stated.

In forming a plan for this purpose I endeavored to put myself in that frame of mind which was the most natural and the most reasonable, and which was certainly the most probable means of securing me from all error. I set out with a perfect distrust of my own abilities, a total renunciation of every speculation of my own, and with a profound reverence for the wisdom of our ancestors, who nave left us the inheritance of so happy a constitution and so flourishing an empire, and what is a thousand times more valuable, the treasury of the maxims and principles which formed the one and obtained the other.

During the reigns of the Kings of Spain of the Austrian family, whenever they were at a loss in the Spanish councils it was common for their statesmen to say that they ought to consult the genius of Philip the Second. The genius of Philip the Second might mislead them, and the issue of their affairs showed that they had not chosen the most perfect standard. But, Sir, I am sure that I shall not be misled when, in a case of constitutional difficulty, I consult the genius of the English constitution. Consulting at that oracle (it was with all due humility and piety) I found four capital examples in a similar case before me, those of Ireland, Wales, Chester, and Durham.

Ireland, before the English conquest, though never governed by a despotic power, had no Parliament. How far the

English Parliament itself was at that time modelled according to the present form is disputed among antiquarians. But we have all the reason in the world to be assured that a form of Parliament, such as England then enjoyed, she instantly communicated to Ireland, and we are equally sure that almost every successive improvement in constitutional liberty as fast as it was made here was transmitted thither. The feudal baronage and the feudal knighthood, the roots of our primitive constitution, were early transplanted into that soil, and grew and flourished there. Magna Charta, if it did not give us originally the House of Commons, gave us at least a House of Commons of weight and consequence. But your ancestors did not churlishly sit down alone to the feast of Magna Charta. Ireland was made immediately a partaker. This benefit of English laws and liberties, I confess, was not at first extended to *all* Ireland. Mark the consequence, English authority and English liberties had exactly the same boundaries. Your Standard could never be advanced an inch before your privileges. Sir John Davis[11] shows beyond a doubt that the refusal of a general communication of these rights was the true cause why Ireland was five hundred years in subduing; and after the vain projects of a military government, attempted in the reign of Queen Elizabeth, it was soon discovered that nothing could make that country English in civility and allegiance but your laws and your forms of legislature. It was not English arms but the English constitution that conquered Ireland. From that time Ireland has ever had a general Parliament, as she had before a partial Parliament. You changed the people, you altered the religion, but you never touched the form or the

---

11. Author of *The True Causes Why Ireland Was Never Entirely Subdued Until the Beginning of His Majesty's Happy Reign*. Published 1604.

vital substance of free government in that kingdom. You deposed kings, you restored them, you altered the succession to theirs as well as to your own crown, but you never altered their constitution, the principle of which was respected by usurpation, restored with the restoration of monarchy, and established, I trust, forever by the glorious Revolution. This has made Ireland the great and flourishing kingdom that it is; and from a disgrace and a burden intolerable to this nation has rendered her a principal part of our strength and ornament. This country cannot be said to have ever formally taxed her. The irregular things done in the confusion of mighty troubles and on the hinge of great revolutions, even if all were done that is said to have been done, form no example. If they have any effect in argument they make an exception to prove the rule. None of your own liberties could stand a moment if the casual deviations from them at such times were suffered to be used as proofs of their nullity. By the lucrative amount of such casual breaches in the constitution judge what the stated and fixed rule of supply has been in that kingdom. Your Irish pensioners would starve if they had no other fund to live on than taxes granted by English authority. Turn your eyes to those popular grants from whence all your great supplies are come, and learn to respect that only source of public wealth in the British empire.

My next example is Wales. This country was said to be reduced by Henry the Third. It was said more truly to be so by Edward the First. But, though then conquered, it was not looked upon as any part of the realm of England. Its old constitution, whatever that might have been, was destroyed, and no good one was substituted in its place. The care of that tract was put into the hands of lords marchers—a form of government of a very singular kind, a strange heterogeneous monster, something between hostility and government; perhaps it has a sort of resemblance, according to the modes of those times, to that of commander-in-chief at present, to whom all civil power is granted as secondary. The manners of the Welsh nation followed the genius of the government; the people were ferocious, restive, savage, and uncultivated, sometimes composed, never pacified. Wales within itself was in perpetual disorder, and it kept the frontier of England in perpetual alarm. Benefits from it to the state there were none. Wales was only known to England by incursion and invasion.

Sir, during that state of things, Parliament was not idle. They attempted to subdue the fierce spirit of the Welsh by all sorts of rigorous laws. They prohibited by statute the sending of all sorts of arms into Wales, as you prohibit by proclamation (with something more of doubt on the legality) the sending arms to America. They disarmed the Welsh by statute, as you attempted (but still with more questions on the legality) to disarm New England by an instruction. They made an Act to drag offenders from Wales into England for trial, as you have done (but with more hardship) with regard to America. By another Act, where one of the parties was an Englishman, they ordained that his trial should be always by English. They made Acts to restrain trade, as you do; and they prevented the Welsh from the use of fairs and markets, as you do the Americans from fisheries and foreign ports. In short, when the statute book was not quite so much swelled as it is now, you find no less than fifteen Acts of penal regulation on the subject of Wales.

Here we rub our hands—a fine body of precedents for the authority of Parliament and the use of it! I admit it fully; and pray add likewise to these precedents that all the while Wales rid this kingdom like an incubus; that it was an unprofitable and oppressive burden; and that an Englishman travelling in that country could not go six yards from the high-road without being murdered.

The march of the human mind is slow. Sir, it was not until after two hundred years discovered that, by an eternal law, Providence had decreed vexation to violence and poverty to rapine. Your ancestors did, however, at length open their eyes to the ill husbandry of injustice. They found that the tyranny of a free people could of all tyrannies the least be endured, and that laws made against a whole nation were not the most effectual methods for securing its obedience. Accordingly, in the twenty-seventh year of Henry VIII, the course was entirely altered. With a preamble stating the entire and perfect rights of the crown of England, it gave to the Welsh all the rights and privileges of English subjects. A political order was established; the military power gave way to the civil; the marches were turned into counties. But that a nation should have a right to English liberties and yet no share at all in the fundamental security of these liberties—the grant of their own property—seemed a thing so incongruous that, eight years after, that is, in the thirty-fifth of that reign, a complete and not ill-proportioned representation by counties and boroughs was bestowed upon Wales by Act of Parliament, From that moment, as by a charm, the tumults subsided, obedience was restored, peace, order, and civilization followed in the train of liberty. When the daystar of the English constitution had arisen in their hearts, all was harmony within and without—

Simul alba nautis

Stella refulsit,
Defluit saxis agitatus humor;
Concidunt venti fugiuntique nubes,
Et minax (quid sic voluere) ponto
Unda recumbit.[12]

The very same year the county palatine of Chester received the same relief from its oppressions and the same remedy to its disorders. Before this time Chester was little less distempered than Wales. The inhabitants, without rights themselves, were the fittest to destroy the rights of others; and from thence Richard II drew the standing army of archers with which for a time he oppressed England. The people of Chester applied to Parliament in a petition penned as I shall read to you: "To the king our sovereign lord, in most humble wise shown unto your excellent Majesty, the inhabitants of your Grace's county palatine of Chester: That where the said county palatine of Chester is and has been always hitherto exempt, excluded, and separated out and from your high court of Parliament, to have any knights and burgesses within the said court; by reason whereof the said inhabitants have hitherto sustained manifold disinheritances, losses, and damages, as well in their lands, goods, and bodies, as in the good, civil, and politic governance and maintenance of the commonwealth of their said country: (2.) And forasmuch as the said

12. "Soon as gleam
    Their stars at sea,
    The lash'd spray trickles from the steep,
    The wind sinks down, the storm-cloud flies.
    The threatening billow on the deep Obedient lies."
                                    —Horace, *Odes*, I, XII, 27.

inhabitants have always hitherto been bound by the acts and statutes made and ordained by your said Highness and your most noble progenitors, by authority of the said court, as far forth as other counties, cities, and boroughs have been, that have had their knights and burgesses within your said court of Parliament, and yet have had neither knight ne burgess there for the said county palatine; the said inhabitants, for lack thereof, have been oftentimes touched and grieved with acts and statutes made within the said court, as well derogatory unto the most ancient jurisdictions, liberties, and privileges of your said county palatine, as prejudicial unto the commonwealth, quietness, rest, and peace of your Grace's most bounden subjects inhabiting within the same."

What did Parliament with this audacious address? Reject it as a libel? Treat it as an affront to Government? Spurn it as a derogation from the rights of legislature? Did they toss it over the table? Did they burn it by the bands of the common hangman? They took the petition of grievance, all rugged as it was, without softening or temperament, unpurged of the original bitterness and indignation of complaint; they made it the very preamble to their Act of address, and consecrated its principle to all ages in the sanctuary of legislation.

Here is my third example. It was attended with the success of the two former. Chester, civilized as well as Wales, has demonstrated that freedom, and not servitude, is the cure of anarchy; as religion, and not atheism, is the true remedy for superstition. Sir, this pattern of Chester was followed in the reign of Charles II with regard to the county palatine of Durham, which is my fourth example. This county had long lain out of the pale of free legislation. So scrupulously was the example of Chester followed that the style of the preamble is nearly the same with that of the Chester Act; and, without affecting the abstract extent of the authority of Parliament, it recognizes the equity of not suffering any considerable district, in which the British subjects may act as a body, to be taxed without their own voice in the grant.

Now if the doctrines of policy contained in these preambles, and the force of these examples in the Acts of Parliament, avail anything, what can be said against applying them with regard to America? Are not the people of America as much Englishmen as the Welsh? The preamble of the Act of Henry VIII says the Welsh speak a language no way resembling that of his Majesty's English subjects. Are the Americans not as numerous? If we may trust the learned and accurate Judge Barrington's account of North Wales, and take that as a standard to measure the rest, there is no comparison. The people cannot amount to above 200,000; not a tenth part of the number in the colonies. Is America in rebellion? Wales was hardly ever free from it. Have you attempted to govern America by penal statutes? You made fifteen for Wales. But your legislative authority is perfect with regard to America; was it less perfect in Wales, Chester, and Durham? But America is virtually represented. What! Does the electric force of virtual representation more easily pass over the Atlantic than pervade Wales, which lies in your neighborhood; or than Chester and Durham, surrounded by abundance of representation that is actual and palpable? But, Sir, your ancestors thought this sort of virtual representation, however ample, to be totally insufficient for the freedom of the inhabitants of territories that are so near, and comparatively so inconsiderable. How then can I think it sufficient for those which are infinitely greater, and infinitely more remote?

You will now, Sir, perhaps imagine, that I am on the point of proposing to you a scheme for a representation of the colonies in Parliament. Perhaps I might be inclined to entertain some such thought; but a great flood stops me in my course. *Opposuit natura*—I cannot remove the eternal barriers of the creation. The thing, in that mode, I do not know to be possible. As I meddle with no theory, I do not absolutely assert the impracticability of such a representation. But I do not see my way to it; and those who have been more confident have not been more successful. However, the arm of public benevolence is not shortened, and there are often several means to the same end. What nature has disjoined in one way, wisdom may unite in another. When we cannot give the benefit as we would wish, let us not refuse it altogether. If we cannot give the principal, let us find a substitute? But how? Where? What substitute?

Fortunately I am not obliged for the ways and means of this substitute to tax my own unproductive invention. I am not even obliged to go to the rich treasury of the fertile framers of imaginary commonwealths; not to the Republic of Plato; not to the Utopia of More; not to the Oceana of Harrington. It is before me—it is at my feet, *and the rude swain treads daily on it with his clouted shoon.*[13] I only wish you to recognize, for the theory, the ancient constitutional policy of this kingdom with regard to representation, as that policy has been declared in Acts of Parliament; and, as to the practice, to return to that mode which a uniform experience has marked out to you as best, and in which you walked with security, advantage, and honor until the year 1763.

---

13. Milton, *Comus*, I, 683.

My resolutions therefore mean to establish the equity and justice of a taxation of America by *grant*, and not by *imposition*. To mark the *legal competency* of the colony assemblies for the support of their government in peace, and for public aids in time of war. To acknowledge that this legal competency has had *a dutiful and beneficial exercise*; and that experience has shown *the benefit of their grants*, and the *futility of Parliamentary taxation as a method of supply*.

These solid truths compose six fundamental propositions. There are three more resolutions corollary to these. If you admit the first set, you can hardly reject the others. But if you admit the first, I shall be far from solicitous whether you accept or refuse the last. I think these six massive pillars will be of strength sufficient to support the temple of British concord. I have no more doubt than I entertain of my existence that, if you admitted these, you would command an immediate peace, and, with but tolerable future management, a lasting obedience in America. I am not arrogant in this confident assurance. The propositions are all mere matters of fact; and if they are such facts as draw irresistible conclusions even in the stating, this is the power of truth and not any management of mine.

Sir, I shall open the whole plan to you, together with such observations on the motions as may tend to illustrate them where they may want explanation. The first is a resolution: "That the colonies and plantations of Great Britain in North America, consisting of fourteen separate governments, and containing two millions and upwards of free inhabitants, have not had the liberty and privilege of electing and sending any knights and burgesses, or others, to represent them in the high court of Parliament." This is a plain matter of fact, necessary to be laid down, and (excepting the description) it is laid down in the language of the constitution; it is taken nearly *verbatim* from Acts of Parliament.

The second is like unto the first: "That the said colonies and plantations have been liable to, and bounden by, several subsidies, payments, rates, and taxes, given and granted by Parliament, though the said colonies and plantations have not their knights and burgesses in the said high court of Parliament, of their own election, to represent the condition of their country; by lack whereof they have been oftentimes touched and grieved by subsidies given, granted, and assented to, in the said court, in a manner prejudicial to the commonwealth, quietness, rest, and peace of the subjects inhabiting within the same." Is this description too hot, or too cold, too strong, or too weak? Does it arrogate too much to the supreme legislature? Does it lean too much to the claims of the people? If it runs into any of these errors, the fault is not mine. It is the language of your own ancient Acts of Parliament.

Non meus hic sermo, sed quae praecepit Ofellus,
Rusticus, abnormis sapiens.[14]

It is the genuine produce of the ancient, rustic, manly, homebred sense of this country. I did not dare to rub off a particle of the venerable rust that rather adorns and preserves than destroys the metal. It would be a profanation to touch with a tool the stones which construct the sacred altar

---

14. "Ofellus shall set forth,
'Twas he that taught me it, a shrewd dear wit,
Though country bred, and for the schools unfit."

—Horace, *Sermones*, II, II, 3.

of peace. I would not violate with modern polish the ingenuous and noble roughness of these truly constitutional materials. Above all things, I was resolved not to be guilty of tampering—the odious vice of restless and unstable minds. I put my foot in the tracks of our forefathers, where I can neither wander nor stumble. Determining to fix articles of peace, I was resolved not to be wise beyond what was written; I was resolved to use nothing else than the form of sound words, to let others abound in their own sense, and carefully to abstain from all expressions of my own. What the law has said, I say. In all things else I am silent. I have no organ but for her words. This, if it be not ingenious, I am sure is safe.

There are indeed words expressive of grievance in this second resolution, which those who are resolved always to be in the right will deny to contain matter of fact, as applied to the present case, although Parliament thought them true with regard to the counties of Chester and Durham. They will deny that the Americans were ever "touched and grieved" with the taxes. If they consider nothing in taxes but their weight as pecuniary impositions, there might be some pretense for this denial. But men may be sorely touched and deeply grieved in their privileges as well as in their purses. Men may lose little in property by the act which takes away all their freedom. When a man is robbed of a trifle on the highway, it is not the twopence lost that constitutes the capital outrage. This is not confined to privileges. Even ancient indulgences withdrawn without offense on the part of those who enjoyed such favors operate as grievances. But were the Americans then not touched and grieved by the taxes, in some measure, merely as taxes? If so, why were they almost all either wholly repealed or exceedingly reduced? Were they not touched and grieved even by the regulating duties[15] of the sixth of George II? Else why were the duties first reduced to one third in 1764, and afterwards to a third of that third in the year 1766? Were they not touched and grieved by the Stamp Act? I shall say they were until that tax is revived. Were they not touched and grieved by the duties of 1767,[16] which were likewise repealed, and which Lord Hillsborough tells you (for the Ministry) were laid contrary to the true principle of commerce? Is not the assurance given by that noble person to the colonies of a resolution to lay no more taxes on them an admission that taxes would touch and grieve them? Is not the resolution of the noble lord in the blue riband, now standing on your journals, the strongest of all proofs that Parliamentary subsidies really touched and grieved them? Else why all these changes, modifications, repeals, assurances, and resolutions?

The next proposition is: "That, from the distance of the said colonies, and from other circumstances, no method hath hitherto been devised for procuring a representation in Parliament for the said colonies." This is an assertion of a fact. I go no further on the paper, though, in my private judgment, a useful representation is impossible; I am sure it is not desired by them, nor ought it perhaps by us—but I abstain from opinions.

The fourth resolution is: "That each of the said colonies hath within itself a body, chosen in part or in the whole by the freemen, freeholders, or other free inhabitants thereof, commonly called the general assembly, or general court, with powers legally to raise, levy, and assess, according to

15. See pp. 115–16, note.

16. See p. 85.

the several usage of such colonies, duties and taxes towards defraying all sorts of public services."

This competence in the colony assemblies is certain. It is proved by the whole tenor of their Acts of supply in all the assemblies, in which the constant style of granting is an "aid to his Majesty"; and Acts granting to the crown have regularly for near a century passed the public offices without dispute. Those who have been pleased paradoxically to deny this right, holding that none but the British Parliament can grant to the crown, are wished to look to what is done not only in the colonies, but in Ireland, in one uniform unbroken tenor every session. Sir, I am surprised that this doctrine should come from some of the law servants of the crown. I say, that if the crown could be responsible, his Majesty—but certainly the ministers, and even these law officers themselves through whose hands the Acts pass biennially in Ireland, or annually in the colonies, are in a habitual course of committing impeachable offences. What habitual offenders have been all presidents of the council, all secretaries of state, all first lords of trade, all attorneys, and all solicitors-general! However, they are safe, as no one impeaches them; and there is no ground of charge against them except in their own unfounded theories.

The fifth resolution is also a resolution of fact: "That the said general assemblies, general courts, or other bodies legally qualified as aforesaid, have at sundry times freely granted several large subsidies and public aids for his Majesty's service, according to their abilities, when required thereto by letter from one of his Majesty's principal secretaries of state; and that their right to grant the same, and their cheerfulness and sufficiency in the said grants, have been at sundry times acknowledge by Parliament." To say nothing of their great expenses in the Indian wars; and not to take their exertion in foreign ones, so high as the supplies in the year 1695; not to go back to their public contributions in the 1710, I shall begin to travel only where the journals give me light, resolving to deal in nothing but fact, authenticated by Parliamentary record, and to build myself wholly on that solid basis.

On the 4th of April, 1748,[17] a committee of this House came to the following resolution:

"Resolved, that it is the opinion of this committee, *That it is just and reasonable* that the several provinces and colonies of Massachusetts Bay, New Hampshire, Connecticut, and Rhode Island be reimbursed the expenses they have been at in taking and securing to the crown of Great Britain the island of Cape Breton and its dependencies."

These expenses were immense for such colonies. They were above £200,000 sterling—money first raised and advanced on their public credit.

On the 28th of January, 1756,[18] a message from the king came to us, to this effect: "His Majesty, being sensible of the zeal and vigor with which his faithful subjects of certain colonies in North America have exerted themselves in defense of his Majesty's just rights and possessions, recommends it to this House to take the same into their consideration, and to enable his Majesty to give them such assistance as may be *a proper reward and encouragement.*" On the 3rd of February, 1756,[19] the House came to a suitable resolution, expressed in words nearly the same

---

17. *Journals* of the House, vol. xxv.

18. Ibid., vol. xxvii.

19. Ibid., vol. xxvii.

as those of the message, but with the further addition, that
the money then voted was as an *encouragement* to the colonies to exert themselves with vigor. It will not be necessary
to go through all the testimonies which your own records
have given to the truth of my resolutions, I will only refer
you to the places in the journals:

> Vol. xxvii: 16th and 19th May, 1757.
> Vol. xxviii: 1st June, 1758; 26th and 30th April, 1759;
> 26th and 31st March, and 28th April, 1760; 9th and
> 20th January, 1761.
> Vol. xxix: 22nd and 26th January, 1762; 14th and 17th
> March, 1763.

Sir, here is the repeated acknowledgment of Parliament that the colonies not only gave but gave to satiety.
This nation has formally acknowledged two things: first,
that the colonies had gone beyond their abilities, Parliament having thought it necessary to reimburse them; secondly, that they had acted legally and laudably in their
grants of money and their maintenance of troops, since the
compensation is expressly given as reward and encouragement. Reward is not bestowed for acts that are unlawful,
and encouragement is not held out to things that deserve
reprehension. My resolution therefore does nothing more
than collect into one proposition what is scattered through
your journals. I give you nothing but your own, and you
cannot refuse in the gross what you have so often acknowledged in detail. The admission of this, which will be so
honorable to them and to you, will indeed be mortal to all
the miserable stories by which the passions of the misguided people have been engaged in an unhappy system. The

people heard, indeed, from the beginning of these disputes one thing continually dinned in their ears, that reason and justice demanded that the Americans, who paid
no taxes, should be compelled to contribute. How did that
fact of their paying nothing stand when the taxing system
began? When Mr. Grenville began to form his system of
American revenue, he stated in this House that the colonies were then in debt two million six hundred thousand
pounds sterling money, and was of opinion they would
discharge that debt in four years. On this state those un-
taxed people were actually subject to the payment of taxes
to the amount of six hundred and fifty thousand a year.
In fact, however, Mr. Grenville was mistaken. The funds
given for sinking the debt did not prove quite so ample as
both the colonies and he expected. The calculation was
too sanguine; the reduction was not completed till some
years after, and at different times in different colonies.
However, the taxes after the war continued too great to
bear any addition with prudence or propriety; and when
the burdens imposed in consequence of former requisitions were discharged our tone became too high to resort
again to requisition. No colony since that time ever has
had any requisition whatsoever made to it.

We see the sense of the crown and the sense of Parliament on the productive nature of a *revenue by grant*. Now
search the same journals for the produce of the *revenue by
imposition*. Where is it? Let us know the volume and the
page; what is the gross, what is the net produce? To what
service is it applied? How have you appropriated its surplus? What, can none of the many skillful index-makers
that we are now employing find any trace of it? Well, let
them and that rest together. But are the journals which say

nothing of the revenue as silent on the discontent? Oh, no, a child may find it. It is the melancholy burden and blot of every page.

I think then I am, from those journals, justified in the sixth and last resolution, which is: "That it hath been found by experience that the manner of granting the said supplies and aids, by the said general assemblies, hath been more agreeable to the said colonies and more beneficial and conducive to the public service than the mode of giving and granting aids in Parliament, to be raised and paid in the said colonies." This makes the whole of the fundamental part of the plan. The conclusion is irresistible. You cannot say that you were driven by any necessity to an exercise of the utmost rights of legislature. You cannot assert that you took on yourselves the task of imposing colony taxes from the want of another legal body that is competent to the purpose of supplying the exigencies of the state without wounding the prejudices of the people. Neither is it true that the body so qualified, and having that competence, had neglected the duty.

The question now, on all this accumulated matter, is, whether you will choose to abide by a profitable experience, or a mischievous theory; whether you choose to build on imagination or fact; whether you prefer enjoyment or hope; satisfaction in your subjects or discontent?

If these propositions are accepted, everything which has been made to enforce a contrary system must, I take it for granted, fall along with it. On that ground I have drawn the following resolution, which, when it comes to be moved, will naturally be divided in a proper manner: "That it may be proper to repeal an Act, made in the seventh year of the reign of his present Majesty, entitled, "An Act for granting certain duties in the British colonies and plantations in America"; for allowing a drawback of the duties of customs upon the exportation from this kingdom of coffee and cocoanuts of the produce of the said colonies or plantations; for discontinuing the drawbacks payable on China earthenware exported to America; and for more effectually preventing the clandestine running of goods in the said colonies and plantations. And that it may be proper to repeal an Act, made in the fourteenth year of the reign of his present Majesty, entitled, An Act to discontinue, in such manner and for such time as are therein mentioned, the landing and discharging, lading or shipping, of goods, wares, and merchandise at the town and within the harbor of Boston, in the province of Massachusetts Bay, in North America. And that it may be proper to repeal an Act, made in the fourteenth year of the reign of his present Majesty, entitled, "An Act for the impartial administration of justice in the cases of persons questioned for any acts done by them in the execution of the law, or for the suppression of riots and tumults, in the province of Massachusetts Bay, in New England." And that it may be proper to repeal an Act, made in the fourteenth year of the reign of his present Majesty, entitled, "An Act for the better regulating the government of the province of Massachusetts Bay, in New England." And, also, that it may be proper to explain and amend an Act, made in the thirty-fifth year of the reign of King Henry the Eighth, entitled, "An Act for the trial of treasons committed out of the king's dominions."

I wish, Sir, to repeal the Boston Port Bill, because (independently of the dangerous precedent of suspending the rights of the subject during the king's pleasure) it was passed, as I apprehend, with less regularity and on more partial principles than it ought. The corporation of

Boston was not heard before it was condemned. Other
towns, full as guilty as she was, have not had their ports
blocked up. Even the restraining bill of the present session
does not go to the length of the Boston Port Act. The
same ideas of prudence, which induced you not to extend equal punishment to equal guilt, even when you were
punishing, induced me, who mean not to chastise but to
reconcile, to be satisfied with the punishment already par-
tially inflicted.

Ideas of prudence and accommodation to circumstances prevent you from taking away the charters of
Connecticut and Rhode Island, as you have taken away
that of Massachusetts colony, though the crown has far
less power in the two former provinces than it enjoyed in
the latter, and though the abuses have been full as great
and as flagrant in the exempted as in the punished. The
same reasons of prudence and accommodation have
weight with me in restoring the charter of Massachusetts
Bay. Besides, Sir, the Act which changes the charter of
Massachusetts is in many particulars so exceptionable,
that if I did not wish absolutely to repeal I would by all
means desire to alter it, as several of its provisions tend
to the subversion of all public and private justice. Such,
among others, is the power in the governor to change the
sheriff at his pleasure, and to make a new returning officer
for every special cause. It is shameful to behold such a
regulation standing among English laws.

The Act for bringing persons accused of committing murder under the orders of Government to England
for trial is but temporary. That Act has calculated the probable duration of our quarrel with the colonies, and is ac-
commodated to that supposed duration. I would hasten the

happy moment of reconciliation, and therefore must, on my principle, get rid of that most justly obnoxious Act.

The Act of Henry the Eighth for the trial of treasons I do not mean to take away, but to confine it to its proper bounds and original intention; to make it expressly for trial of treasons (and the greatest treasons may be committed) in places where the jurisdiction of the crown does not extend.

Having guarded the privileges of local legislature, I would next secure to the colonies a fair and unbiased judicature; for which purpose, Sir, I propose the following resolution: "That, from the time when the general assembly or general court of any colony or plantation in North America shall have appointed by Act of Assembly, duly confirmed, a settled salary to the offices of the chief justice and other judges of the superior court, it may be proper that the said chief justice and other judges of the superior courts of such colony shall hold his and their office and offices during their good behavior; and shall not be removed therefrom, but when the said removal shall be adjudged by his Majesty in council, upon a hearing on complaint from the general assembly, or on a complaint from the governor or council, or the House of Representatives severally, or of the colony in which the said chief justice and other judges have exercised the said offices." The next resolution relates to the courts of Admiralty. It is this: "That it may be proper to regulate the courts of Admiralty or Vice-Admiralty, authorized by the fifteenth chapter of the fourth of George the Third, in such a manner as to make the same more commodious to those who sue, or are sued, in the said courts, and to provide for the more decent maintenance of the judges in the same."

These courts I do not wish to take away; they are in themselves proper establishments. This court is one of the capital securities of the Act of Navigation. The extent of its jurisdiction, indeed, has been increased; but this is altogether as proper, and is indeed on many accounts more eligible where new powers were wanted, than a court absolutely new. But courts incommodiously situated in effect deny justice; and a court partaking in the fruits of its own condemnation is a robber. The Congress complain, and complain justly, of this grievance.

These are the three consequential propositions. I have thought of two or three more, but they come rather too near detail, and to the province of executive government, which I wish Parliament always to superintend, never to assume. If the first six are granted, congruity will carry the latter three. If not, the things that remain unrepealed will be, I hope, rather unseemly encumbrances on the building than very materially detrimental to its strength and stability.

Here, Sir, I should close, but I plainly perceive some objections remain, which I ought, if possible, to remove. The first will be that, in resorting to the doctrine of our ancestors, as contained in the preamble to the Chester Act, I prove too much; that the grievance from a want of representation, stated in that preamble, goes to the whole of legislation as well as to taxation. And that the colonies, grounding themselves upon that doctrine, will apply it to all parts of legislative authority.

To this objection, with all possible deference and humility, and wishing as little as any man living to impair the smallest particle of our supreme authority, I answer, that *the words are the words of Parliament and not mine*; and that all false and inconclusive inferences drawn from them are not mine, for I heartily disclaim any such inference. I have chosen the words of an Act of Parliament, which Mr. Grenville, surely a tolerably zealous and very judicious advocate for the sovereignty of Parliament, formerly moved to have read at your table in confirmation of his tenets. It is true that Lord Chatham considered these preambles as declaring strongly in favor of his opinions. He was a no less powerful advocate for the privileges of the Americans. Ought I not from hence to presume that these preambles are as favorable as possible to both, when properly understood; favorable both to the rights of Parliament and to the privilege of the dependencies of this crown? But, Sir, the object of grievance in my resolution I have not taken from the Chester, but from the Durham Act, which confines the hardship of want of representation to the case of subsidies, and which, therefore, falls in exactly with the case of the colonies. But whether the unrepresented counties were *de jure*, or *de facto*, bound, the preambles do not accurately distinguish; nor indeed was it necessary, for whether *de jure* or *de facto* the legislature thought the exercise of the power of taxing as of right, or as of fact without right, equally a grievance and equally oppressive.

I do not know that the colonies have, in any general way, or in any cool hour, gone much beyond the demand of immunity in relation to taxes. It is not fair to judge of the temper or dispositions of any man or any set of men, when they are composed and at rest from their conduct, or their expressions in a state of disturbance and irritation. It is besides a very great mistake to imagine that mankind follow up practically any speculative principle, either of government or of freedom, as far as it will go in argument and logical illation. We Englishmen stop very short of the principles upon which we support any given part of our constitution, or even the whole of it together, I could easily, if I had not already tired you, give you very striking and convincing instances of ft. This is nothing but what is natural and proper. All government, indeed every human benefit and enjoyment, every virtue, and every prudent act, is founded on compromise and barter. We balance inconveniences, we give and take, we remit some rights that we may enjoy others, and we choose rather to be happy citizens than subtle disputants. As we must give away some natural liberty to enjoy civil advantages, so we must sacrifice some civil liberties for the advantages to be derived from the communion and fellowship of a great empire. But in all fair dealings the thing bought must bear some proportion to the purchase paid. None will barter away the immediate jewel of his soul. Though a great house is apt to make slaves haughty, yet it is purchasing a part of the artificial importance of a great empire too dear to pay for it all essential rights and all the intrinsic dignity of human nature. None of us who would not risk his life rather than fall under a government purely arbitrary. But although there are some among us who think our constitution wants many improvements to make it a complete system of liberty, perhaps none who are of that opinion would think it right to aim at such improvement by disturbing his country and risking everything that is dear to him. In every arduous enterprise we consider what we are to lose as well as what we are to gain, and the more and better stake of liberty every people possess the less they will hazard in a vain attempt to make it more. These are the *cords of man*. Man acts from adequate motives relative to his interest, and not on metaphysical speculations. Aristotle, the great master of reasoning, cautions us, and with great weight and propriety, against this species of delusive geometrical accuracy in moral arguments as the most fallacious of all sophistry.

The Americans will have no interest contrary to the grandeur and glory of England, when they are not oppressed by the weight of it; and they will rather he inclined to respect the acts of a superintending legislature, when they see them the acts of that power which is itself the security, not the rival, of their secondary importance. In this assurance my mind most perfectly acquiesces; and I confess I feel not the least alarm from the discontents which are to arise from putting people at their ease, nor do I apprehend the destruction of this empire from giving, by an act of free grace and indulgence, to two millions of my fellow-citizens some share of those rights upon which I have always been taught to value myself.

It is said, indeed, that this power of granting, vested in American assemblies, would dissolve the unity of the empire, which was preserved entire, although Wales, and Chester, and Durham were added to it. Truly, Mr. Speaker, I do not know what this unity means, nor has it ever been heard of, that I know, in the constitutional policies of this country. The very idea of subordination of parts excludes this notion of simple and undivided unity. England is the head; but she is not the head and the members too. Ireland has ever had from the beginning a separate, but not an independent, legislature, which, far from distracting, promoted the union of the whole. Everything was sweetly and harmoniously disposed through both islands for the conservations of English dominion and the communication of English liberties. I do not see that the same principles might not be carried into twenty islands, ad with the same good effect. This is my model with regard to America, as far as the internal circumstances of the two countries are the same. I know no other unity of this empire than I can draw from its example during these periods, when it seemed to my poor understanding more united than it is now, or than it is likely to be by the present methods.

But since I speak of these methods I recollect, Mr. Speaker, almost too late, that I promised before I finished to say something of the proposition of the noble lord [Lord North] on the floor, which has been so lately received, and stands on your journals. I must be deeply concerned whenever it is my misfortune to continue a difference with the majority of this House. But as the reasons for that difference are in apology for thus troubling you, suffer me to state them in a very few words. I shall compress them into as small a body as I possibly can, having already debated that matter at large when the question was before the committee. First, then, I cannot admit that proposition of a ransom by auction—because it is a mere project. It is a thing new, unheard of, supported by no experience, justified by no analogy, without example of our ancestors or root in the constitution.

It is neither regular Parliamentary taxation, nor colony grant. *Experimentum in corpore vili*, is a good rule, which will ever make me adverse to any trial of experiments on what is certainly the most valuable of all subjects, the peace of this empire.

Secondly, it is an experiment which must be fatal in the end to our constitution. For what is it but a scheme for taxing the colonies in the antechamber of the noble lord and his successors? To settle the quotas and proportions in this House is clearly impossible. You, Sir, may flatter yourself you shall sit a state auctioneer, with your hammer in your hand, and knock down to each colony as it bids. But to settle (on the plan laid down by the noble lord) the true proportional payment for four or five and twenty governments, according to the absolute and the relative wealth of each, and according to the British proportion of wealth and burden, is a wild and chimerical notion. This new taxation must therefore come in by the backdoor of the constitution. Each quota must be brought to this house ready formed; you can neither add nor alter. You must register it. You can do nothing further. For on what grounds can you deliberate either before or after the proposition? You cannot hear the counsel for all these provinces, quarreling each on its own quantity of payment and its proportion to others. If you should attempt it, the committee of provincial ways and means, or by whatever other name it will delight to be called, must swallow up all the time of Parliament.

Thirdly, it does not give satisfaction to the complaint of the colonies. They complain that they are taxed without their consent; you answer that you will fix the sum at which they shall be taxed. That is, you give them the very grievance for the remedy. You tell them indeed that you will leave the mode to themselves. I really beg pardon—it gives me pain to mention it—but you must be sensible that you will not perform this part of the compact. For suppose the colonies were to lay the duties which furnished their contingent upon the importation of your manufactures, you know you would never suffer such a tax to be laid. You know, too, that you would not suffer many other modes of taxation. So that when you come to explain yourself it will be found that you will neither leave to themselves the quantum nor the mode, nor indeed anything. The whole is delusion from one end to the other.

Fourthly, this method of ransom by auction, unless it be *universally* accepted, will plunge you into great and inextricable difficulties. In what year of our Lord are the proportions of payments to be settled? To say nothing of the impossibility that colony agents should have general powers of taxing the colonies at their discretion, consider, I implore you, that the communication by special messages, and orders between these agents and their constituents on each variation of the case, when the parties come to contend together, and to dispute on their relative proportions, will be a matter of delay, perplexity, and confusion that never can have an end.

If all the colonies do not appear at the outcry, what is the condition of those assemblies who offer by themselves or their agents to tax themselves up to your ideas of their proportion? The refractory colonies, who refuse all composition, will remain taxed only to your old impositions, which, however grievous in principle, are trifling as to production. The obedient colonies in this scheme are heavily taxed; the refractory remain unburdened. What will you do? Will you lay new and heavier taxes by Parliament on the disobedient? Pray consider in what way you can do it. You are perfectly convinced that, in the way of taxing, you can do nothing but at the ports. Now suppose it is Virginia that refuses to appear at your auction, while Maryland and North Carolina bid handsomely for their ransom, and are taxed to your quota, how will you put these colonies on a par? Will you tax the tobacco of Virginia? If you do you give its death-wound to your English revenue at home and to one of the very greatest articles of your own foreign trade. If you tax the import of that rebellious colony, what do you tax but your own manufactures, or the goods of some other obedient and already well-taxed colony? Who has said one word on this labyrinth of detail, which bewilders you more and more as you enter into it? Who has presented, who can present you with a clue to lead you out of it? I think, Sir, it is impossible that you should not recollect that the colony bounds are so implicated in one another (you know it by your other experiments in the bill for prohibiting the New England fishery), that you can lay no possible restraints on almost any of them which may not be presently eluded, if you do not confound the innocent with the guilty, and burden those whom, upon every principle, you ought to exonerate. He must be grossly ignorant of America who thinks that, without falling into this confusion of all rules of equity and policy, you can restrain any single colony, especially Virginia and Maryland, the central and most important of them all.[20]

Let it also be considered that, either in the present confusion you settle a permanent contingent, which will and must be trifling, and then you have no effectual revenue; or you change the quota at every exigency, and then on every new repartition you will have a new quarrel.

20. It should be remembered that this is the criticism of an opponent. Governor Pownall, whose authority on American questions was at least equal to Burke's, and who had always shown himself warmly in favor of American liberty, accepted North's proposals as a real basis for compromise (*Parl. Hist.*, xviii. 322). It preserved the suzerain authority of Parliament; it maintained the principle that imperial defense concerned the whole empire; it left taxation to the colonies (see p. 6, note). Lord North's Government in communicating their scheme to the colonies pledged themselves to treat the money-bills of the Assemblies with every possible respect. They never dreamt of such an auction and barter as Burke ridicules.

Reflect, besides, that when you have fixed a quota for
every colony, you have not provided for prompt and punc-
tual payment. Suppose one, two, five, ten years' arrears. You
cannot issue a treasury extent against the failing colony. You
must make new Boston Port Bills, new restraining laws, new
Acts for dragging men to England for trial. You must send
out new fleets, new armies. All is to begin again. From this
day forward the empire is never to know an hour's tranquility. An intestine fire will be kept alive in the bowels of the
colonies which one time or other must consume this whole
empire. I allow indeed that the empire of Germany raises
her revenue and her troops by quotas and contingents; but
the revenue of the empire, and the army of the empire, is
the worst revenue and the worst army in the world.

Instead of a standing revenue, you will therefore have
a perpetual quarrel. Indeed the noble lord who proposed
this project of a ransom by auction seemed himself to be
of that opinion. His project was rather designed for breaking the union of the colonies than for establishing a revenue. He confessed he apprehended that his proposal would
not be to *their taste*. I say this scheme of disunion seems
to be at the bottom of the project; for I will not suspect
that the noble lord meant nothing but merely to delude
the nation by an airy phantom which he never intended
to realize. But whatever his views may be, as I propose the
peace and union of the colonies as the very foundation of
my plan, it cannot accord with one whose foundation is
perpetual discord.

Compare the two. This I offer to give you is plain and
simple, the other full of perplexed and intricate mazes.
This is mild; that harsh. This is found by experience effectual for its purposes; the other is a new project. This is

universal; the other calculated for certain colonies only. This is immediate in its conciliatory operation; the other remote, contingent, full of hazard. Mine is what becomes the dignity of a ruling people; gratuitous, unconditional, and not held out as matter of bargain and sale. I have done my duty in proposing it to you. I have indeed tired you by a long discourse, but this is the misfortune of those to whose influence nothing will be conceded, and who must win every inch of their ground by argument. You have heard me with goodness. May you decide with wisdom! For my part I feel my mind greatly disburdened by what I have done today. I have been the less fearful of trying your patience because on this subject I mean to spare it altogether in future. I have this comfort that in every stage of the American affairs I have steadily opposed the measures that have produced the confusion and may bring on the destruction of this empire. I now go so far as to risk a proposal of my own. If I cannot give peace to my country I give it to my conscience.

But what (says the financier) is peace to us without money? Your plan gives us no revenue. No! But it does— for it secures to the subject the power of refusal; the first of all revenues. Experience is a cheat, and fact a liar, if this power in the subject of proportioning his grant, or of not granting at all, has not been found the richest mine of revenue ever discovered by the skill or by the fortune of man. It does not indeed vote you £152,750:11:2¾ths, nor any other paltry limited sum. But it gives the strong box itself, the fund, the bank, from whence only revenues can arise among a people sensible of freedom: *Posita luditur arca.*[21]

---

21. Juvenal, I, 90; a gambling reference. "Even the strong boxes were staked."

Cannot you in England; cannot you at this time of day; cannot you, a House of Commons, trust to the principle which has raised so mighty a revenue, and accumulated a debt of near 140 millions in this country? Is this principle to be true in England and false everywhere else? Is it not true in Ireland? Has it not hitherto been true in the colonies? Why should you presume that in any country a body duly constituted for any function will neglect to perform its duty and abdicate its trust? Such a presumption would go against all governments in all modes. But in truth this dread of penury of supply from a free assembly has no foundation in nature. For first observe that besides the desire which all men have naturally of supporting the honor of their own Government, that sense of dignity and that security to property which ever attends freedom has a tendency to increase the stock of the free community. Most may be taken where most is accumulated. And what is the soil or climate where experience has not uniformly proved that the voluntary flow of heaped-up plenty, bursting from the weight of its own rich luxuriance, has ever run with a more copious stream of revenue than could be squeezed from the dry busies of oppressed indigence, by the straining of all the politic machinery in the world.

Next we know that parties must ever exist in a free country. We know, too, that the emulations of such parties, their contradictions, their reciprocal necessities, their hopes, and their fears must send them all in their turns to him that holds the balance of the state. The parties are the gamesters; but Government keeps the table, and is sure to be the winner in the end. When this game is played, I really think it is more to be feared that the people will be exhausted than that Government will not be supplied.

Whereas, whatever is got by acts of absolute power ill obeyed, because odious, or by contracts ill kept, because constrained, will be narrow, feeble, uncertain, and precarious. *Ease would retract vows made in pain as violent and void.*[22]

I, for one, protest against compounding our demands; I declare against compounding, for a poor limited sum, the immense, overgrowing, eternal debt, which is due to generous government from protected freedom. And so may I speed in the great object I propose to you, as I think it would not only be an act of injustice, but would be the worst economy in the world to compel the colonies to a sum certain either in the way of ransom or in the way of compulsory compact.

But to clear up my ideas on this subject—a revenue from America transmitted hither—do not delude yourselves—you never can receive it—no, not a shilling. We have experience that from remote countries it is not to be expected. If, when you attempted to extract revenue from Bengal, you were obliged to return in loan[23] what you had taken in imposition, what can you expect from North America? For certainly, if ever there was a country qualified to produce wealth, it is India; or an Institution fit for the transmission, it is the East India Company. America has none of these aptitudes. If America gives you taxable objects on which you lay your duties here, and gives you at the same time a surplus by a foreign sale of her commodities to pay the duties on these objects which you tax at home, she has performed her part to the British revenue. But with regard to her own internal establishments, she may, I doubt not she

22. *Paradise Lost*, IV, 96.

23. See pp. 89–90, note.

will, contribute in moderation. I say in moderation, for she ought not to be permitted to exhaust herself. She ought to be reserved to a war, the weight of which, with the enemies that we are most likely to have, must be considerable in her quarter of the globe. There she may serve you, and serve you essentially.

For that service, for all service, whether of revenue, trade, or empire, my trust is in her interest in the British constitution. My hold of the colonies is in the close affection which grows from common names, from kindred blood, from similar privileges, and equal protection. These are ties which, though light as air, are as strong as links of iron. Let the colonies always keep the idea of their civil rights associated with your government; they will cling and grapple to you, and no force under heaven will be of power to tear them from their allegiance. But let it be once understood that your government may be one thing and their privileges another, that these two things may exist without any mutual relation; the cement is gone, the cohesion is loosened, and everything hastens to decay and dissolution. As long as you have the wisdom to keep the sovereign authority of this country as the sanctuary of liberty, the sacred temple consecrated to our common faith, wherever the chosen race and sons of England worship freedom, they will turn their faces towards you. The more they multiply, the more friends you will have; the more ardently they love liberty, the more perfect will be their obedience. Slavery they can have anywhere. It is a weed that grows in every soil. They may have it from Spain, they may have it from Prussia. But until you become lost to all feeling of your true interest and your natural dignity, freedom they can have from none but you. This is the commodity of price of which you have the monopoly. This is the true act of navigation which binds to you the commerce of the colonies, and through them secures to you the wealth of the world. Deny them this participation of freedom and you break that sole bond which originally made and must still preserve the unity of the empire. Do not entertain so weak an imagination as that your registers and your bonds, your affidavits and your sufferances, your rackets and your clearances are what form the great securities of your commerce. Do not dream that your letters of office, and your instructions, and your suspending clauses are the things that hold together the great contexture of the mysterious whole. These things do not make your government. Dead instruments, passive tools as they are, it is the spirit of the English communion that gives all their life and efficacy to them. It is the spirit of the English constitution which, infused through the mighty mass, pervades, feeds, unites, invigorates, vivifies every part of the empire, even down to the minutest member.

Is it not the same virtue which does everything for us here in England? Do you imagine then that it is the Land Tax Act which raises your revenue, that it is the annual vote in the committee of supply which gives you your army? Or that it is the Mutiny Bill which inspires it with bravery and discipline? No! Surely no! It is the love of the people, it is their attachment to their Government, from the sense of the deep stake they have in such a glorious institution, which gives you your army and your navy, and infuses into both that liberal obedience, without which your army would be a base rabble, and your navy nothing but rotten timber.

All this, I know well enough, will sound wild and chimerical to the profane herd of those vulgar and mechanical politicians, who have no place among us; a sort of people who think that nothing exists but what is gross and material; and who, therefore, far from being qualified to be directors of the great movement of empire, are not fit to turn a wheel in the machine. But to men truly initiated and rightly taught these ruling and master principles which, in the opinion of such men as I have mentioned, have no substantial existence, are in truth everything and all in all. Magnanimity in politics is not seldom the truest wisdom; and a great empire and little minds go ill together. If we are conscious of our situation, and glow with zeal to fill our place as becomes our station and ourselves, we ought to auspicate all our public proceedings on America with the old warning of the Church, *Sursum corda!* We ought to elevate our minds to the greatness of that trust to which the order of Providence has called us. By adverting to the dignity of this high calling, our ancestors have turned a savage wilderness into a glorious empire, and have made the most extensive, and the only honorable conquests, not by destroying, but by promoting the wealth, the number, the happiness of the human race. Let us get an American revenue as we have got an American empire. English privileges have made it all that it is; English privileges alone will make it all it can be.

In full confidence of this unalterable truth, I now (*quod felix faustumque sit*) lay the first stone of the temple of peace; and I move you:

"That the colonies and plantations of Great Britain in North America, consisting of fourteen separate governments, and containing two millions and upwards of free inhabitants, have not had the liberty and privilege of electing and sending any knights and burgesses, or others, to represent them in the High Court of Parliament."

[Upon this Resolution the previous question was put and carried—for the previous question, 270, against it, 78.]

Note.—Most of the arguments brought forward in this speech were repeated by Burke in introducing a bill for "composing the present troubles in America," 16th November, 1775. Burke purposely retained the Declaratory Act, the question of general right not being touched on. Parliament was to enact that no tax was in future to be laid on America, but expressly reserving the right of commercial regulation. Any revenue arising hence, however, was to be disposed of by the colonial assemblies. As the King of England in former times separated the right of taxation from his sovereign prerogative, so, argued Burke, might Parliament now separate it from theirs.—*Parl. Hist.*, vol. xviii.

American Taxation (1774)

During the last session of the last Parliament, on the 19th of April 1774, Mr. Rose Fuller, member for Rye, made the following motion: That an Act made in the seventh year of the reign of his present Majesty, entitled, "An Act for granting certain duties in the British colonies and plantations in America; for allowing a drawback of the duties of customs upon the exportation from this kingdom of coffee and cocoa nuts, of the produce of the said colonies or plantations; for discontinuing the drawbacks payable on china earthenware exported to America; and for more effectually preventing the clandestine running of goods in the said colonies and plantations," might be read.

And the same being read accordingly, he moved, "That this House will, upon this day sevennight, resolve itself into a committee of the whole House, to take into consideration the duty of 3d. per pound weight upon tea, payable in all his Majesty's dominions in America, imposed by the said Act; and also the appropriation of the said duty."[1]

On this latter motion a warm and interesting debate arose, in which Mr. Burke spoke as follows:

Sir, I agree with the honorable gentleman[2] who spoke last that this subject is not new in this House. Very disagreeably to this House, very unfortunately to this nation, and to the peace and prosperity of this whole empire, no topic has been more familiar to us. For nine long years, session after session, we have been lashed round and round this miserable circle of occasional arguments and temporary expedients. I am sure our heads must turn and our stomachs nauseate with them. We have had them in every shape; we have looked at them in every point of view. Invention is exhausted, reason is fatigued, experience has given judgment, but obstinacy is not yet conquered.

The honorable gentleman has made one endeavor more to diversify the form of this disgusting argument. He has thrown out a speech composed almost entirely of challenges. Challenges are serious things; and as he is a man of prudence as well as resolution, I dare say he has very well weighed those challenges before he delivered them. I had long the happiness to sit at the same side of the House, and to agree with the honorable gentleman on all the American questions. My sentiments, I am sure, are well known to him, and I thought I had been perfectly acquainted with his. Though I find myself mistaken, he will still permit me

---

1.   10 Geo. III. c. 17. The Act repealing Townshend's taxes. It should he noticed that the Government, although retaining the 3d. on tea payable in America, hoped, even here, to conciliate America by reducing the duty of 1s. in the pound to which tea was liable in England by three-fifths on re-exportation to the colonies.

2.   Charles Wolfran Cornwall, Esq., lately appointed one of the lords of the treasury.

to use the privilege of an old friendship; he will permit me to apply myself to the House under the sanction of his authority, and, on the various grounds he has measured out, to submit to you the poor opinions which I have formed upon a matter of importance enough to demand the fullest consideration I could bestow upon it.

He has stated to the House two grounds of deliberation; one narrow and simple, and merely confined to the question on your paper, the other more large and more complicated, comprehending the whole series of the Parliamentary proceedings with regard to America, their causes, and their consequences. With regard to the latter ground, he states it as useless, and thinks it may be even dangerous to enter into so extensive a field of inquiry. Yet, to my surprise, he had hardly laid down this restrictive proposition, to which his authority would have given so much weight, when directly, and with the same authority, he condemns it, and declares it absolutely necessary to enter into the most ample historical detail. His zeal has thrown him a little out of his usual accuracy. In this perplexity what shall we do, Sir, who are willing to submit to the law he gives us? He has reprobated in one part of his speech the rule he had laid down for debate in the other; and, after narrowing the ground for all those who are to speak after him, he takes an excursion himself, as unbounded as the subject and the extent of his great abilities.

Sir, when I cannot obey all his laws, I will do the best I can. I will endeavor to obey such of them as have the sanction of his example; and to stick to that rule, which, though not consistent with the other, is the most rational. He was certainly in the right when he took the matter largely. I cannot prevail on myself to agree with him in his censure of his own conduct. It is not, he will give me leave to say, either useless or dangerous. He asserts that retrospect is not wise; and the proper, the only proper, subject of inquiry, is "not how we got into this difficulty, but how we are to get out of it." In other words, we are, according to him, to consult our invention, and to reject our experience. The mode of deliberation be recommends is diametrically opposite to every rule of reason and every principle of good sense established among mankind. For that sense and that reason I have always understood absolutely to prescribe, whenever we are involved in difficulties from the measures we have pursued, that we should take a strict review of those measures, in order to correct our errors, if they should be corrigible; or at least to avoid a dull uniformity in mischief, and the unpitied calamity of being repeatedly caught in the same snare.

Sir, I will freely follow the honorable gentleman in his historical discussion, without the least management for men or measures, further than as they shall seem to me to deserve it. But before I go into that large consideration, because I would omit nothing that can give the House satisfaction, I wish to tread the narrow ground to which alone the honorable gentleman, in one part of his speech, has so strictly confined us.

He desires to know, whether, if we were to repeal this tax, agreeably to the proposition of the honorable gentleman who made the motion, the Americans would not take post on this concession, in order to make a new attack on the next body of taxes; and whether they would not call for a repeal of the duty on wine as loudly as they do now for the repeal of the duty on tea? Sir, I can give no security on this subject. But I will do all that I can, and all that can be fairly demanded. To the experience which the honorable gentleman reprobates in one instant and reverts to in the next—to that *experience*, without the least wavering or hesitation on my part, I steadily appeal; and would to God there was no other arbiter to decide on the vote with which the House is to conclude this day.

When Parliament repealed the Stamp Act in the year 1766, I affirm, first, that the Americans did *not* in consequence of this measure call upon you to give up the former Parliamentary revenue which subsisted in that country, or even any one of the articles which compose it. I affirm, also, that when, departing from the maxims of that repeal, you revived the scheme of taxation and thereby filled the minds of the colonists with new jealousy and all sorts of apprehensions, then it was that they quarreled with the old taxes as well as the new, then it was, and not till then, that they questioned all the parts of your legislative power; and by the battery of such questions have shaken the solid structure of this empire to its deepest foundations.

Of those two propositions I shall, before I have done, give such convincing, such damning proof, that however the contrary may be whispered in circles or bawled in newspapers, they never more will dare to raise their voices in this House. I speak with great confidence. I have reason for it. The ministers are with me. *They* at least are convinced that the repeal of the Stamp Act had not, and that no repeal can have, the consequences which the honorable gentleman who defends their measures is so much alarmed at. To their conduct I refer him for a conclusive answer to this objection. I carry my proof irresistibly into the very body of both Ministry and Parliament, not on any general reasoning growing out of collateral matter, but on the conduct of the honorable gentleman's ministerial friends on the new revenue itself.

The Act of 1767, which grants this tea duty, sets forth in its preamble that it was expedient to raise a revenue in America for the support of the civil government there, as well as for purposes still more extensive. To this support the Act assigns six branches of duties. About two years after this Act passed, the Ministry, I mean the present Ministry, thought it expedient to repeal five of the duties, and to leave (for reasons best known to themselves) only the sixth standing. Suppose any person, at the time of that repeal, had thus addressed the minister [Lord North, then Chancellor of the Exchequer]: "Condemning, as you do, the repeal of the Stamp Act, why do you venture to repeal the duties upon glass, paper, and painters' colors? Let your pretense for the repeal be what it will, are you not thoroughly convinced that your concessions will produce not satisfaction but insolence in the Americans, and that the giving up these taxes will necessitate the giving up of all the rest?" This objection was as palpable then as it is now, and it was as good for preserving the five duties as for retaining the sixth. Besides, the minister will recollect that the repeal of the Stamp Act had but just preceded his repeal, and the ill policy of that measure (had it been so impolitic as it has been represented), and the mischiefs it produced, were quite recent. Upon the principles, therefore, of the honorable gentleman, upon the principles of the minister himself, the minister has nothing at all to answer. He stands condemned by himself, and by all his associates old and new, as a destroyer, in the first trust of finance, of the revenues; and in the first rank of honor, as a betrayer of the dignity of his country.

Most men, especially great men, do not always know their well-wishers. I come to rescue that noble lord out of the hands of those he calls his friends, and even out of his own. I will do him the justice he is denied at home. He has not been this wicked or imprudent man. He knew that a repeal had no tendency to produce the mischiefs which give so much alarm to his honorable friend. His work was not bad in its principle, but imperfect in its execution; and the motion on your paper presses him only to complete a proper plan, which, by some unfortunate and unaccountable error, he had left unfinished.

I hope, Sir, the honorable gentleman who spoke last is thoroughly satisfied, and satisfied out of the proceedings of Ministry on their own favorite Act, that his fears from a repeal are groundless. If he is not, I leave him, and the noble lord who sits by him, to settle the matter as well as they can together; for if the repeal of American taxes destroys all our government in America—he is the man! And he is the worst of all the repealers, because he is the last.

But I hear it rung continually in my ears, now and formerly—"The preamble! What will become of the preamble if you repeal this tax?" I am sorry to be compelled so often to expose the calamities and disgraces of Parliament. The preamble of this law, standing as it now stands, has the lie direct given to it by the provisionary part of the Act, if that can be called provisionary which makes no provision. I should be afraid to express myself in this manner, especially in the face of such a formidable array of ability as is now drawn up before me, composed of the ancient household troops of that side of the House and the new recruits from this, if the matter were not clear and indisputable. Nothing but truth could give me this firmness; but plain truth and clear evidence can be beat down by no ability. The clerk will be so good as to turn to the Act, and to read this favorite preamble:

"*Whereas it is* expedient *that a revenue should be raised in your Majesty's dominions in America, for making a more* certain and adequate *provision for defraying the charge of the* administration of justice, and support of civil government, *in such provinces where it shall be found necessary; and towards* further defraying *the expenses* of defending, protecting, and securing the said dominions."

You have heard this pompous performance. Now where is the revenue which is to do all these mighty things? Five-sixths repealed—abandoned, sunk, gone, lost forever. Does the poor solitary tea duty support the purposes of this preamble? Is not the supply there stated as effectually abandoned as if the tea duty had perished in the general wreck? Here, Mr. Speaker, is a precious mockery—a preamble without an Act—taxes granted in order to be repealed—and the reasons of the grant still carefully kept up! This is raising a revenue in America! This is preserving dignity in England! If you repeal this tax in compliance with the motion, I readily admit that you lose this fair preamble. Estimate your loss in it. The object of the Act is gone already, and all you suffer is the purging the statute-book of the opprobrium of an empty, absurd, and false recital.

It has been said again and again that the five taxes were repealed on commercial principles. It is so said in the paper in my hand,[3] a paper which I constantly carry about, which I have often used, and shall often use again. What is got by this paltry pretense of Commercial principles I know not; for if your government in America is destroyed by the *repeal of taxes*, it is of no consequence upon what ideas the repeal is grounded. Repeal this tax too upon commercial principles if you please. These

3.   Lord Hillsborough's circular letter, see p. 95.

principles will serve as well now as they did formerly. But
you know that, either your objection to a repeal from
these supposed consequences has no validity, or that this
pretense never could remove it. This commercial motive
never was believed by any man, either in America, which
this letter is meant to soothe, or in England, which it is
meant to deceive. It was impossible it should. Because
every man in the least acquainted with the detail of commerce must know that several of the articles on which the
tax was repealed were fitter objects of duties than almost
any other articles that could possibly be chosen, without
comparison more so than the tea that was left taxed, as
infinitely less liable to he eluded by contraband. The tax
upon red and white lead was of this nature. You have,
in this kingdom, an advantage in lead that amounts to
a monopoly. When you find yourself in this situation of
advantage, you sometimes venture to tax even your own
export. You did so soon after the last war, when, upon this
principle, you ventured to impose a duty on coals. In all
the articles of American contraband trade who ever heard
of the smuggling of red lead and white lead? You might,
therefore, well enough, without danger of contraband
and without injury to commerce (if this were the whole
consideration) have taxed these commodities. The same
may be said of glass. Besides, some of the things taxed
were so trivial, that the loss of the objects themselves,
and their utter annihilation out of American commerce,
would have been comparatively as nothing. But is the article of tea such an object in the trade of England as not
to be felt or felt but slightly, like white lead and red lead
and painters' colors? Tea is an object of far other importance. Tea is perhaps the most important object, taking it

with its necessary connections, of any in the mighty circle of our commerce. If commercial principles had been the true motives to the repeal, or had they been at all attended to, tea would have been the last article we should have left taxed for a subject of controversy.

Sir, it is not a pleasant consideration, but nothing in the world can read so awful and so instructive a lesson, as the conduct of Ministry in this business, upon the mischief of not having large and liberal ideas in the management of great affairs. Never have the servants of the state looked at the whole of your complicated interests in one connected view. They have taken things by bits and scraps, some at one time and one pretense, and some at another, just as they pressed, without any sort of regard to their relations or dependencies. They never had any kind of system right or wrong, but only invented occasionally some miserable tale for the day, in order meanly to sneak out of difficulties into which they had proudly strutted. And they were put to all these shifts and devices, full of meanness and full of mischief, in order to pilfer piecemeal a repeal of an Act, which they had not the generous courage, when they found and felt their error, honorably and fairly to disclaim. By such management, by the irresistible operation of feeble councils, so paltry a sum as threepence in the eyes of a financier, so insignificant an article as tea in the eyes of a philosopher, have shaken the pillars of a commercial empire that circled the whole globe.

Do you forget that, in the very last year, you stood on the precipice of general bankruptcy?[4] Your danger was

---

4. The East India Company at this time had become the predominant power in India, and the question arose of what ought to be the relations between the English Government and a private com-

indeed great. You were distressed in the affairs of the East
India Company; and you well know what sort of things are
involved in the comprehensive energy of that significant
appellation. I am not called upon to enlarge to you oil that
danger, which you thought proper yourselves to aggravate
and to display to the world with all the parade of indiscreet
declamation. The monopoly of the most lucrative trades,
and the possession of imperial revenues, had brought you
to the verge of beggary and ruin. Such was your representation—such, in some measure, was your case. The vent
of ten millions of pounds of this commodity, now locked
up by the operation of an injudicious tax and rotting in
the warehouses of the company, would have prevented all
this distress and all that series of desperate measures which

---

pany which had thus acquired immense political importance. A
first step was taken in 1767, when a measure was passed limiting
the dividend which the company might pay to 10 per cent.; and
the directors, terrified by the action of the Government, purchased
temporary exemption from further interference by agreeing to contribute £400,000 to the public revenue. In 1769 this agreement was
renewed for five years. Overwhelmed with debt and burdened with
the cost of a disastrous war against Hyder Ali, the East India Company, in July 1773, had to confess that they were unable to carry
out their engagements. A Parliamentary committee was thereupon
appointed to inquire into the affairs of India, and the publication of
their report in 1773 showed that the company was on the verge of
bankruptcy. Two Acts were thereupon passed by Parliament—the
first affording the company immediate financial assistance, and the
second transforming the center of political power in India to the
Crown. Among other measures taken to help the company was one
allowing them to export tea to America direct, without first landing
it in England, or, if it was so landed and re-exported to America,
remitting the whole duty of a shilling a pound to which it was liable.
As the company had seventeen million pounds of tea stored up in
their warehouses, it was hoped that this license would be of considerable assistance to them.

you thought yourselves obliged to take in consequence of
it. America would have furnished that vent, which no other
part of the world can furnish but America, where tea is
next to a necessary of life, and where the demand grows
upon the supply. I hope our dear-bought East India committees have done us at least so much good as to let us know
that, without a more extensive sale of that article, our East
India revenues and acquisitions can have no certain connection with this country. It is through the American trade
of tea that your East India conquests are to be prevented
from crushing you with their burden. They are ponderous
indeed; and they must have that great country to lean upon,
or they tumble upon your head. It is the same folly that has
lost you at once the benefit of the West and of the East.
This folly has thrown open folding-doors to contraband,
and will be the means of giving the profits of the trade of
your colonies to every nation but yourselves. Never did a
people suffer so much for the empty words of a preamble. It
must be given up. For on what principle does it stand? This
famous revenue stands at this hour on all the debate, as a
description of revenue not as yet known in all the comprehensive (but too comprehensive) vocabulary of finance—*a
preambulary tax*. It is indeed a tax of sophistry, a tax of ped-
antry, a tax of disputation, a tax of war and rebellion, a tax
for anything but benefit to the imposers or satisfaction to
the subject.

Well, but whatever it is, gentlemen, will force the colonists to take the teas. You will force them? Has seven years'
struggle been yet able to force them? Oh but it seems "we
are in the right. The tax is trifling— in effect it is rather
an exoneration than an imposition; three-fourths of the
duty formerly payable on teas exported to America is taken

off, the place of collection is only shifted, instead of the retention of a shilling from the drawback here it is three-pence custom in America." All this, Sir, is very true. But this is the very folly and mischief of the Act. Incredible as it may seem, you know that you have deliberately thrown away a large duty which you held secure and quiet in your hands for the vain hope of getting one three-fourths less, through every hazard, through certain litigation, and pos-sibly through war.

The manner of proceeding in the duties on paper and glass, imposed by the same Act, was exactly in the same spirit. There are heavy excises on those articles when used in England. On export these excises are drawn back. But instead of withholding the drawback, which might have been done with ease, without charge, without possibility of smuggling, and instead of applying the money (money already in your hands) according to your pleasure, you be-gan your operations in finance by flinging away your reve-nue; you allowed the whole drawback on export, and then you charged the duty (which you had before discharged) payable in the colonies, where it was certain the collection would devour it to the bone, if any revenue were ever suf-fered to be collected at all. One spirit pervades and ani-mates the whole mass.

Could anything be a subject of more just alarm to America than to see you go out of the plain highroad of finance, and give up your most certain revenues and your clearest interests, merely for the sake of insulting your col-onies? No man ever doubted that the commodity of tea could bear an imposition of threepence. But no commodity will bear threepence, or will bear a penny, when the general feelings of men are irritated and two millions of people are resolved not to pay. The feelings of the colonies were formerly the feelings of Great Britain. Theirs were formerly the feelings of Mr. Hampden when called upon for the payment of twenty shillings.[5] Would twenty shillings have ruined Mr. Hampden's fortune? No, but the payment of half twenty shillings, on the principle it was demanded, would have made him a slave. It is the weight of that preamble, of which you are so fond, and not the weight of the duty that the Americans are unable and unwilling to bear.

It is then, Sir, upon the *principle* of this measure, and nothing else, that we are at issue. It is a principle of political expediency. Your Act of 1767 asserts that it is expedient to raise a revenue in America; your Act of 1769, which takes away that revenue, contradicts the Act of 1767, and, by something much stronger than words, asserts that it is not expedient. It is a reflection upon your wisdom to persist in a solemn Parliamentary declaration of the expediency of any object for which, at the same time, you make no sort of provision. And pray, Sir, let not this circumstance escape you—it is very material— that the preamble of this Act which we wish to repeal is not *declaratory of a right*, as some gentlemen seem to argue it, it is only a recital of the *expediency* of a certain exercise of a right supposed already to have been asserted; an exercise you are now contending for by ways and means which you confess, though they were obeyed, to be utterly insufficient for their purpose. You are therefore at this moment in the awkward situation

5. John Hampden, the celebrated Parliamentarian, who refused to pay 20s. levied on him for "ship-money," on the ground that Charles I had not obtained Parliamentary authority for the tax. The case was argued before the Exchequer Court in 1638, and seven out of the twelve Judges decided in favor of the king. One of the first Acts of the Long Parliament was to reverse this judgment.

of fighting for a phantom; a quiddity; a thing that wants not only a substance, but even a name for a thing, which is neither abstract right nor profitable enjoyment.

They tell you, Sir, that your dignity is tied to it. I know not how it happens, but this dignity of yours is a terrible encumbrance to you, for it has of late been ever at war with your interest, your equity, and every idea of your policy. Show the thing you contend for to be reason, show it to be common sense; show it to be the means of attaining some useful end, and then I am content to allow it what dignity you please. But what dignity is derived from the perseverance in absurdity is more than ever I could discern. The honorable gentleman has said well—indeed, in most of his *general* observations I agree with him—he says that this subject does not stand as it did formerly. Oh, certainly not! Every hour you continue on this ill-chosen ground your difficulties thicken on you; and therefore my conclusion is, remove from a bad position as quickly as you can. The disgrace and the necessity of yielding, both of them, grow upon you every hour of your delay.

But will you repeal the Act, says the honorable gentleman, at this instant when America is in open resistance to your authority and that you have just revived your system of taxation? He thinks he has driven us into a corner. But thus pent up, I am content to meet him; because I enter the lists supported by my old authority, his new friends, the ministers themselves. The honorable gentleman remembers that about five years ago as great disturbances as the present prevailed in America on account of the new taxes. The ministers represented these disturbances as treasonable; and this House thought proper, on that representation, to make a famous address for a revival, and for a new application of a statute of Henry VIII.[6] We besought the king, in that well-considered address, to inquire into treasons, and to bring the supposed traitors from America to Great Britain for trial. His Majesty was pleased graciously to promise a compliance with our request. All the attempts from this side of the House to resist these violences, and to bring about a repeal, were treated with the utmost scorn. An apprehension of the very consequences now stated by the honorable gentleman was then given as a reason for shutting the door against all hope of such an alteration. And so strong was the spirit for supporting the new taxes that the session concluded with the following remarkable declaration. After stating the vigorous measures which had been pursued, the speech from the throne proceeds:

"*You have assured me of your* firm *support in the* prosecution *of them. Nothing, in my opinion, could be more likely to enable the well-disposed among my subjects in that part of the world effectually to discourage and defeat the designs of the factious and seditious than the hearty concurrence of every branch of the legislature in* maintaining the execution of the laws in every *part of my dominions.*"

After this no man dreamt that a repeal under this Ministry could possibly take place. The honorable gentleman knows as well as I that the idea was utterly exploded by those who sway the House. This speech was made on the ninth day of May, 1769. Five days after this speech, that is, on the 13th of the same month, the public circular letter, a part of which I am going to read to you, was written by Lord Hillsborough, Secretary of State for the Colonies. After reciting the substance of the king's speech, he goes on thus:

"*I can take upon me to assure you, notwithstanding insinuations to the contrary, from men with* factious and seditious views, *that*

6.   The address was moved 15th December, 1768.

His Majesty's present administration have at no time entertained a design to propose to Parliament to lay any further taxes upon America for the purpose of RAISING A REVENUE; *and that it is at present their intention to propose, the next session of Parliament, to take off the duties upon glass, paper, and colors, upon consideration of such duties* having been laid contrary to the true principles of commerce.

"*These have* always *been*, and still are, *the sentiments of His Majesty's* present servants, *and by which their conduct* in respect to America has been governed. *And* His Majesty *relies upon your prudence and fidelity for such an explanation of his measures as may tend to remove the prejudices which have been excited by the misrepresentations of those who are enemies to the peace and prosperity of Great Britain and her colonies; and to re-establish that mutual* confidence and affection *upon which the glory and safety of the British empire depend*."

Here, Sir, is a canonical book of ministerial scripture; the general epistle to the Americans. What does, the gentleman say to it? Here a repeal is promised, promised without condition, and while your authority was actually, resisted. I pass by the public promise of a peer relative to the repeal of taxes by this House. I pass by the use of the king's name in a matter of supply, that sacred and reserved right of the Commons. I conceal the ridiculous figure of Parliament hurling its thunders at the gigantic rebellion of America, and then five days after prostrate at the feet of those assemblies we affected to despise, begging them, by the intervention of our ministerial sureties, to receive our submission and heartily promising amendment. These might have been serious matters formerly, but we are grown wiser than our fathers. Passing therefore from the constitutional consideration to the mere policy, does not this letter imply that the idea of taxing America for the purpose of revenue is an abominable project, when the Ministry suppose that none but *factious* men, and with seditious views, could charge them with it? Does not this letter adopt and sanctify the American distinction of *taxing for a revenue*? Does it not formally reject all future taxation on that principle? Does it not state the ministerial rejection of such principle of taxation, not as the occasional, but the constant opinion of the long's servants? Does it not say (I care not how consistently), but does it not say that their conduct with regard to America has been always governed by this policy? It goes a great deal further. These excellent and trusty servants of the king, justly fearful lest they themselves should have lost all credit with the world, bring out the image of their gracious sovereign from the inmost and most sacred shrine and they pawn him as a security for their promises—"*His Majesty relies* on your prudence and fidelity for such an explanation of *his* measures." These sentiments of the minister and these measures of his Majesty can only relate to the principle and practice of taxing for a revenue, and accordingly Lord Botetourt, stating it as such, did, with great propriety, and in the exact spirit of his instructions, endeavor to remove the fears of the Virginian assembly, lest the sentiments, which it seems (unknown to the world), had *always* been those of the ministers, and by which their conduct *in respect to America had been governed*, should by some possible revolution, favorable to wicked American taxes, be hereafter counteracted. He addresses them in this manner:

"*It may possibly be objected that, as his Majesty's present administration are* not immortal, *their successors may be inclined to attempt to undo what the present ministers shall have attempted to perform; and to that objection I can give but this answer, that it is my firm opinion that the plan I have stated to you will certainly take place, and that it will never be departed from; and so determined am I forever to abide by it, that I will be content to be declared infamous, if I do not, to the last hour of my life, at all times, in all places, and upon all occasions, exert every power with which I either am or ever shall be legally invested in order* to obtain and maintain *for the continent of America that* satisfaction *which I have been authorized to promise this day, by the confidential servants of our gracious sovereign, who to my certain knowledge rates his honor so high* that he would rather part with his crown than preserve it by deceit.

"A glorious and true character! Which (since we suffer his ministers with impunity to answer for his ideas of taxation) we ought to make it our business to enable his Majesty to preserve in all its luster. Let him have character, since ours is no more! Let some part of government be kept in respect!"

This epistle was no the letter of Lord Hillsborough solely, though he held the official pen. It was the letter of the noble lord upon the floor [Lord North] and of all the king's then-ministers, who (with, I think, the exception of two only) are his ministers at this hour. The very first news that a British Parliament heard of what it was to do with the duties which it had given and granted to the king was by the publication of the votes of American assemblies. It was in America that your resolutions were predeclared. It was from thence that we knew to a certainty how much exactly, and not a scruple more or less, we were to repeal. We were unworthy to be let into the secret of our own conduct. The assemblies had *confidential* communications from his Majesty's *confidential* servants. We were nothing but instruments. Do you, after this, wonder that you have no weight and no respect in the colonies? After this, are you surprised that Parliament is every day and everywhere losing (I feel it with sorrow, I utter it with reluctance) that reverential affection which so endearing a name of authority ought ever to carry with it; that you are obeyed solely from respect to the bayonet; and that this House, the ground and pillar of freedom, is itself held up only by the treacherous underpinning and clumsy buttresses of arbitrary power?

If this dignity, which is to stand in the place of just policy and common sense, had been consulted, there was a time for preserving it, and for reconciling it with any concession. If in the session of 1768,[7] that session of idle terror and empty menaces, you had, as you were often pressed to do, repealed these taxes, then your strong operations would have come justified and enforced, in case your concessions had been returned by outrages. But, preposterously, you began with violence; and before terrors could have any effect, either good or bad, your ministers immediately begged pardon, and promised that repeal to the obstinate Americans which they had refused in an easy, good-natured, complying British Parliament. The assemblies, which had been publicly and avowedly dissolved for *their* contumacy, are called together to receive *your* submission. Your ministerial directors blustered like tragic tyrants here, and then went mumping with a sore leg in America, canting and whining, and complaining of faction, which represented them as friends to a revenue from the colonies. I hope nobody in this House will hereafter have the impudence to defend American taxes in the name of Ministry. The

---

7.   When the address for reviving the statute of Henry VIII, referred to above, was carried, as well as resolutions condemning the non-importation agreements and the circular of the Massachusets Assembly.

moment they do, with this letter of attorney in my hand,
I will tell them, in the authorized terms, they are wretches
"with factious and seditious views, enemies to the peace
and prosperity of the mother-country and the colonies,"
and subverters "of the mutual affection and confidence on
which the glory and safety of the British empire depend."

After this letter, the question is no more on propriety
or dignity. They are gone already. The faith of your sovereign is pledged for the political principle. The general
declaration in the letter goes to the whole of it. You must
therefore either abandon the scheme of taxing, or you
must send the ministers tarred and feathered to America
who dared to hold out the royal faith for a renunciation
of all taxes for revenue. Them you must punish or this
faith you must preserve. The preservation of this faith is
of more consequence than the duties on *red lead*, or *white
lead*, or on broken *glass*, or *atlas-ordinary*, or *demy-fine*, or *blue-
royal*, or *bastard*, or *fool's-cap* which you have given up, or
the threepence on tea which you retained. The letter went
stamped with the public authority of this kingdom. The
instructions for the colony government go under no other
sanction, and America cannot believe, and will not obey
you, if you do not preserve this channel of communication
sacred. You are now punishing the colonies for acting on
distinctions held out by that very Ministry which is here
shining in riches, in favor, and in power, and urging the
punishment of the very offense to which they had themselves been the tempters.

Sir, if reasons respecting simply your own commerce,
which is your own convenience, were the sole ground of
the repeal of the five duties, why does Lord Hillsborough,
in disclaiming in the name of the king and Ministry their

ever having had an intent to tax for revenue, mention it as
the means "or re-establishing the confidence and affection
of the colonies"? Is it a way of soothing *others* to assure
them that you will take good care of *yourself*? The medium,
the only medium, for regaining their affection and confidence is, that you will take off something oppressive to
their minds. Sir, the letter strongly enforces that idea; for
though the repeal of the taxes is promised on commercial principles, yet the means of counteracting "the insinuations of men with factious and seditious views" is, by
a disclaimer of the intention of taxing for revenue, as a
constant invariable sentiment and rule of conduct in the
government of America.

I remember that the noble lord on the floor, not in a
former debate to be sure (it would be disorderly to refer
to it, I suppose I read it somewhere), but the noble lord
was pleased to say that he did not conceive how it could
enter into the head of man to impose such taxes as those
of 1767—I mean those taxes which he voted for imposing,
and voted for repealing—as being taxes contrary to all the
principles of commerce laid on *British manufactures*.

I dare say the noble lord is perfectly well read, because
the duty of his particular office requires he should be so,
in all our revenue laws, and in the policy which is to be
collected out of them. Now, Sir, when he had read this
Act of American revenue, and a little recovered from his
astonishment, I suppose he made one step retrograde (it
is but one) and looked at the Act which stands just before
in the statute-book. The American revenue Act is the
forty-fifth chapter; the other to which I refer is the forty-
fourth of the same session. These two Acts are both to the
same purpose—both revenue Acts, both taxing out of the

kingdom, and both taxing British manufactures exported. As the forty-fifth is an Act for raising a revenue in America, the forty-fourth is an Act for raising a revenue in the Isle of Man. The two Acts perfectly agree in all respects, except one. In the Act for taxing the Isle of Man, the noble lord will find, not, as in the American Act, four or five articles, but almost the *whole body* of British manufactures taxed from two and a half to fifteen percent, and some articles, such as that of spirits, a great deal higher. You did not think it uncommercial to tax the whole mass of your manufactures and, let me add, your agriculture too, for, I now recollect, British corn is there also taxed up to ten percent, and this too in the very headquarters, the very citadel of smuggling, the Isle of Man. Now, will the noble lord condescend to tell me why he repealed the taxes on your manufactures sent out to America and not the taxes on the manufactures exported to the Isle of Man? The principle was exactly the same, the objects charged infinitely more extensive, the duties without comparison higher. Why? Why, notwithstanding all his childish pretexts, because the taxes were quietly submitted to in the Isle of Man, and because they raised a flame in America. Your reasons were political, not commercial. The repeal was made, as Lord Hillsborough's letter well expresses it, to regain "the confidence and affection of the colonies, on which the glory and safety of the British empire depend." A wise and just motive surely, if ever there was such. But the mischief and dishonor is that you have no done what you had given the colonies just cause to expect, when your ministers disclaimed the idea of taxes for a revenue. There is nothing simple, nothing manly, nothing ingenuous, open, decisive, or steady in the proceeding, with regard either to the continuance or the repeal of the taxes. The whole has an air of littleness and fraud. The article of tea is slurred over in the circular letter, as it were by accident—nothing is said of a resolution either to keep that tax or to give it up. There is no fair dealing in any part of the transaction.

If you mean to follow your true motive and your public faith, give up your tax on tea for raising a revenue, the principle of which has, in effect, been disclaimed in your name, and which produces you no advantage—no, not a penny. Or, if you choose to go on with a poor pretense instead of a solid reason, and will still adhere to your cant of commerce, you have ten thousand times more strong commercial reasons for giving up this duty on tea than for abandoning the five others that you have already renounced.

The American consumption of teas is annually, I believe, worth £300,000 at the least farthing. If you urge the American violence as a justification of your perseverance in enforcing this tax, you know that you can never answer this plain question: why did you repeal the others given in the same Act while the very same violence subsisted? But you did not find the violence cease upon that concession. No! because the concession was far short of satisfying the principle which Lord Hillsborough had abjured, or even the pretense on which the repeal of the other taxes was announced; and because, by enabling the East India Company to open a shop for defeating the American resolution not to pay that specific tax, you manifestly showed a hankering after the principle of the Act which you formerly had renounced. Whatever road you take leads to a compliance with this motion. It opens to you at the end of every vista. Your commerce, your policy, your promises, your reasons, your pretenses, your consistency, your inconsistency—all jointly oblige you to this repeal.

But still it sticks in our throats—if we go so far, the Americans will go farther. We do not know that. We ought, from experience, rather to presume the contrary. Do we not know for certain that the Americans are going on as fast as possible, while we refuse to gratify them? Can they do more, or can they do worse, if we yield this point? I think this concession will rather fix a turnpike to prevent their further progress. It is impossible to answer for bodies of men. But I am sure the natural effect of fidelity, clemency, kindness in governors is peace, good-will, order, and esteem on the part of the governed. I would certainly, at least, give these fair principles a fair trial, which since the making of this Act to this hour they never have had.

Sir, the honorable gentleman having spoken what he thought necessary upon the narrow part of the subject, I have given him, I hope, a satisfactory answer. He next presses me by a variety of direct challenges and oblique reflections to say something on the historical part. I shall therefore, Sir, open myself fully on that important and delicate subject, not for the sake of telling you a long story (which I know, Mr. Speaker, you are not particularly fond of), but for the sake of the weighty instruction that, I flatter myself, will necessarily result from it. I shall not be longer, if I can help it, than so serious a matter requires.

Permit me then, Sir, to lead your attention very far back, back to the Act of Navigation, the cornerstone of the policy of this country with regard to its colonies. Sir, that policy was, from the beginning, purely commercial, and the commercial system was wholly restrictive. It was the system of a monopoly. No trade was let loose from that constraint but merely to enable the colonists to dispose of what, in the course of your trade, you could not take, or to enable them to dispose of such articles as we forced upon them, and for which, without some degree of liberty, they could not pay. Hence all your specific and detailed enumerations, hence the innumerable checks and counterchecks, hence that infinite variety of paper chains by which you bind together this complicated system of the colonies. This principle of commercial monopoly runs through no less than twenty-nine Acts of Parliament, from the year 1660 to the unfortunate period of 1764.[8]

In all those Acts the system of commerce is established as that from whence alone you proposed to make the colonies contribute (I mean directly and by the operation of your superintending legislative power) to the strength of the empire. I venture to say, that during that whole period, a

---

8.   Under the Navigation Act of 1660, most of the chief products of the colonies were only to be landed at British ports. By a later provision security had to be given on loading that the goods should be so landed. The Act of 1660 further forbade the colonists to import European goods, except in British or colonial ships sailing from British ports; but this restriction was relaxed in the case of salt, which was necessary for the New England fish-curers, and it did not apply to foreign colonies. But in 1733 an Act was passed to prevent the colonists trading with the French West Indies or the Spanish Settlements. This, and the clause in the Navigation Act forbidding the export of tobacco to any country except England, were both largely evaded.

So far as concerns internal manufactures the policy of England was generally repressive. Any form of industry which threatened to compete with production at home was instantly stifled. The Americans were forbidden to export woolens. They were not allowed (1731) to manufacture hats, in which a flourishing trade was springing up. In 1750 the production of hardware was similarly prohibited. Up to 1765 the whaling industry was similarly

Parliamentary revenue from thence was never once in contemplation. Accordingly, in all the number of laws passed with regard to the plantations, the words which distinguish revenue laws specifically as such were, I think, premeditatedly avoided. I do not say. Sir, that a form of words alters the nature of the law or abridges the power of the lawgiver. It certainly does not. However, titles and formal preambles are not always idle words, and the lawyers frequently argue from them. I state these facts to show, not what was your right, but what has been your settled policy. Our revenue laws have usually a *title* purporting their being *grants*, and the words *give* and *grant* usually precede the enacting parts. Although duties were imposed on America in Acts of King Charles II and in Acts of King William, no one title of giving "an aid to his Majesty," or any other of the usual titles to revenue Acts, was to be found in any of them till 1764, nor were the words "give and grant" in any preamble until the sixth of George II.[9]

However, the title of this Act of George II, notwithstanding the words of donation, considers it merely as a regulation of trade, "an Act for the better securing of the trade of his Majesty's sugar colonies in America." This Act was made on a compromise of all, and at the express desire of a part, of the colonies themselves. It was

---

repressed. On the other hand, Parliament encouraged the trade of America in tar, lumber, pitch, and hemp, and the tobacco of Virginia and Maryland enjoyed an absolute monopoly of the home market, maintained by law. While condemning the attempt to monopolize and restrict colonial trade, Adam Smith acknowledged that, at the time, the colonial policy of England was the most liberal in the world.

9.   The Molasses Act, 1733.

therefore in some measure with their consent; and having a title directly purporting only a *commercial regulation*, and being in truth nothing more, the words were passed by, at a time when no jealousy was entertained and things were little scrutinized, Even Governor Bernard, in his second printed letter, dated in 1763, gives it as his opinion that it "was an Act of *prohibition* not of revenue." This is certainly true, that no act avowedly for the purpose of revenue, and with the ordinary title and recital taken together, is found in the statute-book until the year 1764. All before this period stood on commercial regulation and restraint. The scheme of a colony revenue by British authority appeared therefore to the Americans in the light of a great innovation. The words of Governor Bernard's ninth letter, written in November 1765, state this idea very strongly: "It must," says he, "have been supposed, *such an innovation as a Parliamentary taxation* would cause a great *alarm*, and meet with much *opposition* in most parts of America; it was *quite new* to the people, and had no *visible bounds* set to it." After stating the weakness of government there, he says, "Was this a time to introduce *so great a novelty* as a Parliamentary inland taxation in America?" Whatever the right might have been, this mode of using it was absolutely new in policy and practice. Sir, they who are friends to the schemes of American revenue say that the commercial restraint is full as hard a law for America to live under. I think so too. I think it, if uncompensated, to be a condition of as rigorous servitude as men can be subject to. But America bore it from the fundamental Act of Navigation until 1764. Why? Because men do bear the inevitable constitution of their original nature with all its infirmities. The Act of Navigation attended the colonies from their infancy, grew with their growth, and strengthened with their strength. They were confirmed in obedience to it, even more by usage than by law. They scarcely had remembered a time when they were not subject to such restraint. Besides, they were indemnified for it by a pecuniary compensation. Their monopolist happened to be one of the richest men in the world. By his immense capital (primarily employed not for their benefit but his own) they were enabled to proceed with their fisheries, their agriculture, their shipbuilding (and their trade too within the limits), in such a manner as got far the start of the slow, languid operations of unassisted nature. This capital was a hotbed to them. Nothing in the history of mankind is like their progress. For my part, I never cast an eye on their flourishing commerce and their cultivated and commodious life, but they seem to me rather ancient nations grown to perfection through a long series of fortunate events and a train of successful industry, accumulating wealth in many centuries, than the colonies of yesterday, than a set of miserable outcasts, a few years ago, not so much sent as thrown out, on the bleak and barren shore of a desolate wilderness, three thousand miles from all civilized intercourse.

All this was done by England, while England pursued trade and forgot revenue. You not only acquired commerce, but you actually created the very objects of trade in America; and by that creation you raised the trade of this kingdom at least fourfold. America had the compensation of your capital, which made her bear her servitude. She had another compensation, which you are now going to take away from her. She had, except the commercial restraint, every characteristic mark of a free people in all her internal concerns. She had the image of the British constitution. She had the substance. She was taxed by her own representatives. She chose most of her own magistrates. She paid them all. She had in effect the sole disposal of her own internal government. This whole state of commercial servitude and civil liberty, taken together, is certainly not perfect freedom, but comparing it with the ordinary circumstances of human nature it was a happy and a liberal condition.

I know, Sir, that great and not unsuccessful pains have been taken to inflame our minds by an outcry, in this House and out of it, that in America the Act of Navigation neither is, nor ever was, obeyed. But if you take the colonies through, I affirm, that its authority never was disputed, that it was nowhere disputed for any length of time, and, on the whole, that it was well observed. Wherever the Act pressed hard many individuals indeed evaded it. This is nothing. These scattered individuals never denied the law and never obeyed it. Just as it happens whenever the laws of trade, whenever the laws of revenue, press hard upon the people in England, in that case all your shores are full of contraband. Your right to give a monopoly to the East India Company, your right to lay immense duties on French brandy, are not disputed in England. You do not make this charge on any man. But you know that there is not a creek from Pentland Frith to the Isle of Wight in which they do not smuggle immense quantities of teas, East India goods, and brandies. I take it for granted that the authority of Governor Bernard in this point is indisputable. Speaking of these laws as they regarded that part of America now in so unhappy a condition, he says, "I believe they are nowhere better supported than in this province; I do not pretend that it is entirely free from a breach of these laws, but that such a breach, if discovered, is justly punished." What more can you say of the obedience to any laws in any country? An obedience to these laws formed the acknowledgment, instituted by yourselves, for your superiority, and was the payment you originally imposed for your protection.

Whether you were right or wrong in establishing the colonies on the principles of commercial monopoly rather than on that of revenue, is at this day a problem of mere speculation. You cannot have both by the same authority. To join together the restraints of a universal internal and external monopoly with a universal internal and external taxation is an unnatural union—perfect, uncompensated slavery. You have long since decided for yourself and them, and you and they have prospered exceedingly under that decision.

This nation, Sir, never thought of departing from that choice until the period immediately on the close of the last war. Then a scheme of government new in many things seemed to have been adopted. I saw, or I thought I saw, several symptoms of a great change while I sat in your gallery, a good while before I had the honour of a seat in this House. At that period the necessity was established of keeping up no less than twenty new regiments, with twenty colonels capable of seats in this House. This scheme was adopted with very general applause from all sides, at the very time that, by your conquests in America, your danger from foreign attempts in that part of the world was much lessened or indeed rather quite over. When this huge increase of military establishment was resolved on, a revenue was to be found to support so great a burden. Country gentlemen, the great patrons of economy and

the great resisters of a standing armed force, would not
have entered with much alacrity into the vote for so large
and so expensive an army if they had been very sure that
they were to continue to pay for it. But hopes of another
kind were held out to them; and, in particular, I well remember, that Mr. Townshend, in a brilliant harangue on
this subject, did dazzle them by playing before their eyes
the image of a revenue to be raised in America.[10]

Here began to dawn the first glimmerings of this new
colony system. It appeared more distinctly afterwards,
when it was devolved upon a person to whom, on other
accounts, this country owes very great obligations. I do
believe, that he had a very serious desire to benefit the
public. But with no small study of the detail, he did not
seem to have his view, at least equally, carried to the total circuit of our affairs. He generally considered his objects in lights that were rather too detached. Whether the
business of an American revenue was imposed upon him
altogether, whether it was entirely the result of his own
speculation, or, what is more probable, that his own ideas
rather coincided with the instructions he had received—
certain it is that, wit the best intentions in the world, he

10. So far as America is concerned this is surely rather unfair. It is true
that the French had been driven from North America, but they
were firmly planted in the West Indies, and in the not improbable
event of a new war were certain to make an attempt to regain their
lost provinces. Moreover, in 1763, a confederation of Indian tribes
had swept the whole western frontier of Pennsylvania and Virginia,
had surprised and captured every British fort between Ohio and
Lake Erie, and had laid close siege to Forts Detroit and Pittsburg.
The war which followed lasted fourteen months, and the brunt of
it was borne by the English troops and by a contingent from the
southern colonies. Massachusetts absolutely refused to aid their
brethren. Connecticut would send no more than 250 men.

first brought this fatal scheme, into form and established it by Act of Parliament.

No man can believe that at this time of day I mean to lean on the venerable memory of a great man, whose loss we deplore in common. Our little party differences have been long ago composed, and I have acted more with him, and certainly with more pleasure with him, than ever I acted against him. Undoubtedly Mr. Grenville was a first-rate figure in this country. With a masculine understanding, and a stout and resolute heart, he had an application undissipated and unwearied. He took public business, not as a duty which he was to fulfil, but as a pleasure he was to enjoy; and he seemed to have no delight out of this House except in such things as some way related to the business that was to be done within it. If he was ambitious, I will say this for him, his ambition was of a noble and generous strain. It was to raise himself, not by the low, pimping politics of a court, but to win his way to power though the laborious gradations of public service, and to secure to himself a well-earned rank in Parliament by a thorough knowledge of its constitution and a perfect practice in all its business.

Sir, if such a man fell into errors, it must be from defects not intrinsical; they must be rather sought in the particular habits of his life, which, though they do not alter the groundwork of character, yet tinge it with their own hue. He was bred in a profession. He was bred to the law, which is, in my opinion, one of the first and noblest of human sciences, a science which does more to quicken and invigorate the understanding than all the other kinds of learning put together; but it is not apt, except in persons very happily born, to open and to liberalize the mind exactly in the same proportion. Passing from that study he did not go very largely into the world, but plunged into business—I mean into the business of office, and the limited and fixed methods and forms established there. Much knowledge is to be had undoubtedly in that line, and there is no knowledge which is not valuable. But it may be truly said that men too much conversant in office are rarely minds of remarkable enlargement. Their habits of office are apt to give them a turn to think the substance of business not to be much more important than the forms in which it is conducted. These forms are adapted to ordinary occasions, and therefore persons who are nurtured in office do admirably well as long as things go on in their common order; but when the high-roads are broken up, and the waters out, when a new and troubled scene is opened, and the file affords no precedent, then it is that a greater knowledge of mankind and a far more extensive comprehension of things is requisite than ever office gave or than office can ever give. Mr. Grenville thought better of the wisdom and power of human legislation than in truth it deserves. He conceived, and many conceived along with him, that the flourishing trade of this country was greatly owing to law and institution, and not quite so much to liberty; for but too many are apt to believe regulation to be commerce and taxes to be revenue. Among regulations, that which stood first in reputation was his idol. I mean the Act of Navigation. He has often professed it to be so. The policy of that Act is, I readily admit, in many respects well understood. But I do say that, if the Act be suffered to run the full length of its principle and is not changed and modified according to the change of times and the fluctuation of circumstances, it must do great mischief and frequently even defeat its own purpose.

After the war, and in the last years of it, the trade of America had increased far beyond the speculations of the most sanguine imaginations. It swelled out on every side. It filled all its proper channels to the brim. It overflowed with a rich redundance, and breaking its banks on the right and on the left, it spread out upon some places where it was indeed improper, upon others where it was only irregular. It is the nature of all greatness not to be exact, and great trade will always be attended with considerable abuses. The contraband will always keep pace in some measure with the fair trade. It should stand as a fundamental maxim, that no vulgar precaution ought to be employed in the cure of evils which are closely connected with the cause of our prosperity. Perhaps this great person turned his eyes somewhat less than was just towards the incredible increase of the fair trade, and looked with something of too exquisite a jealousy towards the contraband. He certainly felt a singular degree of anxiety on the subject, and even began to act from that passion earlier than is commonly imagined. For while he was First Lord of the Admiralty, though not strictly called upon in his official line, he presented a very strong memorial to the Lords of the Treasury (my Lord Bute was then at the head of the board) heavily complaining of the growth of the illicit commerce in America. Some mischief happened even at that time from this over-earnest zeal. Much greater happened afterwards, when it operated with greater power in the highest department of the finances. The bonds of the Act of Navigation were straitened so much that America was on the point of having no trade, either contraband or legitimate. They found, under the construction and execution then used, the Act no longer tying, but actually strangling them. All this coming with new enumerations of commodities, with regulations which in a manner put a stop to the mutual coasting intercourse of the colonies, with the appointment of courts of Admiralty under various improper circumstances, with a sudden extinction of the paper currencies, with a compulsory provision for the quartering of soldiers—the people of America thought themselves proceeded against as delinquents, or, at best, as people under suspicion of delinquency, and in such a manner as they imagined, their recent services in the war did not at all merit. Any of these innumerable regulations, perhaps, would not have alarmed alone; some might be thought reasonable; the multitude struck them with terror.

But the grand maneuver in that business of new regulating the colonies,[11] was the 15th Act of the fourth

---

11. This refers to the measures taken by Grenville in 1764. Although it is difficult to determine how much smuggling there actually was in America, we are told by Sabine that "nine-tenths probably of all the tea, wine, and fruit, sugar and molasses consumed in the colonies were smuggled." So far as sugar and molasses were concerned the New England colonists had to choose between contraband trade or no trade at all. The Molasses Act of 1733 attempted by prohibitive duties to prevent the plantations from obtaining these articles elsewhere than from the British West Indies. But these islands did not offer a large enough market to carry off the whole of the surplus products of New England, while England herself absolutely shut out the corn and salted provisions of North America, and had only a restricted demand for its timber. These articles, on the other hand, were eagerly sought after by the French West Indies and some of the Spanish colonies. In this trade the New Englanders not only obtained raw materials for the rum with which they supplied West

of George III, which, besides containing several of the matters to which I have just alluded, opened a new principle; and here properly began the second period of the policy of this country with regard to the colonies, by which the scheme of a regular plantation Parliamentary revenue was adopted in theory and settled in practice. A revenue not substituted in the place of, but superadded to, a monopoly, which monopoly was enforced at the same time with additional strictness, and the execution put into military hands.

This Act, Sir, had for the first time the title of "granting

African slave-dealers, but also a supply of the precious metals, with which they purchased goods from the mother-country. The precious metals had become the more necessary to them, because an Act had been carried in this year (1764) restricting their paper currency. Grenville found that the whole customs revenue in America brought in little more than one thousand pounds a year, and he set himself to put it on an entirely new footing. The duties on sugar and molasses were reduced by one-half, the tariff on some other articles was augmented and rearranged, and measures were taken for really seeing that the law was carried out. The jurisdiction of the Admiralty Courts, which tried smuggling cases without a jury, was strengthened and enlarged, warships were stationed off the American, coast, and their officers were made to take the oaths and act as revenue officials, and a circular was issued, requiring the courts to give proper support to revenue officers. The object which lay behind these measures was declared in the preamble of the enacting bill. Parliament declared that it was "expedient to raise a revenue in. America for defraying the expenses of defending, protecting, and securing the same." Everything was thus prepared for the project of maintaining about 10,000 men in America at the expense of the very colonists whose obedience, as well as safety, they were intended to secure. In order to soften the effect of these measures, Grenville made certain regulations peculiarly favorable to American trade. Bounties were given for the cultivation, of flax and hemp. Georgia and South Carolina were allowed to export rice to the French West Indies, and all restrictions were removed from the whale-fishery.

duties in the colonies and plantations of America"; and for the first time it was asserted in the preamble, "that it was *just* and *necessary* that a revenue should be raised there." Then came the technical words of "giving and granting," and thus a complete American Revenue Act was made in all the forms, and with a full avowal of the right, equity, policy, and even necessity of taxing the colonies, without any formal consent of theirs. There are contained also in the preamble to that Act these very remarkable words: the commons, etc.—"being desirous to make *some* provision in the *present* session of Parliament towards *raising* the said revenue." By these words it appeared to the colonies that this Act was but a beginning of sorrows; that every session was to produce something of the same kind, that we were to go on, from day to day, in charging them with such taxes as we pleased, for such a military force as we should think proper. Had this plan been pursued it was evident that the provincial assemblies, in which the Americans felt all their portion of importance and beheld their sole image of freedom, were *ipso facto* annihilated. This ill prospect before them seemed to be boundless in extent and endless in duration. Sir, they were not mistaken. The Ministry valued themselves when this Act passed, and when they gave notice of the Stamp Act, that both of the duties came very short of their ideas of American taxation. Great was the applause of this measure here. In England we cried out for new taxes on America, while they cried out that they were nearly crushed with those which the war and their own grants, had brought upon them.

Sir, it has been said in the debate that when the first American Revenue Act (the Act in 1764 imposing the port-duties) passed, the Americans did not object to the principle. It is true they touched it but very tenderly. It was not a direct attack. They were, it is true, as yet novices, as yet unaccustomed to direct attacks upon any of the rights of Parliament. The duties were port duties, like those they had been accustomed to bear; with this difference, that the title was not the same, the preamble not the same, and the spirit altogether unlike. But of what service is this observation to the cause of those that make it? It is a full refutation of the pretense for their present cruelty to America, for it shows, out of their own mouths, that our colonies were backward to enter into the present vexatious and ruinous controversy.

There is also another circulation abroad (spread with a malignant intention, which I cannot attribute to those who say the same thing in this House) that Mr. Grenville gave the colony agents an option for their assemblies to tax themselves, which they had refused. I find that much stress is laid on this as a fact. However, it happens neither to be true nor possible. I will observe, first, that Mr. Grenville never thought fit to make this apology for himself in the innumerable debates that were had upon the subject. He might have proposed to the colony agents that they should agree in some mode of taxation as the ground of an Act of Parliament. But he never could have proposed that they should tax themselves on requisition, which is the assertion of the day. Indeed, Mr. Grenville well knew that the colony agents could have no general powers to consent to it, and they had no time to consult their assemblies for particular powers before he passed his first Revenue Act. If you compare dates you will find it impossible. Burdened as the agents knew the colonies were at that time, they could not give the least hope of such grants. His

own favorite governor was of opinion that the Americans
were not then taxable objects:

"*Nor was the time less favorable to the* equity *of such a taxation.
I don't mean to dispute the reasonableness of America contributing to
the charges of Great Britain* when she is able; *nor, I believe, would
the Americans themselves have disputed it, at a* proper time and
season. *But it should be considered that the American governments
themselves have, in the prosecution of the late war, contracted very
large debts, which it will take some years to pay off, and in the mean
time occasion very* burdensome taxes for that purpose *only. For
instance, this government, which is as much beforehand as any, raises
every year £37,500 sterling for sinking their debt, and must continue
it for four years longer at least before it will be clear.*"

These are the words of Governor Bernard's letter to a
member of the old Ministry, and which he has since printed. Mr. Grenville could not have made this proposition to
the agents for another reason. He was of opinion, which he
has declared in this House a hundred times, that the colonies could not legally grant any revenue to the crown, and
that infinite mischiefs would be the consequence of such a
power. When Mr. Grenville had passed the first Revenue
Act, and in the same session had made this House come to
a resolution for laying a stamp duty on America, between
that time and the passing the Stamp Act into a law he told
a considerable and most respectable merchant, a member
of this House, whom I am truly sorry I do not now see in
his place, when he represented against this proceeding, that
if the stamp duty was disliked, he was willing to exchange
it for any other equally productive, but that, if he objected
to the Americans being taxed by Parliament, he might save
himself the trouble of the discussion as he was determined
on the measure. This is the fact, and, if you please, I will

mention a very unquestionable authority for it.[12] Thus, Sir, I have disposed of this falsehood. But falsehood has a perennial spring. It is said, that no conjecture could be made of the dislike of the colonies to the principle. This is as untrue as the other. After the resolution of the House, and before the passing of the Stamp Act, the colonies of Massachusetts Bay and New York did send remonstrance, objecting to this mode of Parliamentary taxation. What was the consequence? They were suppressed, they were put under the table, notwithstanding an order of council to the contrary, by the Ministry which composed the very council that had made the order; and thus the House proceeded to its business of taxing without the least regular knowledge of the objections which were made to it. But to give that House its due, it was not over-desirous to receive information or to hear remonstrance. On the 15th February, 1765, while the Stamp Act was under deliberation, they refused with scorn even so much as to receive four petitions presented from so respectable colonies as Connecticut, Rhode Island, Virginia, and Carolina, besides one from the traders of Jamaica. As to the colonies, they had no alternative left to them but to disobey, or to pay the taxes imposed by that Parliament which was not suffered, or did not suffer itself, even to hear them remonstrate upon the subject.

This was the state of the colonies before his Majesty thought fit to change his ministers. It stands upon no

---

12. Burke was mistaken here. In a letter from the Massachusetts Assembly, dated 1764, occurs the following passage: "The actual laying the stamp duty, you say, is deferred till next year, Mr. Grenville being willing to give the provinces their option to raise that or some equivalent tax.... This suspension amounts to this, that if the colonists will not tax themselves as they may be directed the Parliament will tax them."

authority of mine. It is proved by incontrovertible records. The honorable gentleman has desired some of us to lay our hands upon our hearts and answer to his queries upon the historical part of this consideration, and by his manner (as well as my eyes could discern it) he seemed to address himself to me.

Sir, I will answer him as clearly as I am able, and with great openness; I have nothing to conceal. In the year sixty-five, being in a very private station, far enough from any line of business, and not having the honor of a seat in this House, it was my fortune, unknowing and unknown to the then-Ministry, by the intervention of a common friend, to become connected with a very noble person, and at the head of the Treasury department. It was indeed in a situation of little rank and no consequence, suitable to the mediocrity of my talents and pretensions. But a situation near enough to enable me to see, as well as others, what was going on, and I did see in that noble person such sound principles, such an enlargement of mind, such clear and sagacious sense, and such unshaken fortitude, as have bound me, as well as others much better than me, by an inviolable attachment to him from that time forward. Sir, Lord Rockingham very early in that summer received a strong representation from many weighty English merchants and manufacturers, from governors of provinces and commanders of men of war, against almost the whole of the American commercial regulations, and particularly with regard to the total ruin which was threatened to the Spanish trade.[13] I believe, Sir, the noble lord soon saw his way in this business. But he did not rashly determine against Acts which it might be supposed were the result of much deliberation.

---

13. See p. 115, note.

However, Sir, he scarcely began to open the ground when the whole veteran body of office took the alarm. A violent outcry of all (except those who knew and felt the mischief) was raised against any alteration. On one hand, his attempt was a direct violation of treaties and public law; on the other, the Act of Navigation and all the corps of trade laws were drawn up in array against it. The first step the noble lord took was to have the opinion of his excellent, learned, and ever-lamented friend, the late Mr. Yorke, then Attorney-General, on the point of law.[14] When he knew that formally and officially, which in substance he had known before, he immediately dispatched orders to redress the grievance. But I will say it for the then-minister, he is of that constitution of mind that I know he would have issued, on the same critical occasion, the very same orders, if the Acts of trade had been, as they were not, directly against him, and would have cheerfully submitted to the equity of Parliament for his indemnity.

On the conclusion of this business of the Spanish trade, the news of the troubles on account of the Stamp Act arrived in England. It was not until the end of October that these accounts were received. No sooner had the sound of that mighty tempest reached us in England than the whole of the then opposition, instead of feeling humbled by the unhappy issue of their measures, seemed to be infinitely elated, and cried out that the Ministry, from envy to the glory of their predecessors, were prepared to repeal the Stamp Act. Near nine years after, the honorable gentleman takes quite opposite ground, and now challenges me to put my hand to my heart and say whether the Ministry had resolved on the

---

14. Rockingham's policy.

repeal till a considerable time after the meeting of Parliament. Though I do not very well know what the honorable gentleman wishes to infer from the admission or from the denial of this fact, on which he so earnestly adjures me, I do put my hand on my heart and assure him that they *did* not come to a resolution directly to repeal. They weighed this matter as its difficulty and importance required. They considered maturely among themselves. They consulted with all who could give advice or information. It was not determined until a little before the meeting of Parliament; but it was determined, and the main lines of their own plan marked out, before that meeting. Two questions arose—I hope I am not going into a narrative troublesome to the House—

[A cry of, *Go on, go on.*]

The first of the two considerations was, whether the repeal should be total, or whether only partial; taking out everything burdensome and productive, and reserving only an empty acknowledgment, such as a stamp on cards or dice. The other question was, on what principle the Act should be repealed? On this head also two principles were started. One that the legislative rights of this country, with regard to America, were not entire, but had certain restrictions and limitations.[15] The other principle was, that taxes

15. Referring to the position of Chatham, which may he given in his own words: "America being neither really nor virtually represented in Westminster cannot he held legally or constitutionally or reasonably subject to obedience to any money hill of this kingdom.... In every other point of legislation the authority of Parliament is like the north star, fixed for the reciprocal benefit of the parent country and her colonies. The British Parliament has always bound them by her laws, by her regulations of their

of this kind were contrary to the fundamental principles of commerce on which the colonies were founded, and contrary to every idea of political equity; by which equity we are bound, as much as possible, to extend the spirit and benefit of the British constitution to every part of the British dominions. The option, both of the measure and of the principle of repeal, was made before the session, and I wonder how anyone can read the king's speech at the opening of that session without seeing in that speech both the Repeal and the Declaratory Act very sufficiently crayoned out. Those who cannot see this can see nothing.

Surely the honorable gentleman will not think that a great deal less time than was then employed ought to have been spent in deliberation when he considers that the news of the troubles did not arrive till towards the end of October. The Parliament sat to fill the vacancies on the 14th day of December, and on business the 14th of the following January.

Sir, a partial repeal, or, as the *bon ton* of the court then was, a *modification*, would have satisfied a timid, unsystematic,

---

trade and industries, and even in a more absolute interdiction of both...if this power were denied I would not permit them to manufacture a lock of wool, or a horse-shoe, or a hob-nail. But, I repeat, this House has no right to lay an internal tax upon America [*Parl. Hist.*, vol. xvi.). On the other hand, the arguments of Grenville against repeal maybe summarized thus: The Seven Years' War had left eight millions of Englishmen burdened with a debt of £140,000,000. The united debt of about two millions of Americans was now less than £800,000. The annual sum the colonists were asked to contribute in the form of stamp duties was less than £100,000, with an express provision that no part of that sum should he spent on any other object but the defense of the colonies; and the country which refused to bear this small tax was so rich that in three years it had paid off £1,755,000 of its debt."

procrastinating Ministry, as such a measure has since done such a Ministry. A modification is the constant resource of weak, undeciding minds. To repeal by the denial of our right to tax in the preamble (and this, too, did not want advisers) would have cut, in the heroic style, the Gordian knot with a sword. Either measure would have cost no more than a day's debate. But when the total repeal was adopted, and adopted on principles of policy, of equity, and of commerce, this plan made it necessary to enter into many and difficult measures. It became necessary to open a very large field of evidence commensurate to these extensive views. But then this labor did knight's service. It opened the eyes of several to the true state of the American affairs; it enlarged their ideas, it removed prejudices, and it conciliated the opinions and affections of men. The noble lord, who then took the lead in administration, my honorable friend [Mr. Dowdeswell] under me, and a right honorable gentleman [General Conway]—if he will not reject his share, and it was a large one, of this business—exerted the most laudable industry in bringing before you the fullest, most impartial, and least garbled body of evidence that ever was produced to this House.[16] I think the inquiry lasted in the committee for six weeks, and, at its conclusion, this House, by an independent, noble, spirited, and unexpected majority, by a majority that will redeem all the acts ever done by majorities in Parliament, in the teeth of all the old mercenary Swiss of state (i.e., the "king's friends) in despite of all the speculators and augurs of political events, in defiance of the whole embattled legion of veteran pensioners and practiced instruments of a court, gave a total repeal to the

16. The most important witness was Benjamin Franklin.

Stamp Act, and (if it had been so permitted) a lasting peace to this whole empire.

I state, Sir, these particulars because this act of spirit and fortitude has lately been, in the circulation of the season and in some hazarded declamations in this House, attributed to timidity. If, Sir, the conduct of Ministry, in proposing the repeal, had arisen from timidity with regard to themselves, it would have been greatly to be condemned. Interested timidity disgraces as much in the cabinet, as personal timidity does in the field. But timidity, with regard to the well-being of our country, is heroic virtue. The noble lord who then conducted affairs, and his worthy colleagues, while they trembled at the prospect of such distresses as you have since brought upon yourselves, were not afraid steadily to look in the face that glaring and dazzling influence at which the eyes of eagles have blenched. He looked in the face one of the ablest, and, let me say, not the most scrupulous, oppositions that perhaps ever was in this House, and withstood it, unaided by even one of the usual supports of administration. He did this when he repealed the Stamp Act. He looked in the face of a person he had long respected and regarded, and whose aid was then particularly wanting—I mean Lord Chatham.[17] He did this when he passed the Declaratory Act.

It is now given out, for the usual purposes by the usual emissaries, that Lord Rockingham did not consent to the repeal of this Act until he was bullied into it by Lord Chatham; and the reporters have gone so far as publicly to assert, in a hundred companies, that the honorable gentleman under the gallery [General Conway], who proposed

---

17. See p. 123–24, note.

the repeal in the American committee, had another set of resolutions in his pocket directly the reverse of those he moved. These artifices of a desperate cause are at this time spread abroad with incredible care, in every part of the town, from the highest to the lowest companies, as if the industry of the circulation were to make amends for the absurdity of the report.

Sir, whether the noble lord is of a complexion to be bullied by Lord Chatham, or by any man, I must submit to those who know him. I confess, when I look back to that time, I consider him as placed in one of the most trying situations in which, perhaps, any man ever stood. In the House of Peers there were very few of the Ministry, out of the noble lord's own particular connection (except Lord Egmont, who acted, as far as I could discern, an honorable and manly part), that did not look to some other future arrangement, which warped his politics. There were in both Houses new and menacing appearances that might very naturally drive any other than a most resolute minister from his measure or from his station. The household troops openly revolted. The allies of Ministry (those, I mean, who supported some of their measures, but refused responsibility for any) endeavored to undermine their credit, and to take ground that must be fatal to the success of the very cause which they would be thought to countenance. The question of the repeal was brought on by Ministry in the committee of this House in the very instant when it was known that more than one court negotiation was carrying on with the heads of the opposition. Everything, upon every side, was full of traps and mines. Earth below shook, heaven above menaced; all the elements of ministerial safety were dissolved. It was in the midst of this chaos of plots and counter-plots, it was in the midst of this complicated warfare against public opposition and private treachery, that the firmness of that noble person was put to the proof. He never stirred from his ground—no, not an inch. He remained fixed and determined in principle, in measure, and in conduct. He practiced no managements. He secured no retreat. He sought no apology.

I will likewise do justice, I ought to do it, to the honorable gentleman who led us in this House [General Conway]. Far from the duplicity wickedly charged on him, he acted his part with alacrity and resolution. We all felt inspired by the example he gave us, down even to myself, the weakest in that phalanx. I declare for one, I knew well enough (it could not be concealed from anybody) the true state of things; but, in my life, I never came with so much spirits into this House. It was a time for a *man* to act in. We had powerful enemies; but we had faithful and determined friends, and a glorious cause. We had a great battle to fight; but we had the means of fighting—not as now, when our arms are tied behind us. We did fight that day, and conquer.

I remember, Sir, with a melancholy pleasure, the situation of the honorable gentleman [General Conway] who made the motion for the repeal; in that crisis, when the whole trading interest of this empire, crammed into your lobbies, with a trembling and anxious expectation, waited, almost to a winter's return of light, their fate from your resolutions. When at length you had determined in their favor, and your doors, thrown open, showed them the figure of their deliverer in the well-earned triumph of his important victory, from the whole of that grave multitude there arose an involuntary burst of gratitude and transport. They jumped

upon him like children on a long absent father. They clung
about him as captives about their redeemer. All England, all
America, joined to his applause. Nor did he seem insensible
to the best of all earthly rewards, the love and admiration
of his fellow citizens. *Hope elevated, and joy brightened his crest.*[18]
I stood near him, and his face, to use the expression of the
Scripture of the first martyr, "his face was as if it had been
the face of an angel." I do not know how others feel, but if I
had stood in that situation, I would never have exchanged it
for all that kings in their profusion could bestow. I did hope
that that day's danger and honor would have been a bond
to hold us all together for ever. But, alas l that, with other
pleasing visions, is long since vanished.

Sir, this act of supreme magnanimity has been represented as if it had been a measure of an administration
that, having no scheme of their own, took a middle line, pil-
fered a bit from one side and a bit from the other. Sir, they
took *no* middle lines. They differed fundamentally from the
schemes of both parties; but they preserved the objects of
both. They preserved the authority of Great Britain. They
preserved the equity of Great Britain. They made the
Declaratory Act; they repealed the Stamp Act. They did
both *fully*, because the Declaratory Act was *without qualification*, and the repeal of the Stamp Act *total*. This they did in
the situation I have described.

Now, Sir, what will the adversary say to both these Acts?
If the principle of the Declaratory Act was not good, the
principle we are contending for this day is monstrous. If the
principle of the repeal was not good, why are we not at war
for a real, substantial, effective revenue? If both were bad,

---

18. *Paradise Lost*, IX, 633.

why has this Ministry incurred all the inconveniences of both and of all schemes? Why have they enacted, repealed, enforced, yielded, and now attempt to enforce again?

Sir, I think I may as well now as at any other time speak to a certain matter of fact, not wholly unrelated to the question under your consideration. We, who would persuade you to revert to the ancient policy of this kingdom, labor under the effect of this short current phrase, which the court leaders have given out to all their corps in order to take away the credit of those who would prevent you from that frantic war you are going to wage upon your colonies. Their cant is this: "All the disturbances in America have been created by the repeal of the Stamp Act." I suppress for a moment my indignation at the falsehood, baseness, and absurdity of this most audacious assertion. Instead of remarking on the motives and character of those who have issued it for circulation, I will clearly lay before you the state of America antecedently to that repeal, after the repeal, and since the renewal of the schemes of American taxation.

It is said that the disturbances, if there were any, before the repeal were slight, and without difficulty or inconvenience might have been suppressed. For an answer to this assertion I will send you to the great author and patron of the Stamp Act, who certainly meaning well to the authority of this country and fully apprised of the state of that, made, before a repeal was so much as agitated in this House, the motion which is on your journals, and which, to save the clerk the trouble of turning to it, I will now read to you. It was for an amendment to the address of the 17th of December, 1765: "*To express our just resentment and indignation at the* outrages, tumults, and insurrections *which have been excited and carried on in North America; and at the resistance given, by* open *and* rebellious *force, to the execution of the laws in that part of his Majesty's dominions. And to assure his Majesty, that his faithful Commons, animated with the warmest duty and attachment to his royal person and government, will firmly and effectually support his Majesty in all such measures as shall be necessary for preserving and supporting the legal dependence of the colonies on the mother-country,*" etc. etc.

Here was certainly a disturbance preceding the repeal, such a disturbance as Mr. Grenville thought necessary to qualify by the name of an *insurrection* and the epithet of a *rebellious* force—terms much stronger than any by which those who then supported his motion have ever since thought proper to distinguish the subsequent disturbances in America. They were disturbances which seemed to rum and his friends to justify as strong a promise of support as hath been usual to give in the beginning of a war with the most powerful and declared enemies. When the accounts of the American governors came before the House, they appeared stronger even than the warmth of public imagination had painted them; so much stronger, that the papers on your table bear me out in saying, that all the late disturbances, which have been at one time the minister's motives for the repeal of five out of six of the new court taxes, and are now his pretenses for refusing to repeal that sixth, did not amount—why do I compare them?—no, not to a tenth part of the tumults and violence which prevailed long before the repeal of that Act.

Ministry cannot refuse the authority of the commander-in-chief, General Gage, who, in his letter of the 4th of November, from New York, thus represents the state of things: "*It is difficult to say, from the* highest to the lowest, *who has not been accessory to this* insurrection, *either by writing or* mutual agreements, *to oppose the Act, by what they are pleased to term all legal opposition to it. Nothing effectual has been proposed, either to prevent or quell the tumult.* The rest of the provinces are in the same situation *as to a positive refusal to take the stamps; and threatening those who shall take them* to plunder and murder them; *and this affair stands* in all the provinces, *that unless the Act, from its own nature, enforces itself, nothing but a* very *considerable military force can do it."*

It is remarkable, Sir, that the persons who formerly trumpeted forth the most loudly the violent resolutions of the assemblies, the universal insurrections, the seizing and burning the stamped papers, the forcing stamp officers to resign their commissions under the gallows, the rifling and pulling down of the houses of magistrates, and the expulsion from their country of all who dared to write or speak a single word in defense of the powers of Parliament—those very trumpeters are now the men that represent the whole as a mere trifle, and choose to date all the disturbances from the repeal of the Stamp Act, which put an end to them. Hear your officers abroad, and let them refute this shameless falsehood, who, in all their correspondence, state the disturbances as owing to their true causes, the discontent of the people from the taxes. You have this evidence in your own archives—and it will give you complete satisfaction, if you are not so far lost to all Parliamentary ideas of information as rather to credit the lie of the day than the records of your own House.

Sir, this vermin of court reporters, when they are forced into day upon one point, are sure to burrow in another; but they shall have no refuge—I will make them bolt out of all their holes. Conscious that they must be baffled, when they attribute a precedent disturbance to a subsequent measure, they take other ground, almost as absurd, but very common in modern practice and very wicked, which is, to attribute the ill effect of ill-judged conduct to the arguments which had been used to dissuade us from it. They say that the opposition made in Parliament to the Stamp Act at the time of its passing encouraged the Americans to their resistance. This has even formally appeared in print in a regular volume, from an advocate of that faction, a Dr. Tucker.[19] This Dr. Tucker is already a dean, and his earnest labors in this vineyard will, I suppose, raise him to a bishopric. But this assertion too, just like the rest, is false. In all the papers which have loaded your table, in all the vast crowd of verbal witnesses that appeared at your bar, witnesses which were indiscriminately produced from both sides of the House, not the least hint of such a cause of disturbance has ever appeared. As to the fact of a strenuous opposition to the Stamp Act, I sat as a stranger in your gallery when the Act was under consideration. Far from anything inflammatory, I never heard a more languid debate

---

19. Tucker, Dean of Gloucester, one of the best economic writers of his time. He was a bitter Tory, and had no sympathy with the colonists; but he pointed out that even if America was separated from England, the Americans would continue to patronise English markets because they were the cheapest in the world. Since, then, the colonies would do nothing for their own defense, were in a condition of smothered rebellion, and were always ready to take advantage of the difficulties of the mother-country, they were a source of political weakness, and there was no object in retaining them.

The views of Adam Smith were much the same, though he came to a different conclusion. After showing that the system of trade monopoly was injurious to England as well as to the colonies, that the "mercantile" colonial policy had been mainly responsible for the last two wars and was likely to cause more, he points out that a peaceful separation would have many advantages. Great Britain would not only be saved the cost of the peace establishment in the

in this House. No more than two or three gentlemen, as I remember, spoke against the Act, and that with great reserve and remarkable temper. There was but one division in the whole progress of the bill; and the minority did not reach to more than 39 or 40. In the House of Lords I do not recollect that there was any debate or division at all. I am sure there was no protest. In fact, the affair passed with so very, very little noise, that in town they scarcely knew the nature of what you were doing. The opposition to the bill in England never could have done this mischief, because there scarcely ever was less of opposition to a bill of consequence.

Sir, the agents and distributors of falsehoods have, with their usual industry, circulated another lie of the same nature with the former. It is this: that the disturbances arose from the account which had been received in America of the change in the Ministry. No longer awed, it seems, with the spirit of the former rulers, they thought themselves a match for what our calumniators chose to qualify by the name of so feeble a Ministry as succeeded. Feeble in one sense these men certainly may be called; for, with all their efforts, and they have made many, they have not been able to resist the distempered vigor and insane alacrity with

---

colonies, but might settle -with them such a treaty of commerce which would effectually secure to her a free trade more advantageous than her present monopoly; at the same time the good feeling between the two great branches of the English race, which was rapidly turning into hatred, might be revived. "Such a measure," however, "never was, and never will he, adopted by any nation in the world." Dismissing this solution, therefore, he agreed with Grenville that America ought to contribute to her own defense, and that Parliament, as the depositary of Imperial power, had the right to determine what they ought to pay. Since the colonists refused to be taxed by a body in which they were not represented, colonial representatives ought to be admitted into Parliament.

which you are rushing to your ruin. But it does so happen, that the falsity of this circulation is (like the rest) demonstrated by indisputable dates and records.

So little was the change known in America, that the letters of your governors, giving an account of these disturbances long after they had arrived at their highest pitch, were all directed to the *old Ministry*, and particularly to the *Earl of Halifax*, the Secretary of State corresponding with the colonies, without once in the smallest degree intimating the slightest suspicion of any ministerial revolution whatsoever. The Ministry was not changed in England until the 10th day of July, 1765. On the 14th of the preceding June, Governor Fauquier from Virginia writes thus—and writes thus to the Earl of Halifax: "*Government is set at* defiance, *not having strength enough in her hands to enforce obedience to the laws of the community. The private distress which every man feels, increases the* general dissatisfaction *at the duties laid by the* Stamp Act, *which breaks out and shows itself upon every trifling occasion.*" The general dissatisfaction had produced some time before, that is, on the 29th of May, several strong public resolves against the Stamp Act; and those resolves are assigned by Governor Bernard as the cause of the *insurrections* in Massachusetts Bay, in his letter of the 15th of August, still addressed to the Earl of Halifax, and he continued to address such accounts to that minister quite to the 7th of September of the same year. Similar accounts, and of as late a date, were sent from other governors, and all directed to Lord Halifax. Not one of these letters indicates the slightest idea of a change, either known or even apprehended.

Thus are blown away the insect race of courtly falsehoods! Thus perish the miserable inventions of the

wretched runners for a wretched cause, which they have
fly-blown into every weak and rotten part of the country,
in vain hopes that when their maggots had taken wing
their importunate buzzing might sound something like the
public voice!

Sir, I have troubled you sufficiently with the state of
America before the repeal. Now I turn to the honorable
gentleman who so stoutly challenges us to tell, whether,
after the repeal, the provinces were quiet? This is coming
home to the point. Here I meet him directly, and answer
most readily, *They were quiet.* And I, in my turn, challenge
him to prove when, and where, and by whom, and in what
numbers, and with what violence, the other laws of trade,
as gentlemen assert, were violated in consequence of your
concession? Or that even your other revenue laws were attacked? But I quit the vantage-ground on which I stand,
and where I might leave the burden of the proof, upon him:
I walk down upon the open plain, and undertake to show
that they were not only quiet, but showed many unequivocal marks of acknowledgment and gratitude. And to give
him every advantage, I select the obnoxious colony of Massachusetts Bay, which at this time (but without hearing her)
is so heavily a culprit before Parliament[20]—I will select their
proceedings even under circumstances of no small irritation. For, a little imprudently I must say, Governor Bernard
mixed in the administration of the lenitive of the repeal no
small acrimony arising from matters of a separate nature.
Yet see, Sir, the effect of that lenitive, though mixed with
these bitter ingredients, and how this rugged people can
express themselves on a measure of concession.

---

20. This refers to the famous throwing of the tea into Boston Harbor
and the penal measures passed in consequence of it.

"*If it is not in our power,*" say they in their address to Governor Bernard, "*in so full a manner as will be expected, to show our respectful gratitude to the mother-country, or to make a dutiful and affectionate return to the indulgence of the king and Parliament, it shall be no fault of ours; for this we intend, and hope we shall be able fully to effect.*"

Would to God that this temper had been cultivated, managed, and set in action! Other effects than those which we have since felt would have resulted from it. On the requisition for compensation to those who had suffered from the violence of the populace, in the same address they say, "*The recommendation enjoined by Mr. Secretary Conway's letter, and in consequence thereof made to us, we will embrace the first convenient opportunity to consider and act upon.*" They did consider; they did act upon it. They obeyed the requisition. I know the mode has been chicaned upon, but it was substantially obeyed; and much better obeyed than I fear the Parliamentary requisition of this session will be, though enforced by all your rigor and backed with all your power. In a word, the damages of popular fury were compensated by legislative gravity. Almost every other part of America in various ways demonstrated their gratitude. I am bold to say that so sudden a calm recovered after so violent a storm is without parallel in history. To say that no other disturbance should happen from any other cause is folly. But as far as appearances went, by the judicious sacrifice of one law you procured an acquiescence in all that remained. After this experience nobody shall persuade me, when a whole people are concerned, that acts of leniency are not means of conciliation.

I hope the honorable gentleman has received a fair and full answer to his question.

I have done with the third period of your policy, that of your repeal, and the return of your ancient system, and your ancient tranquility and concord. Sir, this period was not as long as it was happy. Another scene was opened, and other actors appeared on the stage. The state, in the condition I have described it, was delivered into the hands of Lord Chatham—a great and celebrated name, a name that keeps the name of this country respectable in every other on the globe. It may be truly called:

Clarum et venerabile nomen
Gentibus, et multum nostrae quod proderat urbi.[21]

Sir, the venerable age of this great man, his merited rank, his superior eloquence, his splendid qualities, his eminent services, the vast space he fills in the eye of mankind, and, more than all the rest, his fall from power, which, like death, canonizes and sanctifies a great character, will not suffer me to censure any part of his conduct. I am afraid to flatter him; I am sure I am not disposed to blame him. Let those who have betrayed him by their adulation insult him with their malevolence. But what I do not presume to censure I may have leave to lament. For a wise man, he seemed to me at that time to be governed too much by general maxims. I speak with the freedom of history, and I hope without offense. One or two of these maxims, flowing from an opinion not the most indulgent to our unhappy species, and surely a little too general, led him into measures that were greatly mischievous to himself, and for that reason among others fatal to his country; measures, the effects of which, I

21. Lucan, IX, V, 202. "An illustrious name, venerable to the world, and one which has much helped our city."

am afraid, are forever incurable. He made an administration, so chequered and speckled; he put together a piece of joinery, so crossly indented and whimsically dovetailed; a cabinet so variously inlaid; such a piece of diversified mosaic; such a tessellated pavement without cement; here a bit of black stone, and there a bit of white; patriots and courtiers, long's friends and republicans; Whigs and Tories; treacherous friends and open enemies—that it was indeed a very curious show, but utterly unsafe to touch, and unsure to stand on. The colleagues whom he had assorted at the same boards stared at each other, and were obliged to ask, "Sir, your name?—Sir, you have the advantage of me—Mr. Such-a-one—I beg a thousand pardons—" I venture to say, it did so happen that persons had a single office divided between them, who had never spoke to each other in their lives until they found themselves, they knew not how, pigging together, heads and points, in the same truckle-bed.[22]

Sir, in consequence of this arrangement, having put so much the larger part of his enemies and opposers into power, the confusion was such that his own principles could not possibly have any effect or influence in the conduct of affairs. If ever he fell into a fit of the gout, or if any other cause withdrew him from public cares, principles directly the contrary were sure to predominate. When he had executed his plan he had not an inch of ground to stand upon. When he had accomplished his scheme of administration he was no longer a minister.

When his face was hid but for a moment his whole system was on a wide sea, without chart or compass. The

---

22. Supposed to allude to the Right Honorable Lord North and George Cooke, Esq., who were made joint paymasters in the summer of 1766, on the removal of the Rockingham, administration.

gentlemen, his particular friends, who, with the names of various departments of Ministry, were admitted to seem as if they acted a part under him, with a modesty that becomes all men, and with a confidence in him which was justified even in its extravagance by his superior abilities, had never, in any instance, presumed upon any opinion of their own. Deprived of his guiding influence, they were whirled about, the sport of every gust, and easily driven into any port; and as those who joined with them in manning the vessel were the most directly opposite to his opinions, measures, and character, and far the most artful and most powerful of the set, they easily prevailed, so as to seize upon the vacant, unoccupied, and derelict minds of his friends; and instantly they turned the vessel wholly out of the course of his policy. As if it were to insult as well as to betray him, even long before the close of the first session of his administration, when everything was publicly transacted, and with great parade, in his name, they made an Act declaring it highly just and expedient to raise a revenue in America. For even then, Sir, even before this splendid orb was entirely set, and while the western horizon was in a blaze with his descending glory, on the opposite quarter of the heavens arose another luminary, and for his hour became lord of the ascendant.

This light too is passed and set forever. You understand, to be sure, that I speak of Charles Townshend, officially the reproducer of this fatal scheme, whom I cannot even now remember without some degree of sensibility. In truth, Sir, he was the delight and ornament of this House, and the charm of every private society which he honored with his presence. Perhaps there never arose in this country, nor in any country, a man of a more pointed and finished wit; nor (where his passions were not concerned) of a more refined, exquisite, and penetrating judgment. If he had not so great a stock, as some have had who flourished formerly, of knowledge long treasured up, he knew better by far than any man I ever was acquainted with how to bring together within a short time all that was necessary to establish, to illustrate, and to decorate that side of the question he supported. He stated his matter skillfully and powerfully. He particularly excelled in a most luminous explanation and display of his subject. His style of argument was neither trite and vulgar nor subtle and abstruse. He hit the House just between wind and water. And not being troubled with too anxious a zeal for any matter in question, he was never more tedious, or more earnest, than the preconceived opinions and present temper of his hearers required, to whom he was always in perfect unison. He conformed exactly to the temper of the House, and he seemed to guide, because he was also sure to follow it.

I beg pardon, Sir, if, when I speak of this and of other great men, I appear to digress in saying something of their characters. In this eventful history of the revolutions of America, the characters of such men are of much importance. Great men are the guideposts and landmarks in the state. The credit of such men at court, or in the nation, is the sole cause of all the public measures. It would be an invidious thing (most foreign, I trust, to what you think my disposition) to remark the errors into which the authority of great names has brought the nation, without doing justice at the same time to the great qualities whence that authority arose. The subject is instructive to those who wish to form themselves on whatever of excellence has gone before them.

There are many young members in the House (such of late has been the rapid succession of public men) who never saw that prodigy, Charles Townshend, nor of course know what a ferment he was able to excite in everything by the violent ebullition of his mixed virtues and failings. For failings he had undoubtedly—many of us remember them; we are this day considering the effect of them. But he had no failings which were not owing to a noble cause, to an ardent, generous, perhaps an immoderate, passion for fame—a passion which is the instinct of all great souls. He worshipped that goddess wheresoever she appeared; but he paid his particular devotions to her in her favorite habitation, in her chosen temple, the House of Commons. Besides the characters of the individuals that compose our body, it is impossible, Mr. Speaker, not to observe that this House has a collective character of its own. That character too, however imperfect, is not unamiable. Like all great public collections of men, you possess a marked love of virtue and an abhorrence of vice. But among vices, there is none which the House abhors in the same degree with *obstinacy*. Obstinacy, Sir, is certainly a great vice; and in the changeful state of political affairs it is frequently the cause of great mischief. It happens, however, very unfortunately, that almost the whole line of the great and masculine virtues, constancy, gravity, magnanimity, fortitude, fidelity, and firmness, are closely allied to this disagreeable quality, of which you have so just an abhorrence, and, in their excess, all these virtues very easily fall into it. He who paid such a punctilious attention to all your feelings certainly took care not to shock them by that vice which is the most disgustful to you.

That fear of displeasing those who ought most to be pleased betrayed him sometimes into the other extreme. He had voted, and, in the year 1765, had been an advocate, for the Stamp Act. Things and the disposition of men's minds were changed. In short, the Stamp Act began to be no favorite in this House. He therefore attended at the private meeting, in which the resolutions moved by a right honorable gentleman were settled, resolutions leading to the repeal. The next day he voted for that repeal, and he would have spoken for it too if an illness (not, as was then given out, a political, but to my knowledge a very real illness) had not prevented it.

The very next session, as the fashion of this world passes away, the repeal began to be in as bad an odor in this House as the Stamp Act had been in the session before. To conform to the temper which began to prevail, and to prevail mostly among those most in power, he declared very early in the winter that a revenue must be had out of America. Instantly he was tied down to his engagements by some who had no objection to such experiments when made at the cost of persons for whom they had no particular regard. The whole body of courtiers drove him onward. They always talked as if the king stood in a sort of humiliated state until something of the kind should be done.

Here this extraordinary man, then Chancellor of the Exchequer, found himself in great straits. To please universally was the object of his life, but to tax and to please, no more than to love and to be wise, is not given to men. However, he attempted it. To render the tax palatable to the partisans of American revenue, he had a preamble stating the necessity of such a revenue. To close with the American distinction, this revenue was *external* or port duty; but again, to soften it to the other party, it was a duty of *supply*. To gratify the *colonists*, it was laid on British

manufactures; to satisfy the *merchants of Britain*, the duty
was trivial, and (except that on tea, which touched only
the devoted East India Company) on none of the grand
objects of commerce. To counterwork the American contraband, the duty on tea was reduced from a shilling to
threepence. But to secure the favor of those who would
tax America, the scene of collection was changed, and,
with the rest, it was levied in the colonies. What need I
say more? This fine-spun scheme had the usual fate of all
exquisite policy. But the original plan of the duties and the
mode of executing that plan both arose singly and solely
from a love of our applause. He was truly the child of the
House. He never thought, did, or said anything, but with a
view to you. He every day adapted himself to your disposition, and adjusted himself before it as at a looking-glass.

He had observed (indeed it could not escape him) that
several persons, infinitely his inferiors in all respects, had
formerly rendered themselves considerable in this House
by one method alone. They were a race of men (I hope
in God the species is extinct) who, when they rose in their
place, no man living could divine, from any known adherence to parties, to opinions, or to principles, from any
order or system in their politics, or from any sequel or connection in their ideas, what part they were going to take
in any debate. It is astonishing how much this uncertainty,
especially at critical times, called the attention of all parties
on such men. All eyes were fixed on them, all ears open
to hear them; each party gaped, and looked alternately
for their vote, almost to the end of their speeches. While
the House hung in this uncertainty, now the *hear hims* rose
from this side—now they reechoed from the other; and
that party to whom they fell at length from their tremulous

and dancing balance always received them in a tempest of applause. The fortune of such men was a temptation too great to be resisted by one to whom a single whiff of incense withheld gave much greater pain than he received delight hi the clouds of it which daily rose about him from the prodigal superstition of innumerable admirers. He was a candidate for contradictory honors, and his great aim was to make those agree in admiration of him who never agreed in anything else.

Hence arose this unfortunate Act, the subject of this day's debate; from a disposition which, after making an American revenue to please one, repealed it to please others, and again revived it in hopes of pleasing a third, and of catching something in the ideas of all.

This Revenue Act of 1767 formed the fourth period of American policy. How we have fared since then—what woeful variety of schemes have been adopted; what enforcing and what repealing; what bullying and what submitting; what doing and undoing; what straining and what relaxing; what assemblies dissolved for not obeying and called again without obedience; what troops sent out to quell resistance and, on meeting that resistance, recalled; what shiftings and changes and jumblings of all kinds of men at home, which left no possibility of order, consistency, vigor, or even so much as a decent unity of color in any one public measure—it is a tedious, irksome task. My duty may call me to open it out some other time; on a former occasion[23] I tried your temper on a part of it, for the present I shall forbear.

After all these changes and agitations, your immediate

---

23. Resolutions in May 1770.

situation upon the question on your paper is at length brought to this. You have an Act of Parliament, stating that "it is *expedient* to raise a revenue in America." By a partial repeal you annihilated the greatest part of that revenue which this preamble declares to be so expedient. You have substituted no other in the place of it. A Secretary of State has disclaimed, in the king's name, all thoughts of such a substitution in future. The principle of this disclaimer goes to what has been left as well as what has been repealed. The tax which lingers after its companions (under a preamble declaring an American revenue expedient, and for the sole purpose of supporting the theory of that preamble) militates with the assurance authentically conveyed to the colonies, and is an exhaustless source of jealousy and animosity. On this state, which I take to be a fair one, not being able to discern any grounds of honor, advantage, peace, or power, for adhering either to the Act or to the preamble, I shall vote for the question which leads to the repeal of both.

If you do not fall in with this motion, then secure something to fight for consistent in theory and valuable in practice. If you must employ your strength, employ it to uphold you in some honorable right or some profitable wrong. If you are apprehensive that the concession recommended to you, though proper, should be a means of drawing on you further but unreasonable claims, why then employ your force in supporting that reasonable concession against those unreasonable demands. You will employ it with more grace, with better effect, and with great probable concurrence of all the quiet and rational people in the provinces, who are now united with, and hurried away by, the violent—having indeed different dispositions, but a common interest. If you apprehend that on a concession you shall be pushed by metaphysical process to the extreme lines and argued out of your whole authority, my advice is this: when you have recovered your old, your strong, your tenable position, then face about—stop short, do nothing more, reason not at all; oppose the ancient policy and practice of the empire as a rampart against the speculations of innovators on both sides of the question, and you will stand on great, manly, and sure ground. On this solid basis fix your machines, and they will draw worlds towards you.

Your ministers, in their own and his Majesty's name, have already adopted the American distinction of internal and external duties. It is a distinction, whatever merit it may have, that was originally moved by the Americans themselves, and I think they will acquiesce in it, if they are not pushed with too much logic and too little sense, in all the consequences. That is, if external taxation be understood, as they and you understand it, when you please, to be not a distinction of geography, but of policy; that it is a power for regulating trade, and not for supporting establishments. The distinction, which is as nothing with regard to right, is of most weighty consideration in practice. Recover your old ground and your old tranquility—try it—I am persuaded the Americans will compromise with you. When confidence is once restored, the odious and suspicious *summum jus* will perish of course. The spirit of practicability, of moderation, and mutual convenience will never call in geometrical exactness as the arbitrator of amicable settlement. Consult and follow your experience. Let not the long story with which I have exercised your patience prove fruitless to your interests.

For my part, I should choose (if I could have my wish) that the proposition of the honorable gentleman [Mr.

Fuller] for the repeal could go to America without the attendance of the penal bills.[24] Alone I could almost answer for its success. I cannot be certain of its reception in the bad company it may keep. In such heterogeneous assortments, the most innocent person will lose the effect of his innocence. Though you should send out this angel of peace, yet you are sending out a destroying angel too; and what would be the effect of the conflict of these two adverse spirits, or which would predominate in the end, is what I dare not say: whether the lenient measures would cause American passion to subside, or the severe would increase its fury—all this is in the hand of Providence. Yet now, even now, I should confide in the prevailing virtue and efficacious operation of leniency, though working in darkness and in chaos, in the midst of all this unnatural and turbid combination, I should hope it might produce order and beauty in the end.

Let us, Sir, embrace some system or other before we end this session. Do you mean to tax America and to draw a productive revenue from thence? If you do, speak out; name, fix, ascertain this revenue; settle its quantity; define its objects; provide for its collection; and then fight when you have something to fight for, if you murder, rob; if you kill, take possession: and do not appear in the character of madmen as well as assassins, violent, vindictive, bloody, and tyrannical, without an object. But may better counsels guide you!

Again and again revert to your own principles—seek peace and ensue it—leave America, if she has taxable

---

24. The Acts closing the port of Boston, remodeling the charter of Massachusetts, and empowering magistrates to transfer trials for murder or other capital offenses to England.

matter in her, to tax herself. I am not here going into the distinctions of rights, not attempting to mark their boundaries. I do not enter into these metaphysical distinctions; I hate the very sound of them. Leave the Americans as they anciently stood, and these distinctions, born of our unhappy contest, will die along with it. They and we, and their and our ancestors, have been happy under that system. Let the memory of all actions in contradiction to that good old mode, on both sides, be extinguished forever. Be content to hind America by laws of trade; you have always done it. Let this be your reason for binding their trade. Do not burden them by taxes; you were not used to do so from the beginning. Let this be your reason for not taxing. These are the arguments of states and kingdoms. Leave the rest to the schools, for there only they may be discussed with safety. But if, intemperately, unwisely, fatally, you sophisticate and poison the very source of government, by urging subtle deductions and consequences odious to those you govern, from the unlimited and illimitable nature of supreme sovereignty, you will teach them by these means to call that sovereignty itself in question. When you drive him hard, the boar will surely turn upon the hunters. If that sovereignty and their freedom cannot be reconciled, which will they take? They will cast your sovereignty in your face. Nobody will be argued into slavery. Sir, let the gentlemen on the other side call forth all their ability, let the best of them get up and tell me, what on character of liberty the Americans have, and what one brand of slavery they are free from, if they are bound in their property and industry by all the restraints you can imagine on commerce, and at the same time are made pack-horses of every tax you choose to impose, without the least share in granting them. When they bear the burdens of unlimited monopoly, will you bring them to bear the burdens of unlimited revenue too? The Englishman in America will feel that this is slavery—that it is *legal* slavery will be no compensation either to his feelings of his understanding.

A noble lord [Lord Carmarthen], who spoke some time ago, is full of the fire of ingenuous youth; and when he has modelled the ideas of a lively imagination by further experience he will be an ornament to his country in either House. He has said that the Americans are our children, and how can they revolt against their parent? He says that if they are not free in their present state, England is not free, because Manchester and other considerable places are not represented. So then, because some towns in England are not represented, America is to have no representative at all. They are "our children"; but when children ask for bread we are not to give a stone. Is it because the natural resistance of things and the various mutations of time hinder our Government, or any scheme of government, from being any more than a sort of approximation to the right, is it therefore that the colonies are to recede from it infinitely? When this child of ours wishes to assimilate to its parent and to reflect with a true filial resemblance the beauteous countenance of British liberty, are we to turn to them the shameful parts of our constitution? Are we to give them our weakness for their strength? Our opprobrium for their glory? And the slough of slavery, which we are not able to work off, to serve them for their freedom?

If this be the case, ask yourselves this question—will they be content in such a state of slaver? If not, look to the consequences. Reflect how you are to govern a people who think they ought to be free and think they are not. Your scheme yields no revenue, it yields nothing but discontent, disorder, disobedience; and such is the state of America, that after wading up to your eyes in blood, you could only end just where you began; that is, to tax where no revenue is to be found, to—my voice fails me; my inclination indeed carries me no farther—all is confusion beyond it.

Well, Sir, I have recovered a little, and before I sit down I must say something to another point with which gentlemen urge us. What is to become of the Declaratory Act asserting the entireness of British legislative authority if we abandon the practice of taxation?

For my part I look upon the rights stated in that Act exactly in the manner in which I viewed them on its very first proposition, and which I have often taken the liberty, with great humility, to lay before you. I look, I say, on the imperial rights of Great Britain and the privileges which the colonists ought to enjoy under these rights to be just the most reconcilable things in the world.[25] The Parliament of Great Britain sits at the head of her extensive empire in two capacities: one as the local legislature of this island, providing for all things at home, immediately, and by no other instrument than the executive power; the other, and I think her nobler capacity, is what I call her *imperial character*,

---

25. The views here stated were supported by prominent colonists. Even Otis, who won fame by denouncing the writs of assistance issued in 1761 and later to authorize revenue officers to make general searches, wrote in 1765 that "the supreme legislature represents the whole society or community, as well as the dominions of the realm, and this is the true reason why the dominions are justly bound by such Acts of Parliament as name them. This is implied in the idea of a supreme sovereign power; and if the Parliament had not such authority the colonies would be independent, which none but rebels, fools, or madmen will contend for." —*Answer to the Halifax Libel*, p. 167.

in which, as from the throne of heaven, she superintends all the several inferior legislatures, and guides and controls them all, without annihilating any. As all these provincial legislatures are only coordinate to each other, they ought all to be subordinate to her; else they can neither preserve mutual peace, nor hope for mutual justice, nor effectually afford mutual assistance. It is necessary to coerce the negligent, to restrain the violent, and to aid the weak and deficient by the overruling plentitude of her power. She is never to intrude into the place of the others, while they are equal to the common ends of their institution. But in order to enable Parliament to answer all these ends of provident and beneficent superintendence, her powers must be boundless. The gentlemen who think the powers of Parliament limited, may please themselves to talk of requisitions. But suppose the requisitions are not obeyed? What! Shall there be no reserved power in the empire,[26] to supply a deficiency which may weaken, divide, and dissipate the whole? We are engaged in war, the Secretary of State calls upon the colonies to contribute; some would do it, I think most would cheerfully furnish whatever is demanded; one or two, suppose, hang back, and, easing themselves, let the stress of the draft lie on the others—surely it is proper, that some authority might legally say, "Tax yourselves for the common supply, or Parliament will do it for you." This backwardness was, as I am told, actually the case of Pennsylvania for some short time towards the beginning of the last war, owing to some internal dissensions in the colony. But whether the fact were so, or otherwise, the case is equally to be provided for by a competent sovereign power. But then this ought to be no

---

26. On the question of taxation Burke subsequently modified his attitude.

ordinary power, nor ever used in the first instance. This is what I meant, when I have said at various times that I consider the power of taxing in Parliament as an instrument of empire and not as a means of supply.

Such, Sir, is my idea of the constitution of the British empire, as distinguished from the constitution of Britain; and on these grounds I think subordination and liberty may be sufficiently reconciled through the whole, whether to serve a refining speculatist or a factious demagogue, I know not, but enough surely for the ease and happiness of man.

Sir, while we held this happy course, we drew more from the colonies than all the impotent violence of despotism ever could extort from them. We did this abundantly in the last war. It has never been once denied—and what reason have we to imagine that the colonies would not have proceeded in supplying government as liberally, if you had not stepped in and hindered them from contributing, by interrupting the channel in which their liberality flowed with so strong a course, by attempting to take, instead of being satisfied to receive? Sir William Temple says that Holland has loaded itself with ten times the impositions which it revolted from Spain, rather than submit to. He says true. Tyranny is a poor provider. It knows neither how to accumulate nor how to extract.

I charge therefore to this new and unfortunate system the loss not only of peace, of union, and of commerce, but even of revenue, which its friends are contending for. It is morally certain that we have lost at least a million of free grants since the peace. I think we have lost a great deal more, and that those who look for a revenue from the provinces never could have pursued, even in that light, a course more directly repugnant to their purposes.

Now, Sir, I trust I have shown, first on that narrow ground which the honorable gentleman measured, that you are likely to lose nothing by complying with the motion, except what you have lost already. I have shown afterwards, that in time of peace you flourished in commerce, and, when war required it, had sufficient aid from the colonies while you pursued your ancient policy; that you threw everything into confusion when you made the Stamp Act; and that you restored everything to peace and order when you repealed it. I have shown that the revival of the system of taxation has produced the very worst effects, and that the partial repeal has produced, not partial good, but universal evil. Let these considerations, founded on facts not one of which can be denied, bring us back to our reason by the road of our experience.

I cannot, as I have said, answer for mixed measures; but surely this mixture of leniency would give the whole a better chance of success. When you once regain confidence, the way will be clear before you. Then you may enforce the Act of Navigation when it ought to be enforced. You will yourselves open it where it ought still further to be opened. Proceed in what you do, whatever you do, from policy and not from rancor. Let us act like men, let us act like statesmen. Let us hold some sort of consistent conduct. It is agreed that a revenue is not to be had in America. If we lose the profit, let us get rid of the odium.

On this business of America I confess I am serious even to sadness. I have had but one opinion concerning it since I sat, and before I sat, in Parliament. The noble lord [Lord North] will, as usual, probably attribute the part taken by me and my friends in this business to a desire of getting his places. Let him enjoy this happy and original idea. If I deprived him of it, I should take away most of his wit and all his argument. But I had rather bear the brunt of all his wit, and indeed blows much heavier, than stand answerable to God for embracing a system that tends to the destruction of some of the very best and fairest of his works. But I know the map of England as well as the noble lord [Lord North], or as any other person, and I know that the way I take is not the road to preferment. My excellent and honorable friend under me on the floor [Mr. Dowdeswell] has trod that road with great toil for upwards of twenty years together. He is not yet arrived at the noble lord's destination. However, the tracks of my worthy friend are those I have ever wished to follow, because I know they lead to honor. Long may we tread the same road together, whoever may accompany us, or whoever may laugh at us on our journey! I honestly and solemnly declare, I have in all seasons adhered to the system of 1766, for no other reason than that I think it laid deep in your truest interest—and that, by limiting the exercise, it fixes on the firmest foundations a real, consistent, well-grounded authority in Parliament. Until you come back to that system there will be no peace for England.

Speech at His Arrival at Bristol Before the Election in That City (1774)

Gentlemen, I am come hither to solicit in person, that favor which my friends have hitherto endeavored to procure for me, by the most obliging, and to me the most honorable, exertions.

I have so high an opinion of the great trust which you have to confer on this occasion; and, by long experience, so just a diffidence in my abilities to fill it in a manner adequate even to my own ideas, that I should never have ventured of myself to intrude into that awful situation. But since I am called upon by the desire of several respectable fellow-subjects, as I have done at other times, I give up my fears to their wishes. Whatever my other deficiencies may be, I do not know what it is to be wanting to my friends.

I am not fond of attempting to raise public expectation by great promises. At this time, there is much cause to consider, and very little to presume. We seem to be approaching to a great crisis in our affairs, which calls for the whole wisdom of the wisest among us, without being able to assure ourselves, that any wisdom can preserve us from many and great inconveniences. You know I speak of our unhappy contest with America. I confess, it is a matter on which I look down as from a precipice. It is difficult in itself, and it is rendered more intricate by a great variety of plans of conduct. I do not mean to enter into them. I will not suspect a want of good intention in framing them. But however pure the intentions of their authors may have been, we all know that the event has been unfortunate. The means of recovering our affairs are not obvious. So many great questions of commerce, of finance, of constitution, and of policy, are involved in this American deliberation, that I dare engage for nothing, but that I shall give it, without any predilection to former opinions, or any sinister bias whatsoever, the most honest and impartial consideration of which I am capable. The public has a full right to it; and this great city, a main pillar in the commercial interest of Great Britain, must totter on its base by the slightest mistake with regard to our American measures.

Thus much, however, I think it not amiss to lay before you; that I am not, I hope, apt to take up or lay down my opinions lightly. I have held, and ever shall maintain, to the best of my power, unimpaired and undiminished, the just, wise, and necessary constitutional superiority of Great Britain. This is necessary for America as well as for us. I never mean to depart from it. Whatever may be lost by it, I avow it. The forfeiture even of your favor, if by such a declaration I could forfeit it, though the first object of my ambition, never will make me disguise my sentiments on this subject.

But I have ever had a clear opinion, and have ever held a constant correspondent conduct, that this superiority is consistent with all the liberties a sober and spirited American ought to desire. I never mean to put any colonist, or any human creature, in a situation not becoming a freeman. To reconcile British superiority with American liberty shall be my great object, as far as my little faculties extend. I am far from thinking that both, even yet, may not be preserved.

When I first devoted myself to the public service, I considered how I should render myself fit for it; and this I did by endeavoring to discover what it was that gave this country the rank it holds in the world. I found that our prosperity and dignity arose principally, if not solely, from two sources; our constitution, and commerce. Both these I have spared no study to understand, and no endeavor to support.

The distinguishing part of our constitution is its liberty. To preserve that liberty inviolate, seems the particular duty and proper trust of a member of the House of Commons. But the liberty, the only liberty I mean, is a liberty connected with order; that not only exists along with order and virtue, but which cannot exist at all without them. It inheres in good and steady government, as in its substance and vital principle.

The other source of our power is commerce, of which you are so large a part, and which cannot exist, no more than your liberty, without a connection with many virtues. It has ever been a very particular and a very favorite object of my study, in its principles, and in its details. I think many here are acquainted with the truth of what I say. This I know, that I have ever had my house open, and my poor services ready, for traders and manufacturers of every denomination. My favorite ambition is to have those services acknowledged. I now appear before you to make trial, whether my earnest endeavors have been so wholly oppressed by the weakness of my abilities, as to be rendered insignificant in the eyes of a great trading city; or whether you choose to give a weight to humble abilities, for the sake of the honest exertions with which they are accompanied. This is my trial today. My industry is not on trial. Of my industry I am sure, as far as my constitution of mind and body admitted.

When I was invited by many respectable merchants, freeholders, and freemen of this city, to offer them my services, I had just received the honor of an election at another place, at a very great distance from this. I immediately opened the matter to those of my worthy constituents who were with me, and they unanimously advised me not to decline it. They told me that they had elected me with a view to the public service; and as great questions relative to our commerce and colonies were imminent, that in such matters I might derive authority and support from the representation of this great commercial city; they desired me therefore to set off without delay, very well persuaded that I never could forget my obligations to them, or to my friends, for the choice they had made of me. From that time to this instant I have not slept; and if I should have the honor of being freely chosen by you, I hope I shall be as far from slumbering or sleeping when your service requires me to be awake, as I have been in coming to offer myself a candidate for your favor.

Speech to the Electors of Bristol

On his being declared by the sheriffs, duly elected one of the representatives in Parliament for that city, on Thursday the 3rd of November, 1774.

Gentlemen, I cannot avoid sympathizing strongly with the feelings of the gentleman who has received the same honor that you have conferred on me. If he, who was bred and passed his whole life among you; if he, who through the easy gradations of acquaintance, friendship, and esteem, has obtained the honor, which seems of itself, naturally and almost insensibly, to meet with those who, by the even tenor of pleasing manners and social virtues, slide into the love and confidence of their fellow-citizens; if he cannot speak but with great emotion on this subject, surrounded as he is on all sides with his old friends; you will have the goodness to excuse me, if my real, unaffected embarrassment prevents me from expressing my gratitude to you as I ought.

I was brought hither under the disadvantage of being unknown, even by sight, to any of you. No previous canvas was made for me. I was put in nomination after the poll was opened. I did not appear until it was far advanced. If, under all these accumulated disadvantages, your good opinion has carried me to this happy point of success; you will pardon me, if I can only say to you collectively, as I said to you individually, simply, and plainly, I thank you—I am obliged to you—I am not insensible of your kindness.

This is all that I am able to say for the inestimable favor you have conferred upon me. But I cannot be satisfied, without saying a little more in defense of the right you have to confer such a favor. The person that appeared here as counsel for the candidate, who so long and so earnestly solicited your votes, thinks proper to deny, that a very great part of you have any votes to give. He fixes a standard period of time in his own imagination, not what the law defines, but merely what the convenience of his client suggests, by which he would cut off, at one stroke, all those freedoms which are the dearest privileges of your corporation; which the common law authorizes; which your magistrates are compelled to grant; which come duly authenticated into this court; and are saved in the clearest words, and with the most religious care and tenderness, in that very act of Parliament, which was made to regulate the elections by freemen, and to prevent all possible abuses in making them.

I do not intend to argue the matter here. My learned counsel has supported your cause with his usual ability; the worthy sheriffs have acted with their usual equity, and I have no doubt, that the same equity, which dictates the return, will guide the final determination. I had the honor, in conjunction with many far wiser men, to contribute a very small assistance, hut, however, some assistance, to the forming the judicature which is to try such questions. It would be unnatural in me to doubt the justice of that court, in the trial of my own cause, to which I have been so active to give jurisdiction over every other.

I assure the worthy freemen, and this corporation, that, if the gentleman perseveres in the intentions which his present warmth dictates to him, I will attend their cause with diligence, and I hope with effect. For, if I know anything of myself, it is not my own interest in it, but my full conviction, that induces me to tell you—*I think there is not a shadow of doubt in the case.*

I do not imagine that you find me rash in declaring myself, or very forward in troubling you. From the beginning to the end of the election, I have kept silence in all matters of discussion. I have never asked a question of a voter on the other side, or supported a doubtful vote on my own. I respected the abilities of my managers; I relied on the candor of the court. I think the worthy sheriffs will bear me witness, that I have never once made an attempt to impose upon their reason, to surprise their justice, or to ruffle their temper. I stood on the hustings (except when I gave my thanks to those who favored me with their votes) less like a candidate, than an unconcerned spectator of a public proceeding. But here the face of things is altered. Here is an attempt for a general *massacre* of suffrages; an attempt, by a promiscuous carnage of *friends* and *foes*, to exterminate above two thousand votes, including *seven hundred foiled for the gentleman himself, who now complains*, and who would destroy the friends whom he has obtained, only because he cannot obtain as many of them as he wishes.

How he will be permitted, in another place, to stultify and disable himself, and to plead against his own acts, is another question. The law will decide it. I shall only speak of it as it concerns the propriety of public conduct in this city. I do not pretend to lay down rules of decorum for other gentlemen. They are best judges of the mode of proceeding that will recommend them to the favor of their fellow-citizens. But I confess I should look rather awkward, if I had been the *very first to produce the new copies of freedom*, if I had persisted in producing them to the last; if I had ransacked, with the most unremitting industry and the most penetrating research, the remotest corners of the kingdom to discover them; if I were then, all at once, to turn short, and declare, that I had been sporting all this while with the right of election; and that I had been drawing out a poll, upon no sort of rational grounds, which disturbed the peace of my fellow-citizens for a month together—I really, for my part, should appear awkward under such circumstances.

It would be still more awkward in me, if I were gravely to look the sheriffs in the face, and to tell them, they were not to determine my cause on my own principles, not to make the return upon those votes upon which I had rested my election. Such would be my appearance to the court and magistrates.

But how should I appear to the *voters* themselves? If I had gone round to the citizens entitled to freedom, and squeezed them by the hand—"Sir, I humbly beg your vote—I shall be eternally thankful—may I hope for the honor of your support?—Well!—come—we shall see you at the council-house." If I were then to deliver them to my managers, pack them into tallies, vote them off in court, and when I heard from the bar—"Such a one only! And such a one forever!—he's my man!"—"Thank you, good

Sir—Hah! My worthy friend! Thank you kindly—that's an honest fellow—how is your good family?" While these words were hardly out of my mouth, if I should have wheeled round at once, and told them, "Get you gone, you pack of worthless fellows! You have no votes—you are usurpers! You are intruders on the rights of real freemen! I will have nothing to do with you! You ought never to have been produced at this election, and the sheriffs ought not to have admitted you to poll."

Gentlemen, I should make a strange figure if my conduct had been of this sort. I am not so old an acquaintance of yours as the worthy gentleman. Indeed I could not have ventured on such land of freedoms with you. But I am bound, and I will endeavor, to have justice done to the rights of freemen; even though I should, at the same lime, be obliged to vindicate the former[1] part of my antagonist's conduct against his own present inclinations.

I owe myself, in all things, to *all* the freemen of this city. My particular friends have a demand on me that I should not deceive their expectations. Never was cause or man supported with more constancy, more activity, more spirit. I have been supported with a zeal indeed and heartiness in my friends, which (if their object had been at all proportioned to their endeavors) could never be sufficiently commended. They supported me upon the most liberal principles. They wished that the members for Bristol should be chosen for the city, and for their country at large, and not for themselves.

So far they are not disappointed. If I possess nothing else, I am sure I possess the temper that is fit for your

---

1. Mr. Brickdale opened his poll, it seems, with a tally of those very kind of freemen, and voted many hundreds of them.

service. I know nothing of Bristol, but by the favors I have received, and the virtues I have seen exerted in it.

I shall ever retain, what I now feel, the most perfect and grateful attachment to my friends—and I have no enmities; no resentment. I never can consider fidelity to engagements, and constancy in friendships, but with the highest approbation; even when those noble qualities are employed against my own pretensions. The gentleman, who is not so fortunate as I have been in this contest, enjoys in this respect a consolation full of honor both to himself and to his friends. They have certainly left nothing undone for his service.

As for the trifling petulance, which the rage of party stirs up in little minds, though it should show itself even in this court, it has not made the slightest impression on me. The highest flight of such clamorous birds is winged in an inferior reign of the air. We hear them, and we look upon them, just as you, gentlemen, when you enjoy the serene air on your lofty rocks, look down upon the gulls that skim the mud of your river, when it is exhausted of its tide.

I am sorry I cannot conclude without saying a word on a topic touched upon by my worthy colleague. I wish that topic had been passed by at a time when I have so little leisure to discuss it. But since he has thought proper to throw it out, I owe you a clear explanation of my poor sentiments on that subject.

He tells you that "the topic of instructions has occasioned much altercation and uneasiness in this city"; and he expresses himself (if I understand him rightly) in favor of the coercive authority of such instructions.

Certainly, gentlemen, it ought to be the happiness and glory of a representative to live in the strictest union, the closest correspondence, and the most unreserved communication with his constituents. Their wishes ought to have great weight with him; their opinion, high respect; their business, unremitted attention. It is his duty to sacrifice his repose, his pleasures, his satisfactions, to theirs; and above all, ever, and in all cases, to prefer their interest to his own. But his unbiased opinion, his mature judgment, his enlightened conscience, he ought not to sacrifice to you, to any man, or to any set of men living. These he does not derive from your pleasure; no, nor from the law and the constitution. They are a trust from Providence, for the abuse of which he is deeply answerable. Your representative owes you, not his industry only, but his judgment; and he betrays, instead of serving you, if he sacrifices it to your opinion.

My worthy colleague says his will ought to be subservient to yours. If that be all, the thing is innocent. If government were a matter of will upon any side, yours, without question, ought to be superior. But government and legislation are matters of reason and judgment, and not of inclination; and what sort of reason is that, in which the determination precedes the discussion; in which one set of men deliberate, and another decide; and where those who form the conclusion are perhaps three hundred miles distant from those who hear the arguments?

To deliver an opinion is the right of all men; that of constituents is a weighty and respectable opinion, which a representative ought always to rejoice to hear, and which he ought always most seriously to consider. But *authoritative* instructions, *mandates* issued, which the member is bound blindly and implicitly to obey, to vote, and to argue for, though contrary to the clearest conviction of his judgment and conscience—these are things utterly unknown to the laws of this land, and which arise from a fundamental mistake of the whole order and tenor of our constitution.

Parliament is not a *congress* of ambassadors from different and hostile interests, which interests each must maintain, as an agent and advocate, against other agents and advocates; but Parliament is a *deliberative* assembly of *one* nation, with *one* interest, that of the whole; where, not local purposes, not local prejudices, ought to guide, but the general good, resulting from the general reason of the whole. You choose a member indeed; but when you have chosen him, he is not member of Bristol, but he is a member of *Parliament*. If the local constituent should have an interest, or should form a hasty opinion, evidently opposite to the real good of the rest of the community, the member for that place ought to be as far, as any other, from any endeavor to give it effect. I beg pardon for saying so much on this subject. I have been unwillingly drawn into it; but I shall ever use a respectful frankness of communication with you. Your faithful friend, your devoted servant, I shall be to the end of my life: a flatterer you do not wish for. On this point of instructions, however, I think it scarcely possible we ever can have any sort of difference. Perhaps I may give you too much, rather than too little, trouble.

From the first hour I was encouraged to court your favor, to this happy day of obtaining it, I have never promised you anything but humble and persevering endeavors to do my duty. The weight of that duty, I confess, makes me tremble; and whoever well considers what it is, of all things in the world, will fly from what has the least likeness to a positive and precipitate engagement. To be a good member of Parliament is, let me tell you, no easy task; especially at this time, when there is so strong a disposition to run into the perilous extremes of servile compliance or wild popularity. To unite circumspection with vigor, is absolutely necessary; but it is extremely difficult. We are now members for a rich commercial *city*; this city, however, is but a part of a rich commercial *nation*, the interests of which are various, multiform, and intricate. We are members for that great nation, which however is itself but part of a great *empire*, extended by our virtue and our fortune to the farthest limits of the east and of the west. All these widespread interests must be considered, must be compared; must be reconciled, if possible. We are members for a *free* country, and surely we all know that the machine of a free constitution is no simple thing, but as intricate and as delicate as it is valuable. We are members in a great and ancient *monarchy*; and we must preserve religiously the true legal rights of the sovereign, which form the keystone that binds together the noble and well-constructed arch of our empire and our constitution. A constitution made up of balanced powers must ever be a critical thing. As such I mean to touch that part of it which comes within my reach. I know my inability, and I wish for support from every quarter. In particular I shall aim at the friendship, and shall cultivate the best correspondence, of the worthy colleague you have given me.

I trouble you no further than once more to thank you all; you, gentlemen, for your favors; the candidates, for their temperate and polite behavior; and the sheriffs, for a conduct which may give a model for all who are in public stations.

LETTERS AND ADDRESSES

Letter to the
Marquis of Rockingham
(August 23, 1775)

My dear Lord,—

When I was last in town, I wrote a short letter, by Mr. Thesiger. But I opened all I had in my thoughts so fully to Lord John Cavendish, who was then setting out for the north, that I do not know whether it be necessary to trouble your lordship any further upon the unhappy subject of that letter and conversation. However, if I did not write something on that subject, I should be incapable of writing at all. It has, I confess, taken entire possession of my mind.

We are, at length, actually involved in that war which your lordship, to your infinite honor, has made so many efforts to keep at a distance. It has come upon us in a manner more disagreeable and unpromising than the most gloomy prognostic had ever foretold it. Your lordship's observation on the general temper of the nation at this crisis is certainly just. If any indication is to be taken from external appearances, the king is entirely satisfied with the present state of his government. His spirits at his levees, at the play, everywhere, seem to be remarkably good. His ministers, too, are perfectly at their ease. Most of them are amusing themselves in the country, while England is disfurnished of its forces in the face of armed Europe, and Gibraltar and Minorca are delivered over to the custody of foreigners. They are at their ease relative to the only point which could give them anxiety—they are assured of their places.

As to the good people of England, they seem to partake every day, more and more, of the character of that administration which they have been induced to tolerate. I am satisfied, that within a few years there has been a great change in the national character. We seem no longer that eager, inquisitive, jealous, fiery people, which we have been formerly, and which we have been a very short time ago. The people look back, without pleasure or indignation; and forward, without hope or fear. No man commends the measures which have been pursued, or expects any good from those which are in preparation; but it is a cold, languid opinion, like what men discover in affairs that do not concern them. It excites to no passion; it prompts to no action.

In all this state of things I find my observation and intelligence perfectly agree with your lordship's. In one point, indeed, I have the misfortune to differ. I do not think that weeks, or even months, or years, will bring the monarch, the ministers, or the people, to feeling. To bring the people to a feeling, such a feeling, I mean, as tends to amendment or alteration of system, there must be plan and management. All direction of public humor and opinion must originate in a few. Perhaps a good deal of that humor and opinion must be owing to such direction. Events supply materials; times furnish dispositions; but conduct alone can bring them to bear to any useful purpose. I never yet knew an instance of any general temper in the nation that might not have been tolerably well traced to some particular persons. If things are left to themselves, it is my clear opinion that a nation may slide down fair and softly from the highest point of grandeur and prosperity to the lowest state of imbecility and meanness, without any one's marking a particular period in this declension, without asking a question about it, or in the least speculating on any of the innumerable acts which have stolen in this silent and insensible revolution. Every event so prepares the subsequent, that, when it arrives, it produces no surprise, nor any extraordinary alarm. I am certain that if pains, great and immediate pains, are not taken to prevent it, such must be the fate of this country. We look to the merchants in vain—they are gone from us, and from themselves. They consider America as lost, and they look to administration for an indemnity. Hopes are accordingly held out to them, that some equivalent for their debts will he provided. In the meantime, the leading men among them are kept full fed with contracts, and remittances, and jobs of all descriptions; and they are indefatigable in their endeavors to keep the others quiet, with the prospect of their share in those emoluments, of which they see their advisers already so amply in possession. They all, or the greatest number of them, begin to snuff the cadaverous *haut goût* of lucrative war. War, indeed, is become a sort of substitute for commerce. The freighting business never was so lively, on account of the prodigious taking up for transport service. Great orders for provisions and stores of all kinds, new clothing for the troops and the intended six thousand Canadians, puts life into the woolen manufacture; and a number of men of war, ordered to be equipped, has given a pretense for such a quantity of nails and other iron work, as to keep the midland parts tolerably quiet. All this, with the incredible increase of the northern market since the peace between Russia and the Porte, keeps up the spirits of the mercantile world, and induces them to consider the American war, not so much their calamity, as their resource in an inevitable distress. This is the state of *most*, not of *all* the merchants.

All this, however, would not be of so much consequence. The great evil and danger will be the full and decided engagement of Parliament in this war. Then we shall be thoroughly dipped, and then there will be no way of getting out, but by disgracing England, or enslaving America. In that state, ministry has a lease of power, as long as the war continues. The hinge between war and peace is, indeed, a dangerous juncture to ministers; but a determined state of the one or the other is a pretty safe position. When their cause, however absurdly, is made the cause of the nation, the popular cry will be with them. The style will be that their hands must be strengthened by an unreserved confidence. When that cry is once raised, and raised it infallibly will be, if not prevented, the puny voice of reason will not be heard. As sure as we have now an existence, if the meeting of Parliament should catch your lordship and your friends in an unprepared state, nothing but disgrace and ruin can attend the cause you are at the head of. Parliament will plunge over head and ears. They will vote the war with every supply of domestic and foreign force. They will pass an act of attainder; they will lay their hands upon the press. The ministers will even procure addresses from those very merchants who, last session, harassed them with petitions; and then what is left for us, but to spin out of our bowels, under the frowns of the court and the hisses of the people, the little slender thread of a peevish and captious opposition, unworthy of our cause and ourselves, and without credit, concurrence, or popularity in the nation!

I hope I am as little awed out of my senses by the fear of vulgar opinion, as most of my acquaintance. I think, on a fair occasion, I could look it in the face; but speaking of the prudential consideration, we know that all opposition is absolutely crippled, if it can obtain no kind of support without doors. If this should be found impracticable, I must revert to my old opinion, that much the most effectual and much the most honorable course is, without the obligation of a formal secession, to absent ourselves from Parliament. My experience is worth nothing, if it has not made it as clear to me as the sun, that, in affairs like these, a feeble opposition is the greatest service which can be done to ministry; and surely, if there be a state of decided disgrace, it is to add to the power of your enemies by every step you take to distress them.

I am confident that your lordship considers my importunity with your usual goodness. You will not attribute my earnestness to any improper cause. I shall, therefore, make no apology for urging, again and again, how necessary it is for your lordship and your great friends most seriously to take under immediate deliberation what you are to do in this crisis. Nothing like it has happened in your political life. I protest to God, I think that your reputation, your duty, and the duty and honor of us all, who profess your sentiments, from the highest to the lowest of us, demand at this time one honest, hearty effort, in order to avert the heavy calamities that are impending; to keep our hands from blood, and, if possible, to keep the poor, giddy, thoughtless people of our country from plunging headlong into this impious war. If the attempt is necessary, it is honorable. You will, at least, have the comfort that nothing has been left undone, on your part, to prevent the worst mischief that can befall the public. Then, and not before, you may shake the dust from your feet, and leave the people and their leaders to their own conduct and fortune.

I see, indeed, many, many difficulties in the way; but we have known as great, or greater, give way to a regular series of judicious and active exertions. This is no time for taking public business in their course and order, and only as a part in the scheme of life, which comes and goes at its proper periods, and is mixed in with occupations and amusements. It calls for the whole of the best of us; and everything else, however just or even laudable at another time, ought to give way to this great, urgent, instant concern. Indeed, my dear lord, you are called upon in a very peculiar manner. America is yours. You have saved it once, and you may very possibly save it again. The people of that country are worth preserving; and preserving, if possible, to England. I believe your lordship remembers that last year or the year before, I am not sure which, you fixed your quarters for a while in London, and sent circular letters to your friends who were concerned in the business on which you came to town. It was on occasion of the Irish absentee-tax. Your friends met, and the attempt was defeated. It may be worth your lordship's consideration, whether you ought not, as soon as possible, to draw your principal friends together. It may be then examined, whether a larger meeting might not be expedient, to see whether some plan could not be thought of for doing something in the counties and towns. The October meeting at Newmarket will be too late in the

year, and then the business of the meeting would take up
too much time from the other.

It might be objected to doing anything in this imma-
ture condition of the public temper, that the interests of
your lordship's friends might suffer in making an attempt,
which might be vigorously and rather generally opposed
and counterworked. On ordinary occasions this might be a
matter of very serious consideration. The risk ought to be
proportioned to the object; but this is no ordinary occasion.
In the first place, I lay it down that the present state of opposition is so bad, that the worst judged and most untimely
exertions would only vary the mode of its utter dissolution.
Such a state of things justifies every hazard. But, supposing
our condition better, what is an interest cultivated for, but
its aptness for public purposes? And for what public purpose do gentlemen wait, that will be more worthy of the use
of all the interests they have? I should certainly consider the
affair as desperate, if your success in such an effort depended on anything like a unanimous concurrence in the nation.
But in times of trouble, this is impossible. In such times, it
is not necessary. A minority cannot make or carry on a war;
but a minority, well composed and acting steadily, may clog
a war in such a manner, as to make it not very easy to proceed. When you once begin to show yourselves, many will
be animated to join you, who are now faint and uncertain.
Your adversaries will raise the spirit of your friends; and
the very contest will excite that concern and curiosity in
the nation, the want of which is now the worst part of the
public distemper.

Lord John has given your lordship an account of the
scheme we talked over, for reviving the importance of the
city of London, by separating the sound from the rotten

contract-hunting part of the mercantile interest, uniting it with the corporation, and joining both to your lordship.

There are now some facilities attending such a design. Lord Chatham is, in a manner, out of the question; and the court have lost, in him, a sure instrument of division in every public contest. Baker was chiefly relied on for our main part in this work. He was willing to do his part; but lo! he is called away to another part; and if he is not yet married to Miss Conyers, he will in a very few days. This puts us back. Nothing I believe can be done in it till the Duke of Portland comes to town; and then we shall have a center to turn upon. Hand, of Leeds, and some other friends, might feel the pulse of the people of Leeds and the adjacent country. Jack Lee would not let his assistance be wanting on such an occasion, and in such a cause; but if Sir George Savile could be persuaded to come forward....

I must instantly set off for Bristol. The enclosed will let your lordship see the necessity of it. The horrid expense of these expeditions would keep me at home; but that city is going headlong to the dust, through the maneuvers of the court and of the Tory party; but principally through the absurd and paltry behavior of my foolish colleague. I shall be there on the 28th for the assizes; as appearing to go on a particular occasion, may give me an excuse for not continuing long in that quarter.

I have seen J. D. and Penn. The former, I believe, has suffered himself to be made a tool; your lordship will soon see him. The latter is steady for America. His account of the determined spirit and resolution of the people there agrees with that which we have generally received. He brings a very decent and manly petition from the congress. It mentions no specific conditions, but, in general, it is for peace. Lord Chatham is the idol, as usual. I find by Penn that, in America, they have scarce any idea of the state of men and parties here, nor who are their friends or foes. To this he attributes much of their nonsense about the declaratory act.

Just as I finished this sentence, the paper gives an account (to which I cannot help giving some credit) that a great battle is fought near Boston, to the disadvantage of the unhappy Americans. Though this would add much to the difficulties of our present conduct, it makes no change in the necessity of doing something effectual before the meeting of Parliament.

Your lordship will have the goodness to present, etc, etc.

EDM. BURKE.

Letter to the
Marquis of Rockingham[†]

My dear Lord,—

I am afraid that I ought rather to beg your pardon for troubling you at all in this season of repose, than to apologize for having been so long silent on the approaching business. It comes upon us, not indeed in the most agreeable manner; but it does come upon us, and, I believe, your friends in general are in expectation of finding your Lordship resolved in what way you are to meet it. The deliberation is full of difficulties, but the determination is necessary.

The affairs of America seem to be drawing towards a crisis. The Howes are at this time in possession of, or are

---

[†] This Letter, with the two Addresses which follow it, was written upon occasion of a proposed secession from Parliament of the members in both Houses who had opposed the measures of government, in the contest between this country and the colonies in North America, from the time of the repeal of the Stamp Act. It appears, from an endorsement written by Mr. Burke on the manuscript, that he warmly recommended the measure, but (for what reasons is not stated) it was not adopted.

able to awe, the whole middle coast of America, from Delaware to the western boundary of Massachusetts Bay; the naval barrier on the side of Canada is broken, a great tract of country is open for the supply of the troops, the river Hudson opens a way into the heart of the provinces, and nothing can, in all probability, prevent an early and offensive campaign. What the Americans *have* done is, in their circumstances, truly astonishing; it is, indeed, infinitely more than I expected from them. But having done so much, for some short time I began to entertain an opinion that they might do more. It is now, however, evident that they cannot look standing armies in the face. They are inferior in everything, even in numbers; I mean in the number of those whom they keep in constant duty and in regular pay. There seem, by the best accounts, not to be above 10,000 or 12,000 men, at most, in their grand army. The rest are militia, and not wonderfully well composed or disciplined. They decline a general engagement, prudently enough, if their object had been to make the war attend upon a treaty of good terms of subjection; but when they look further, this will not do. An army that is obliged at all times and in all situations to decline an engagement may delay their ruin, but can never defend their country. Foreign assistance they have little, or none, nor are likely soon to have more. France, in effect, has no king, nor any minister accredited enough, either with the court or nation, to undertake a design of great magnitude.

In this state of things, I persuade myself, Franklin is come to Paris to draw from that court a definitive and satisfactory answer concerning the support of the colonies. If he cannot get such an answer (and I am of opinion that at present he cannot), then it is to be presumed he is authorized to negotiate with Lord Stormont on the basis of dependence on the Crown. This I take to be his errand, for I never can believe that he is come thither as a fugitive from his cause in the hour of its distress, or that he is going to conclude a long life, which has brightened every hour it has continued, with so foul and dishonorable a flight. On this supposition, I thought it not wholly impossible that the Whig party might be made a sort of mediators of the peace. It is unnatural to suppose that, in making an accommodation, the Americans should not choose rather to give credit to those who all along have opposed the measure of ministers, than to throw themselves wholly on the mercy of their bitter, uniform, and systematic enemies. It is indeed the victorious enemy that has the terms to offer; the vanquished party and their friends are, both of them, reduced in their power; and it is certain that those who are utterly broken and subdued have no option. But as this is hardly yet the case of the Americans, in this middle state of their affairs (much impaired, but not perfectly ruined), one would think it must be their interest to provide, if possible, some further security for the terms which they may obtain from their enemies. If the Congress could be brought to declare in favor of those terms, for which 100 members of the House of Commons voted last year, with some civility to the party which held out those terms, it would undoubtedly have an effect to revive the cause of our liberties in England, and to give the colonies some sort of mooring and anchorage in this country. It seemed to me that Franklin might be made to feel the propriety of such a step, and, as I have an acquaintance with him, I had a strong desire of taking a turn to Paris. Everything else failing, one might obtain a better knowledge of the general aspect of affairs abroad than, I believe, any of us possess at present. The Duke of Portland approved the idea. But when I had conversed with the very few of your Lordship's friends who were in town, and considered a little more maturely the constant temper and standing maxims of the party, I laid aside the design, not being desirous of risking the displeasure of those for whose sake alone I wished to take that fatiguing journey at this severe season of the year.

The Duke of Portland has taken with him some heads of deliberation, which were the result of a discourse with his Grace and Mr. Montagu at Burlington House. It seems essential to the cause, that your Lordship meet your friends with some settled plan either of action or inaction. Your friends will certainly require such a plan, and I am sure the state of affairs requires it, whether they call for it or not. As to the measure of a secession with reasons, after rolling the matter in my head a good deal, and turning it a hundred ways, I confess I still think it the most advisable, notwithstanding the serious objections that lie against it, and indeed the extreme uncertainty of all political measures, especially at this time. It provides for your honor. I know of nothing else that can so well do this: it is something, perhaps all, that can be done in our present situation. Some precaution, in this respect, is not without its motives. That very estimation, for which you have sacrificed everything else, is in some danger of suffering in the general wreck; and perhaps it is likely to suffer the more, because you have hitherto confided more than was quite prudent in the clearness of your intentions, and in the solidity of the popular judgment upon them. The former, indeed, is out of the power of events; the latter is full of levity, and the very creature of fortune. However, such as it is (and for one I do not

think I am inclined to overvalue it), both our interest and
our duty make it necessary for us to attend to it very carefully, so long as we act a part in public. The measure you
take for this purpose may produce no immediate effect; but
with regard to the party, and the principles for whose sake
the party exists, all hope of their preservation or recovery
depends upon your preserving your reputation.

By the conversation of some friends, it seemed as
if they were willing to fall in with this design, because it
promised to emancipate them from the servitude of irksome business, and to afford them an opportunity of re-
tiring to ease and tranquility. If that be their object in the
secession and addresses proposed, there surely never were
means worse chosen to gain their end; and if this be any
part of their project, it were a thousand times better it were
never undertaken. The measure is not only unusual, and as
such critical, but it is in its own nature strong and vehement
in a high degree. The propriety, therefore, of adopting it
depends entirely upon the spirit with which it is supported and followed. To pursue violent measures with languor
and irresolution is not very consistent in speculation, and
not more reputable or safe in practice. If your Lordship's
friends do not go to this business with their whole hearts, if
they do not feel themselves uneasy without it, if they do not
undertake it with a certain degree of zeal, and even with
warmth and indignation, it had better be removed wholly
out of our thoughts. A measure of less strength, and more
in the beaten circle of affairs, if supported with spirit and
industry, would be, on all accounts, infinitely more eligible.
We have to consider what it is that, in this undertaking, we
have against us; we have the weight of King, Lords, and
Commons, in the other scale; we have against us, within a

trifle, the whole body of the law; we oppose the more considerable part of the landed and mercantile interests; we contend, in a manner, against the whole church; we set our faces against great armies flushed with victory, and navies who have tasted of civil spoil, and have a strong appetite for more; our strength, whatever it is, must depend, for a good part of its effect, upon events not very probable. In such a situation, such a step requires not only great magnanimity but unwearied activity and perseverance, with a good deal too of dexterity and management, to improve every accident in our favor.

The delivery of this paper may have very important consequences. It is true that the court may pass it over in silence, with a real or affected contempt. But this I do not think so likely. If they do take notice of it, the mildest course will be such an address from Parliament as the House of Commons made to the king on the London remonstrance in the year 1769. This address will be followed by addresses of a similar tendency from all parts of the kingdom, in order to overpower you with what they will endeavor to pass as the united voice and sense of the nation. But if they intend to proceed further, and to take steps of a more decisive nature, you are then to consider, not what they may legally and justly do, but what a Parliament, omnipotent in power, influenced with party rage and personal resentment, operating under the implicit military obedience of court discipline, is capable of. Though they have made some successful experiments on juries, they will hardly trust enough to them to order a prosecution for a supposed libel. They may proceed in two ways; either by an *impeachment*, in which the Tories may retort on the Whigs (but with better success, though in a worse cause) the proceedings in the case of Sacheverel, or they may, without this form, proceed, as against the Bishop of Rochester, by a bill of pains and penalties more or less grievous. The similarity of the cases, or the justice, is (as I said) out of the question. The mode of proceeding has several very ancient, and very recent, precedents. None of these methods is impossible. The court may select three or four of the most distinguished among you for their victims; and therefore nothing is more remote from the tendency of the proposed act than any idea of retirement or repose. On the contrary, you have all of you, as principals or auxiliaries, a much better and more desperate conflict, in all probability, to undergo than any you have been yet engaged in. The only question is, whether the risk ought to be run for the chance (and it is no more) of recalling the people of England to their ancient principles, and to that personal interest which formerly they took in all public affairs? At any rate, I am sure it is right, if we take this step, to take it with a full view of the consequences, and with minds and measures in a state of preparation to meet them. It is not becoming that your boldness should arise from a want of foresight. It is more reputable, and certainly it is more safe, too, that it should be grounded on the evident necessity of encountering the dangers which you foresee.

Your Lordship will have the goodness to excuse me, if I state in strong terms the difficulties attending a measure, which on the whole I heartily concur in. But as, from my want of importance, I can be personally little subject to the most trying part of the consequences, it is as little my desire to urge others to dangers in which I am myself to have so inconsiderable a share.

If this measure should be thought too great for our strength, or the dispositions of the times, then the point will

be to consider what is to be done in Parliament. A weak, irregular, desultory, peevish opposition there will be, as much
too little as the other may be too big. Our scheme ought
to be such as to have in it a succession of measures, else it
is impossible to secure anything like a regular attendance;
opposition will otherwise always carry a disreputable air.
Neither will it be possible, without that attendance, to persuade the people that we are in earnest. Above all, a motion
should be well digested for the first day. There is one thing
in particular I wish to recommend to your Lordship's consideration; that is, the opening of the doors of the House
of Commons. Without this, I am clearly convinced, it will
be in the power of ministry to make our opposition appear
without doors just in what light they please. To obtain a
gallery is the easiest thing in the world, if we are satisfied
to cultivate the esteem of our adversaries by the resolution
and energy with which we act against them, but if their
satisfaction and good humor be any part of our object, the
attempt, I admit, is idle.

I had some conversation, before I left town, with the D.
of M. He is of opinion, that, if you adhere to your resolution of seceding, you ought not to appear on the first day
of the meeting. He thinks it can have no effect except to
break the continuity of your conduct, and thereby to weak-
en and fritter away the impression of it. It certainly will
seem odd to give solemn reasons for a discontinuance of
your attendance in Parliament, after having two or three
times returned to it, and immediately after a vigorous act
of opposition. As to trials of the temper of the House, there
have been of that sort so many already that I see no reason
for making another that would not hold equally good for
another after that; particularly, as nothing has happened in

the least calculated to alter the disposition of the House. If the secession were to be general, such an attendance, followed by such an act, would have force; but being in its nature incomplete and broken, to break it further by retreats and returns to the chase must entirely destroy its effect. I confess I am quite of the D. of M.'s opinion in this point.

I send your Lordship a corrected copy of the paper; your Lordship will be so good to communicate it, if you should approve of the alterations, to Lord J. C. and Sir G. S. I showed it to the D. of P. before his Grace left town, and at his, the D. of P.'s desire, I have sent it to the D. of R. The principal alteration is in the pages last but one. It is made to remove a difficulty which had been suggested to Sir G. S., and which he thought had a good deal in it. I think it much the better for that alteration. Indeed it may want still more corrections, in order to adapt it to the present or probable future state of things.

What shall I say in excuse for this long letter, which frightens me when I look back upon it? Your Lordship will take it, and all in it, with your usual incomparable temper, which carries you through so much both from enemies and friends. My most humble respects to Lady K., and, believe me, with the highest regard, ever, etc.

E. B.

I hear that Dr. Franklin has had a most extraordinary reception at Paris from all ranks of people.

Beaconsfield, Monday night, Jan. 6, 1777.

An Address to the King[†]

We, your Majesty's most dutiful and loyal subjects, several of the peers of the realm, and several members of the House of Commons chosen by the people to represent them in Parliament, do in our individual capacity, but with hearts filled with a warm affection to your Majesty, with a strong attachment to your royal house, and with the most unfeigned devotion to your true interest, beg leave, at this crisis of your affairs, in all humility to approach your royal presence.

While we lament the measures adopted by the public councils of the kingdom, we do not mean to question the legal validity of their proceedings. We do not desire to appeal from them to any person whatsoever. We do not dispute the conclusive authority of the bodies in which we have a place over all their members. We know that it is our ordinary duty to submit ourselves to the determinations of

---

†   See p. 181, note.

the majority in everything except what regards the just defense of our honor and reputation. But the situation into which the British empire has been brought, and the conduct to which we are reluctantly driven in that situation, we hold ourselves bound by the relation in which we stand both to the Crown and the people clearly to explain to your Majesty and our country.

We have been called upon in the speech from the throne at the opening of this session of Parliament, in a manner peculiarly marked, singularly emphatic, and from a place from whence anything implying censure falls with no common weight, to concur in unanimous approbation of those measures which have produced our present distresses, and threaten us in future with others far more grievous. We trust, therefore, that we shall stand justified in offering to our sovereign and the public our reasons for persevering inflexibly in our uniform dissent from every part of those measures. We lament them from an experience of their mischief, as we originally opposed them from a sure foresight of their unhappy and inevitable tendency.

We see nothing in the present events in the least degree sufficient to warrant an alteration in our opinion. We were always steadily averse to this civil war—not because we thought it impossible that it should be attended with victory, but because we were fully persuaded that in such a contest victory would only vary the mode of our ruin; and, by making it less immediately sensible, would render it the more lasting and the more irretrievable. Experience had but too fully instructed us in the possibility of the reduction of a free people to slavery by foreign mercenary armies. But we had a horror of becoming the instruments in a design of which, in our turn, we might become the victims. Knowing the inestimable value of peace, and the contemptible value of what was sought by war, we wished to compose the distractions of our country, not by the use of foreign arms, but by prudent regulations in our own domestic policy. We deplored, as your Majesty has done in your speech from the throne, the disorders which prevail in your empire, but we are convinced that the disorders of the people in the present time and in the present place are owing to the usual and natural cause of such disorders at all times and in all places where such have prevailed—the misconduct of government; that they are owing to plans laid in error, pursued with obstinacy, and conducted without wisdom.

We cannot attribute so much to the power of faction, at the expense of human nature, as to suppose, that in any part of the world a combination of men, few in number, not considerable in rank, of no natural hereditary dependencies, should be able, by the efforts of their policy alone, or the mere exertion of any talents, to bring the people of your American dominions into the disposition which has produced the present troubles. We cannot conceive that, without some powerful concurring cause, any management should prevail on some millions of people, dispersed over an whole continent, in thirteen provinces, not only unconnected, but in many particulars of religion, manners, government, and local interest totally different and adverse, voluntarily to submit themselves to a suspension of all the profits of industry and all the comforts of civil life, added to all the evils of an unequal war carried on with circumstances of the greatest asperity and rigor. This, Sir, we conceive, could never have happened but from a general sense of some grievance, so radical in its nature, and so spreading in its effects, as to poison all the ordinary satisfactions of life, to discompose the frame of society, and to convert into fear and hatred that habitual reverence ever paid by mankind to an ancient and venerable government.

That grievance is as simple in its nature, and as level to the most ordinary understanding, as it is powerful in affecting the most languid passions; it is "AN ATTEMPT MADE TO DISPOSE OF THE PROPERTY OF A WHOLE PEOPLE WITHOUT THEIR CONSENT."

Your Majesty's English subjects in the colonies, possessing the ordinary faculties of mankind, know that to live under such a plan of government is not to live in a state of freedom. Your English subjects in the colonies, still impressed with the ancient feelings of the people from whom they are derived, cannot live under a government which does not establish freedom as its basis.

This scheme, being therefore set up in direct opposition to the rooted and confirmed sentiments and habits of thinking of a whole people, has produced the effects which ever must result from such a collision of power and opinion. For we beg leave, with all duty and humility, to represent to your Majesty (what we fear has been industriously concealed from you), that it is not merely the opinion of a very great number, or even of the majority, but the universal sense of the whole body of the people in those provinces, that the practice of taxing in the mode, and on the principles, which have been lately contended for and enforced, is subversive of all their rights.

This sense has been declared, as we understand on good information, by the unanimous voice of all their assemblies; each assembly also, on this point, is perfectly unanimous within itself. It has been declared as fully by the actual voice of the people without these assemblies as by the constructive voice within them; as well by those in that country who addressed as by those who remonstrated; and it is as much the avowed opinion of those who have hazarded their all rather than take up arms against your Majesty's forces, as of those who have run the same risk to oppose them. The difference among them is, not on the grievance, but on the mode of redress; and we are sorry to say that they, who have conceived hopes from the placability of the ministers, who influence the public councils of this kingdom, disappear in the multitude of those who conceive that passive compliance only confirms and emboldens oppression.

The sense of a whole people, most gracious sovereign, never ought to be condemned by wise and beneficent rulers; whatever may be the abstract claims, or even rights, of *the supreme power*. We have been too early instructed, and too long habituated to believe, that the only firm seat of all authority is in the minds, affections, and interests of the people, to change our opinions on the theoretic reasonings of speculative men, or for the convenience of a mere temporary arrangement of state. It is not consistent with equity or wisdom to set at defiance the general feelings of great communities, and of all the orders which compose them. Much power is tolerated, and passes unquestioned, where much is yielded to opinion. All is disputed where everything is enforced.

Such are our sentiments on the duty and policy of conforming to the prejudices of a whole people, even where the foundation of such prejudices may be false or disputable. But permit us to lay at your Majesty's feet our deliberate judgment on the real merits of that principle, the violation of which is the known ground and origin of these troubles. We assure your Majesty that, on our parts, we should think ourselves unjustifiable as good citizens, and not influenced by the true spirit of Englishmen, if, with any effectual means of prevention in our hands, we were to submit to taxes to which we did not consent, either directly, or by a representation of the people, securing to us the substantial benefit of an absolutely free disposition of our own property in that important case. And we add, Sir, if fortune, instead of blessing us with a situation where we may have daily access to the propitious presence of a gracious prince, had fixed us in settlements on the remotest part of the globe, we must carry these sentiments with us, as part of our being persuaded, that the distance of situation would render this privilege in the disposal of property but the more necessary. If no provision had been made for it, such provision ought to be made or permitted. Abuses of subordinate authority increase, and all means of redress lessen, as the distance of the subject removes him from the seat of the supreme power. What, in those circumstances, can save him from the last extremes of indignity and oppression but something left in his own hands, which may enable him to conciliate the favor and control the excesses of government? When no means of power to awe or to oblige are possessed, the strongest ties which connect mankind in every relation, social and civil, and which teach them mutually to respect each other, are broken. Independency, from that moment, virtually exists. Its formal declaration will quickly follow. Such must be our feelings for ourselves; we are not in possession of another rule for our brethren.

When the late attempt practically to annihilate that inestimable privilege was made, great disorders and tumults very unhappily and very naturally arose from it. In this state of things we were of opinion that satisfaction ought instantly to be given; or that, at least, the punishment of the disorder ought to be attended with the redress of the grievance. We were of opinion that if our dependencies had so outgrown the positive institutions made for the preservation of liberty in this kingdom that the operation of their powers was become rather a pressure than a relief to the subjects in the colonies, wisdom dictated that the spirit of the constitution should rather be applied to their circumstances, than its authority enforced with violence in those very parts where its reason became wholly inapplicable.

Other methods were then recommended, and followed, as infallible means of restoring peace and order. We looked upon them to be, what they have since proved to be, the cause of inflaming discontent into disobedience, and resistance into revolt: the subversion of solemn fundamental charters, on a suggestion of abuse, without citation, evidence, or hearing; the total suspension of the commerce of a great maritime city, the capital of a great maritime province, during the pleasure of the Crown; the establishment of a military force, not accountable to the ordinary tribunals of the country in which it was kept up—these and other proceedings at that time, if no previous cause of dissension had subsisted, were sufficient to produce great troubles. Unjust at all times, they were then irrational.

We could not conceive, when disorders had arisen from the complaint of one violated right, that to violate every other was the proper means of quieting an exasperated people. It seemed to us absurd and preposterous to hold out, as the means of calming a people in a state of extreme inflammation, and ready to take up arms, the austere law which a rigid conqueror would impose, as the sequel of the most decisive victories.

Recourse, indeed, was at the same time had to force; and we saw a force sent out, enough to menace liberty, but not to awe opposition; tending to bring odium on the civil power, and contempt on the military; at once to provoke and encourage resistance. Force was sent out not sufficient to hold one town; laws were passed to inflame thirteen provinces.

This mode of proceeding by harsh laws and feeble armies could not be defended on the principle of mercy and forbearance. For mercy, as we conceive, consists, not in the weakness of the means, but in the benignity of the ends. We apprehend that mild measures may be powerfully enforced; and that acts of extreme rigor and injustice may be attended with as much feebleness in the execution as severity in the formation.

In consequence of these terrors, which, falling upon some, threatened all, the colonies made a common cause with the sufferers; and proceeded, on their part, to acts of resistance. In that alarming situation, we besought your Majesty's ministers to entertain some distrust of the operation of coercive measures, and to profit of their experience. Experience had no effect. The modes of legislative rigor were construed, not to have been erroneous in their policy, but too limited in their extent. New severities were adopted. The fisheries of your people in America followed their charters, and their mutual combination to defend what they thought their common rights brought on a total prohibition of their mutual commercial intercourse. No distinction of persons or merits was observed—the peaceable and the mutinous, friends and foes, were alike involved, as if the rigor of the laws had a certain tendency to recommend the authority of the legislator.

While the penal laws increased in rigor, and extended

in application over all the colonies, the direct force was applied but to one part. Had the great fleet and foreign army since employed been at that time called for, the greatness of the preparation would have declared the magnitude of the danger. The nation would have been alarmed, and taught the necessity of some means of reconciliation with our countrymen in America, who, whenever they are provoked to resistance, demand a force to reduce them to obedience full as destructive to us as to them. But Parliament and the people, by a premeditated concealment of their real situation, were drawn into perplexities which furnished excuses for further armaments; and while they were taught to believe themselves called to suppress a riot, they found themselves involved in a mighty war.

At length British blood was spilled by British hands—a fatal era, which we must ever deplore, because, your empire will forever feel it. Your Majesty was touched with a sense of so great a disaster. Your paternal breast was affected with the sufferings of your English subjects in America. In your speech from the throne, in the beginning of the session of 1775, you were graciously pleased to declare yourself inclined to relieve their distresses, and to pardon their errors. You felt their sufferings under the late penal acts of Parliament. But your ministry felt differently. Not discouraged by the pernicious effects of all they had hitherto advised, and notwithstanding the gracious declaration of your Majesty, they obtained another act of Parliament, in which the rigors of all the former were consolidated, and embittered by circumstances of additional severity and outrage. The whole trading property of America (even unoffending shipping in port) was indiscriminately and irrecoverably given, as the plunder of foreign enemies, to the sailors of your navy. This property was put out of the reach of your mercy. Your people were despoiled; and your navy, by a new, dangerous, and prolific example, corrupted with the plunder of their countrymen. Your people in that part of your dominions were put, in their general and political as well as their personal capacity, wholly out of the protection of your government.

Though unwilling to dwell on all the improper modes of carrying on this unnatural and ruinous war, and which have led directly to the present unhappy separation of Great Britain and its colonies, we must beg leave to represent two particulars, which we are sure must have been entirely contrary to your Majesty's order or approbation. Every course of action in hostility, however that hostility may be just or merited, is not justifiable or excusable. It is the duty of those who claim to rule over others not to provoke them beyond the necessity of the case, nor to leave stings in their minds which must long rankle, even when the appearance of tranquility is restored. We therefore assure your Majesty, that it is with shame and sorrow we have seen several acts of hostility, which could have no other tendency than incurably to alienate the minds of your American subjects. To excite, by a proclamation issued by your Majesty's governor, a universal insurrection of negro lives in any of the colonies, is a measure full of complicated horrors, absolutely illegal, suitable neither to the practice of war nor to the laws of peace. Of the same quality we look upon all attempts to bring down on our subjects an irruption of those fierce and cruel tribes of savages and cannibals, in whom the vestiges of human nature are nearly effaced by ignorance and barbarity. They are not fit allies for your Majesty in a war with your people. They are not fit instruments of an English government. These, and many other acts, we disclaim as having advised or approved when done; and we clear ourselves to your Majesty, and to all civilized nations, from any such participation whatever, before or after the fact, in such unjustifiable and horrid proceedings.

But there is one weighty circumstance which we lament equally with the causes of war, and with the modes of carrying it on—that no disposition whatsoever towards peace or reconciliation has ever been shown by those who have directed the public councils of this kingdom, either before the breaking out of these hostilities, or during the unhappy continuance of them. Every proposition made in your Parliament to remove the original cause of these troubles, by taking off taxes, obnoxious for their principle or their design, has been overruled; every bill, brought in for quiet, rejected even on the first proposition. The petitions of the colonies have not been admitted even to a hearing. The very possibility of public agency, by which such petitions could authentically arrive at Parliament, has been evaded and chicaned away. All the public declarations which indicate anything resembling a disposition to reconciliation, seem to us loose, general, equivocal, capable of various meanings or of none; and they are accordingly construed differently, at different times, by those on whose recommendation they have been made, being wholly unlike the precision and stability of public faith, and bearing no mark of that ingenuous simplicity, and native candor and integrity, which formerly characterized the English nation.

Instead of any relaxation of the claim of taxing at the discretion of Parliament, your ministers have devised a new mode of enforcing that claim, much more effectual for the oppression of the colonies, though not for your Majesty's service, both as to the quantity and application, than any of the former methods; and their mode has been expressly held out by ministers, as a plan not to be departed from by the House of Commons, and as the very condition on which the legislature is to accept the dependence of the colonies.

At length, when, after repeated refusals to hear or to conciliate, an act, dissolving your government by putting your people in America out of your protection, was passed, your ministers suffered several months to elapse without affording to them, or to any community, or any individual among them, the means of entering into that protection even on unconditional submission, contrary to your Majesty's gracious declaration from the throne, and in direct violation of the public faith.

We cannot, therefore, agree to unite in new severities against the brethren of our blood for their asserting an independency, to which, we know in our conscience, they have been necessitated by the conduct of those very persons who now make use of that argument to provoke us to a continuance and repetition of the acts, which in a regular series have led to this great misfortune.

The reasons, dread Sir, which have been used to justify this perseverance in a refusal to hear or conciliate, have been reduced into a sort of Parliamentary maxims which we do not approve. The first of these maxims is, "that the two Houses ought not to receive (as they have hitherto refused to receive) petitions containing matter derogatory to any part of the authority they claim." We conceive this maxim, and the consequent practice, to be unjustifiable by reason of the practice of other sovereign powers, and that it must be productive, if adhered to, of a total separation between this kingdom and its dependencies. The supreme power, being in ordinary cases the ultimate judge, can, as we conceive, suffer nothing in having any part of his rights excepted to, or even discussed, before himself. We know that sovereigns in other countries, where the assertion of absolute regal power is as high as the assertion of absolute power in any politic body can possibly be here, have received many petitions in direct opposition to many of their claims of prerogative; have listened to them; condescended to discuss and to give answers to them. This refusal to admit even the discussion of any part of an undefined prerogative will naturally tend to annihilate any privilege that can be claimed by every inferior dependent community, and every subordinate order in the state.

The next maxim, which has been put as a bar to any plan of accommodation, is, "that no offer of terms of peace ought to be made before Parliament is assured that these terms will be accepted." On this we beg leave to represent to your Majesty, that if in all events the policy of this kingdom is to govern the people in your colonies as a free people, no mischief can possibly happen from a declaration to them, and to the world, of the manner and form in which Parliament proposes that they shall enjoy the freedom it protects. It is an encouragement to the innocent and meritorious that they at least shall enjoy those advantages which they patiently expected, rather from the benignity of Parliament than their own efforts. Persons more contumacious may also see that they are resisting terms of perhaps greater freedom and happiness than they are now in arms to obtain. The glory and propriety of offered mercy is neither tarnished nor weakened by the folly of those who refuse to take advantage of it.

We cannot think that the declaration of independency makes any natural difference in the reason and policy of

the offer. No prince out of the possession of his dominions, and become a sovereign *de jure* only, ever thought it
derogatory to his rights or his interests to hold out to his
former subjects a distinct prospect of the advantages to be
derived from his readmission, and a security for some of
the most fundamental of those popular privileges in vindication of which he had been deposed. On the contrary,
such offers have been almost uniformly made under similar circumstances. Besides, as your Majesty has been graciously pleased, in your speech from the throne, to declare
your intention of restoring your people in the colonies to a
state of law and liberty, no objection can possibly lie against
defining what that law and liberty are; because those who
offer, and those who are to receive, terms frequently differ most widely, and most materially, in the signification of
these words, and in the objects to which they apply.

To say that we do not know, at this day, what the grievances of the colonies are (be they real or pretended), would
be unworthy of us. But while we are thus waiting to be informed of what we perfectly know, we weaken the powers
of the commissioners; we delay, perhaps we lose, the happy
hour of peace; we are wasting the substance of both countries; we are continuing the effusion of human, of Christian, of English blood.

We are sure that we must have your Majesty's heart
along with us, when we declare in favor of mixing something conciliatory with our force. Sir, we abhor the idea
of making a conquest of our countrymen. We wish that
they may yield to well ascertained, well authenticated, and
well secured terms of reconciliation; not that your Majesty
should owe the recovery of your dominions to their total waste and destruction. Humanity will not permit us to

entertain such a desire; nor will the reverence we bear to the civil rights of mankind make us even wish that questions of great difficulty, of the last importance, and lying deep in the vital principles of the British constitution, should be solved by the arms of foreign mercenary soldiers.

It is not, Sir, from a want of the most inviolable duty to your Majesty, not from a want of a partial and passionate regard to that part of your empire in which we reside, and which we wish to be supreme, that we have hitherto withstood all attempts to render the supremacy of one part of your dominions inconsistent with the liberty and safety of all the rest. The motives of our opposition are found in those very sentiments which we are supposed to violate. For we are convinced beyond a doubt that a system of dependence, which leaves no security to the people for any part of their freedom in their own hands, cannot be established in any inferior member of the British empire, without consequentially destroying the freedom of that very body in favor of whose boundless pretensions such a scheme is adopted. We know and feel that arbitrary power over distant regions is not within the competence, nor to be exercised agreeably to the forms, or consistently with the spirit, of great popular assemblies. If such assemblies are called to a nominal share in the exercise of such power, in order to screen, under general participation, the guilt of desperate measures, it tends only the more deeply to corrupt the deliberative character of those assemblies, in training them to blind obedience; in habituating them to proceed upon grounds of fact, with which they can rarely be sufficiently acquainted, and in rendering them executive instruments of designs, the bottom of which they cannot possibly fathom.

To leave any real freedom to Parliament, freedom must be left to the colonies. A military government is the only substitute for civil liberty. That the establishment of such a power in America will utterly ruin our finances (though its certain effect) is the smallest part of our concern. It will become an apt, powerful, and certain engine for the destruction of our freedom here. Great bodies of armed men, trained to a contempt of popular assemblies representative of an English people; kept up for the purpose of exacting impositions without their consent, and maintained by that exaction; instruments in subverting, without any process of law, great ancient establishments and respected forms of governments; set free from, and therefore above, the ordinary English tribunals of the country where they serve; these men cannot so transform themselves, merely by crossing the sea, as to behold with love and reverence, and submit with profound obedience to the very same things in Great Britain which in America they had been taught to despise, and had been accustomed to awe and humble. All your Majesty's troops, in the rotation of service, will pass through this discipline, and contract these habits. If we could flatter ourselves that this would not happen, we must be the weakest of men; we must be the worst, if we were indifferent whether it happened or not. What, gracious sovereign, is the empire of America to us, or the empire of the world, if we lose our own liberties? We deprecate this last of evils. We deprecate the effect of the doctrines which must support and countenance the government over conquered Englishmen.

As it will be impossible long to resist the powerful and equitable arguments in favor of the freedom of these unhappy people that are to be drawn from the principle of our own liberty, attempts will be made, attempts have been made, to ridicule and to argue away this principle, and to inculcate into the minds of your people other maxims of government and other grounds of obedience, than those which have prevailed at and since the glorious revolution. By degrees, these doctrines, by being convenient, may grow prevalent. The consequence is not certain, but a general change of principles rarely happens among a people without leading to a change of government.

Sir, your throne cannot stand secure upon the principles of unconditional submission and passive obedience; on powers exercised without the concurrence of the people to be governed; on acts made in defiance of their prejudices and habits; on acquiescence procured by foreign mercenary troops, and secured by standing armies. These may possibly be the foundation of other thrones: they must be the subversion of yours. It was not to passive principles in our ancestors that we owe the honor of appearing before a sovereign who cannot feel that he is a prince without knowing that we ought to be free. The revolution is a departure from the ancient course of the descent of this monarchy. The people at that time re-entered into their original rights; and it was not because a positive law authorized what was then done, but because the freedom and safety of the subject, the origin and cause of all laws, required a proceeding paramount and superior to them. At that ever-memorable and instructive period, the letter of the law was superseded in favor of the substance of liberty. To the free choice therefore, of the people, without either king or Parliament, we owe that happy establishment, out of which both king and Parliament were regenerated. From that great principle of liberty have originated the statutes, confirming and ratifying the establishment from which your Majesty derives your right to rule over us. Those statutes have not given us our liberties; our liberties have produced them. Every hour of your Majesty's reign your title stands upon the very same foundation on which it was at first laid; and we do not know a better on which it can possibly be placed.

Convinced, Sir, that you cannot have different fights and a different security in different parts of your dominions, we wish to lay an even platform for your throne; and to give it an unmovable stability, by laying, it on the general freedom of your people; and by securing to your Majesty that confidence and affection in all parts of your dominions which makes your best security and dearest title in this the chief seat of your empire.

Such, Sir, being among us the foundation of monarchy itself, much more clearly and much more peculiarly is it the ground of all Parliamentary power. Parliament is a security provided for the protection of freedom, and not a subtle fiction contrived to amuse the people in its place. The authority of both Houses can still less than that of the Crown he supported upon, different principles in different places; so as to be for one part of your subjects a protector of liberty, and for another a fund of despotism, through which prerogative is extended by occasional powers, whenever an arbitrary will finds itself straitened by the restrictions of law. Had it seemed good to Parliament to consider itself as the indulgent guardian and strong protector of the freedom of the subordinate popular assemblies, instead of exercising its powers to their annihilation, there is no doubt that it never could have been their inclination, because not their interest, to raise questions on the extent of Parliamentary rights; or to enfeeble privileges which were the security of their own. Powers, evident from necessity, and not suspicious from an alarming mode or purpose in the exertion, would, as formerly they were, be cheerfully submitted to; and these would have been fully sufficient for conservation of unity in the empire, and for directing its wealth to one common center. Another use has produced other consequences; and a power which refuses to be limited by moderation must either be lost, or find other more distinct and satisfactory limitations.

As for us, a supposed, or, if it could be, a real, participation in arbitrary power would never reconcile our minds to its establishment. We should be ashamed to stand before your Majesty boldly asserting, in our own favor, inherent rights which bind and regulate the Crown itself, and yet insisting on the exercise, in our own persons, of a more arbitrary sway over our fellow-citizens and fellow-freemen.

These, gracious sovereign, are the sentiments which we consider ourselves as bound, in justification of our present conduct, in the most serious and solemn manner to lay at your Majesty's feet. We have been called by your Majesty's writs and proclamations, and we have been authorized, either by hereditary privilege, or the choice of your people, to confer and treat with your Majesty, in your highest councils, upon the arduous affairs of your kingdom. We are sensible of the whole importance of the duty which this constitutional summons implies. We know the religious punctuality of attendance which, in the ordinary course, it demands. It is no light cause which, even for a time, could persuade us to relax in any part of that attendance. The British empire is in convulsions which threaten its dissolution. Those particular proceedings which cause and inflame this disorder, after many years' incessant struggle, we find ourselves wholly unable to oppose, and unwilling to behold. All our endeavors having proved fruitless, we are fearful at this time of irritating, by contention, those passions which we have found it impracticable to compose by reason. We cannot permit ourselves to countenance, by the appearance of a silent assent, proceedings fatal to the liberty and unity of the empire; proceedings which exhaust the strength of all your Majesty's dominions, destroy all trust and dependence of our allies, and leave us both at home and abroad exposed to the suspicious mercy and uncertain inclinations of our neighbor and rival powers; to whom, by this desperate course, we are driving our countrymen for protection, and with whom we have forced them into connections, and may bind them by habits and by interest—an evil which no victories that may be obtained, no severities which may be exercised, ever will or can remove.

If but the smallest hope should from any circumstances appear of a return to the ancient maxims and true policy of this kingdom, we shall with joy and readiness return to our attendance, in order to give our hearty support to whatever means may be left for alleviating the complicated evils which oppress this nation.

If this should not happen, we have discharged our consciences by this faithful representation to your Majesty and our country; and, however few in number, or however we may be overborne by practices, whose operation is but too powerful, by the revival of dangerous, exploded principles, or by the misguided zeal of such arbitrary factions as formerly prevailed in this kingdom, and always to its detriment and disgrace, we have the satisfaction of standing forth and recording our names in assertion of those principles whose operation has, in better times, made your Majesty a great prince, and the British dominions a mighty empire.

Address to the British Colonists in North America

The very dangerous crisis into which the British empire, is brought, as it accounts for, so it justifies, the unusual step we take in addressing ourselves to you.

The distempers of the state are grown to such a degree of violence and malignity as to render all ordinary remedies vain and frivolous. In such a deplorable situation an adherence to the common forms of business appears to us rather as an apology to cover a supine neglect of duty, than the means of performing it in a manner adequate to the exigency that presses upon us. The common means we have already tried, and tried to no purpose. As our last resource, we turn ourselves to you. We address you merely in our private capacity: vested with no other authority than what will naturally attend those, in whose declarations of benevolence you have no reason to apprehend any mixture of dissimulation or design.

We have this title to your attention: we call upon it in a moment of the utmost importance to us all. We find, with infinite concern, that arguments are used to persuade you of the necessity of separating yourselves from your ancient connection with your parent country, grounded on a supposition that a general principle of alienation and enmity to you had pervaded the whole of this kingdom; and that there does no longer subsist between you and us any common and kindred principles, upon which we can possibly unite consistently with those ideas of liberty in which you have justly placed your whole happiness.

If this fact were true, the inference drawn from it would be irresistible. But nothing is less founded. We admit, indeed, that violent addresses have been procured with uncommon pains by wicked and designing men, purporting to be the genuine voice of the whole people of England; that they have been published by authority here, and made known to you by proclamations, in order, by despair and resentment, incurably to poison your minds against the origin of your race, and to render all cordial reconciliation between us utterly impracticable. The same wicked men, for the same bad purposes, have so far surprised the justice of Parliament, as to cut off all communication betwixt us, except what is to go in their own fallacious and hostile channel.

But we conjure you by the invaluable pledges, which have hitherto united, and which we trust will hereafter lastingly unite us, that you do not suffer yourselves to be persuaded, or provoked, into an opinion, that you are at war with this nation. Do not think, that the whole, or even the uninfluenced majority, of Englishmen in this island are enemies to their own blood on the American continent. Much delusion has been practiced; much corrupt influence treacherously employed. But still a large, and we trust the largest and soundest, part of this kingdom perseveres in the most perfect unity of sentiments, principles, and affections, with you. It spreads out a large and liberal platform of common liberty, upon which we may all unite forever. It abhors the hostilities which have been carried on against you, as much as you who feel the cruel effect of them. It has disclaimed, in the most solemn manner, at the foot of the throne itself, the addresses, which tended to irritate your sovereign against his colonies. We are persuaded that even many of those who unadvisedly have put their hands to such intemperate and inflammatory addresses, have not at all apprehended to what such proceedings naturally lead; and would sooner die, than afford them the least countenance, if they were sensible of their fatal effects on the union and liberty of the empire.

For ourselves, we faithfully assure you that we have ever considered you as rational creatures, as free agents, as men willing to pursue, and able to discern, your own true interest. We have wished to continue united with you, in order that a people of one origin and one character should be directed to the rational objects of government by joint counsels, and protected in them by a common force. Other subordination in you we require none. We have never pressed that argument of general union to the extinction of your local, natural, and just privileges. Sensible of what is due both to the dignity and weakness of man, we have never wished to place over you any government, over which, in great fundamental points, you should have no sort of check or control in your own hands, or which should be repugnant to your situation, principles, and character.

No circumstances of fortune, you may be assured, will ever induce us to form, or tolerate, any such design. If the disposition of Providence (which we deprecate) should even prostrate you at our feet, broken in power and in spirit, it would be our duty and inclination to revive, by every practical means, that free energy of mind, which a fortune unsuitable to your virtue had damped and dejected, and to put you voluntarily in possession of those very privileges which you had in vain attempted to assert by arms. For we solemnly declare, that although we should look upon a separation from you as a heavy calamity (and the heavier, because we know you must have your full share in it), yet we had much rather see you totally independent of this Crown and kingdom, than joined to it by so unnatural a conjunction as that of freedom with servitude; a conjunction which, if it were at all practicable, could not fail in the end of being more mischievous to the peace, prosperity, greatness, and power of this nation, than beneficial, by an enlargement of the bounds of nominal empire.

But because, brethren, these professions are general, and such as even enemies may make, when they reserve to themselves the construction of what servitude and what liberty are, we inform you, that we adopt your own standard of the blessing of free government. We are of opinion that you ought to enjoy the sole and exclusive right of freely granting, and applying to the support of your administration, what God has freely granted as a reward to your industry. And we do not confine this immunity from exterior coercion in this great point solely to what regards your local establishment, but also to what may be thought proper for the maintenance of the whole empire. In this resource we cheerfully trust and acquiesce, satisfied by evident reason that no other expectation of revenue can possibly be given by free men, and knowing, from an experience uniform both on yours and on our side of the ocean, that such an expectation has never yet been disappointed. We know of no road to your coffers but through your affections.

To manifest our sentiments the more clearly to you and to the world on this subject, we declare our opinion, that if no revenue at all (which, however, we are far from supposing) were to be obtained from you to this kingdom, yet as long as it is our happiness to be joined with you in bonds of fraternal charity and freedom, with an open and flowing commerce between us, one principle of enmity and friendship pervading, and one right of war and peace directing, the strength of the whole empire, we are likely to be, at least, as powerful as any nation, or as any combination of nations, which in the course of human events may be formed against us. We are sensible that a very large proportion of the wealth and power of every empire must necessarily be thrown upon the presiding state. We are sensible that such a state ever has borne, and ever must bear, the greatest part, and sometimes the whole, of the public expenses, and we think her well indemnified for that (rather apparent than real) inequality of charge, in the dignity and preeminence she enjoys, and in the superior opulence which, after all charges defrayed, must necessarily remain at the center of affairs. Of this principle we are not without evidence in our remembrance (not yet effaced) of the glorious and happy days of this empire. We are, therefore, incapable of that prevaricating style, by which, when taxes without your consent are to be extorted from you, this nation is represented as in the lowest state of impoverishment and public distress; but when we are called upon to oppress you by force of arms, it is painted as scarcely feeling its impositions, abounding with wealth, and inexhaustible in its resources.

We also reason and feel as you do on the invasion of your charters. Because the charters comprehend the essential forms by which you enjoy your liberties, we regard them as most sacred, and by no means to be taken away or altered without process, without examination, and without hearing, as they have lately been. We even think that they ought by no means to be altered at all but at the desire of the greater part of the people who live under them. We cannot look upon men as delinquents in the mass; much less are we desirous of lording over our brethren, insulting their honest pride, and wantonly overturning establishments judged to be just and convenient by the public wisdom of this nation at their institution, and which long and inveterate use has taught you to look up to with affection and reverence. As we disapproved of the proceedings with regard to the forms of your constitution, so we are equally tender of every leading principle of free government. We never could think with approbation of putting the military power out of the coercion of the civil justice in the country where it acts.

We disclaim also any sort of share in that other measure which has been used to alienate your affections from this country, namely, the introduction of foreign mercenaries. We saw their employment with shame and regret, especially in numbers so far exceeding the English forces as in effect to constitute vassals who have no sense of freedom and strangers who have no common interest or feelings as the arbiters of our unhappy domestic quarrel.

We likewise saw with shame the African slaves, who had been sold to you on public faith, and under the sanction of acts of Parliament, to be your servants and your guards, employed to cut the throats of their masters.

You will not, we trust, believe that, born in a civilized country, formed to gentle manners, trained in a merciful religion, and living in enlightened and polished times where even foreign hostility is softened from its original sternness, we could have thought of letting loose upon you, our late beloved brethren, these fierce tribes of savages and cannibals, in whom the traces of human nature are effaced by ignorance and barbarity. We rather wished to have joined with you in bringing gradually that unhappy part of mankind into civility, order, piety, and virtuous discipline, than to have confirmed their evil habits, and increased their natural ferocity, by fleshing them in the slaughter of you, whom our wiser and better ancestors had sent into the wilderness, with the express view of introducing, along with our holy religion, its humane and charitable manners. We do not hold that all things are lawful in war. We should think that every barbarity, in fire, in wasting, in murders, in tortures, and other cruelties too horrible, and too full of turpitude, for Christian mouths to utter, or ears to hear, if done at our instigation by those who we know will make war thus if they make it at all, to be to all intents and purposes as if done by ourselves. We clear ourselves to you our brethren, to the present age, and to future generations, to our king and our country, and to Europe, which as a spectator beholds this tragic scene, of every part or share in adding this last and worst of evils to the inevitable mischiefs of a civil war.

We do not call you rebels and traitors. We do not call for the vengeance of the Crown against you. We do not know how to qualify millions of our countrymen, contending with one heart for an admission to privileges which we have ever thought our own happiness and honor, by odious and unworthy names. On the contrary, we highly revere the principles on which you act, though we lament some of their effects. Armed as you are, we embrace you as our friends, and as our brethren, by the best and dearest ties of relation.

We view the establishment of the English colonies on principles of liberty as that which is to render this kingdom venerable to future ages. In comparison of this we regard all the victories and conquests of our warlike ancestors, or of our own times, as barbarous, vulgar distinctions, in which many nations, whom we look upon with little respect or value, have equaled if not far exceeded us. This is the peculiar and appropriated glory of England. Those who *have and who hold* to that foundation of common liberty, whether on this or on your side of the ocean, we consider as the true, and the only true, Englishmen. Those who depart from it, whether there or here, are attainted, corrupted in blood, and wholly fallen from their original rank and value. They are the real rebels to the fair constitution and just supremacy of England.

We exhort you, therefore, to cleave for ever to those principles, as being the true bond of union in this empire; and to show, by a manly perseverance, that the sentiments of honor, and the rights of mankind, are not held by the uncertain events of war, as you have hitherto shown a glorious and affecting example to the world that they are not dependent on the ordinary conveniences and satisfactions of life.

Knowing no other arguments to be used to men of liberal minds, it is upon these very principles, and these alone, we hope and trust that no flattering and no alarming circumstances shall permit you to listen to the seductions of those who would alienate you from your dependence on the Crown and Parliament of this kingdom. That very liberty, which you so justly prize above all things, originated here, and it may be very doubtful whether, without being constantly fed from the original fountain, it can be at all perpetuated or preserved in its native purity and perfection. Untried forms of government may, to unstable minds, recommend themselves even by their novelty. But you will do well to remember that England has been great and happy under the present limited monarchy (subsisting in more or less vigor and purity) for several hundred years. None but England can communicate to you the benefits of such a constitution. We apprehend you are not now, nor for ages are likely to be, capable of that form of constitution in an independent state. Besides, let us suggest to you our apprehensions that your present union (in which we rejoice, and which we wish long to subsist) cannot always subsist without the authority and weight of this great and long-respected body, to equipoise, and to preserve you among yourselves in a just and fair equality. It may not even be impossible that a long course of war with the administration of this country may be but a prelude to a series of wars and contentions among yourselves, to end, at length (as such scenes have too often ended), in a species of humiliating repose, which nothing but the preceding calamities would reconcile to the dispirited few who survived them. We allow that even this evil is worth the risk to men of honor, when rational liberty is at stake, as in the present case we confess and lament that it is. But if ever a real security, by Parliament, is given against the terror or the abuse of unlimited power, and after such security given you should persevere in resistance, we leave you to consider whether the risk is not incurred without an object, or incurred for an object infinitely diminished by such concessions in its importance and value.

As to other points of discussion, when these grand fundamentals of your grants and charters are once settled and ratified by clear Parliamentary authority, as the ground for peace and forgiveness on our side, and for a manly and liberal obedience on yours, treaty and a spirit of reconciliation will easily and securely adjust whatever may remain. Of this we give you our word, that so far as we are at present concerned, and if by any event we should become more concerned hereafter, you may rest assured, upon the pledges of honor not forfeited, faith not violated, and uniformity of character and profession not yet broken, we at least, on these grounds, will never fail you.

Respecting your wisdom, and valuing your safety, we do not call upon you to trust your existence to your enemies. We do not advise you to an unconditional submission. With satisfaction we assure you that almost all in both Houses (however unhappily they have been deluded, so as not to give any immediate effect to their opinion) disclaim that idea. You can have no friends in whom you cannot rationally confide. But Parliament is your friend from the moment in which, removing its confidence from those who have constantly deceived its good intentions, it adopts the sentiments of those who have made sacrifices (inferior indeed to yours), but have, however, sacrificed enough to demonstrate the sincerity of their regard and value for your liberty and prosperity.

Arguments may be used to weaken your confidence in that public security, because, from some unpleasant appearances, there is a suspicion that Parliament itself is somewhat fallen from its independent spirit. How far this supposition may be founded in fact we are unwilling to determine. But we are well assured from experience, that even if all were true that is contended for (and in the extent, too, in which it is argued) yet as long as the solid and well-disposed forms of this constitution remain, there ever is within Parliament itself a power of renovating its principles, and effecting a self-reformation, which no other plan of government has ever contained. This constitution has therefore admitted innumerable improvements, either for the correction of the original scheme, or for removing corruptions, or for bringing its principles better to suit those changes which have successively happened in the circumstances of the nation, or in the manners of the people.

We feel that the growth of the colonies is such a change of circumstances, and that our present dispute is an exigency as pressing as any whichever demanded a revision of our government. Public troubles have often called upon this country to look into its constitution. It has ever been bettered by such a revision. If our happy and luxuriant increase of dominion, and our diffused population, have outgrown the limits of a constitution made for a contracted object, we ought to bless God, who has furnished us with this noble occasion for displaying our skill and beneficence in enlarging the scale of rational happiness, and of making the politic generosity of this kingdom as extensive as its fortune. If we set about this great work, on both sides, with the same conciliatory turn of mind, we may now, as in former times, owe even to our mutual mistakes, contentions, and animosities, the lasting concord, freedom, happiness, and glory of this empire.

Gentlemen, the distance between us, with other obstructions, has caused much misrepresentation of our mutual sentiments. We, therefore, to obviate them as well as we are able, take this method of assuring you of our thorough

detestation of the whole war, and particularly the mercenary and savage war carried on or attempted against you:
our thorough abhorrence of all addresses adverse to you,
whether public or private; our assurances of an invariable
affection towards you; our constant regard to your privileges and liberties; and our opinion of the solid security
you ought to enjoy for them, under the paternal care and
nurture of a protecting Parliament.

Though many of us have earnestly wished that the authority of that august and venerable body, so necessary in
many respects to the union of the whole, should be rather
united by its own equity and discretion, than by any bounds
described by positive laws and public compacts; and though
we felt the extreme difficulty, by any theoretical limitations,
of qualifying that authority so as to preserve one part and
deny another; and though you (as we gratefully acknowledge) had acquiesced most cheerfully under that prudent
reserve of the constitution, at that happy moment, when
neither you nor we apprehended a further return of the
exercise of invidious powers, we are now as fully persuaded
as you can be, by the malice, inconstancy, and perverse in-
quietude of many men, and by the incessant endeavors of
an arbitrary faction, now too powerful, that our common
necessities do require a full explanation and ratified security
for your liberties and our quiet.

Although his Majesty's condescension in committing
the direction of his affairs into the hands of the known
friends of his family, and of the liberties of all his people,
would, we admit, be a great means of giving repose to your
minds, as it must give infinite facility to reconciliation, yet
we assure you, that we think, with such a security as we
recommend, adopted from necessity, and not choice, even

by the unhappy authors and instruments of the public mis-
fortunes, that the terms of reconciliation, if once accepted
by Parliament, would not be broken. We also pledge ourselves to you, that we should give, even to those unhappy
persons, a hearty support in effectuating the peace of the
empire; and every opposition in an attempt to cast it again
into disorder.

When that happy hour shall arrive, let us in all affection
recommend to you the wisdom of continuing, as in former times, or even in a more ample measure, the support
of your government, and even to give to your administration some degree of reciprocal interest in your freedom.
We earnestly wish you not to furnish your enemies, here
or elsewhere, with any sort of pretexts for reviving quarrels by too reserved and severe or penurious an exercise of
those sacred rights, which no pretended abuse in the exercise ought to impair, nor, by overstraining the principles of
freedom, to make them less compatible with those haughty
sentiments in others, which the very same principles may
be apt to breed in minds not tempered with the utmost equity and justice.

The well-wishers of the liberty and union of this empire salute you, and recommend you most heartily to the
Divine protection.

Letter to
John Farr and John Harris, Esqrs.
(Sheriffs of the City of Bristol),
On the Affairs of America
(1777)

Gentlemen,—

I have the honor of sending you the two last Acts which have been passed with regard to the troubles in America. These Acts are similar to all the rest which have been made on the same subject. They operate by the same principle, and they are derived from the very same policy. I think they complete the number of this sort of statutes to nine. It affords no matter for very pleasing reflection to observe that our subjects diminish as our laws increase.

If I have the misfortune of differing with some of my fellow citizens on this great and arduous subject, it is no small consolation to me that I do not differ from you. With you I am perfectly united. We are heartily agreed in our detestation of a civil war. We have ever expressed the most unqualified disapprobation of all the steps which have led to it, and of all those which tend to prolong it. And I have no doubt that we feel exactly the same emotions of grief and shame in all its miserable consequences, whether they

appear, on the one side or the other, in the shape of victories or defeats, of captures made from the English on the
continent or from the English in these islands, of legislative
regulations which subvert the liberties of our brethren or
which undermine our own.

Of the first of these statutes (that for the letter of marque)
I shall say little. Exceptionable as it may be, and as I think it is
in some particulars, it seems the natural, perhaps necessary,
result of the measures we have taken and the situation we are
in. The other (for a partial suspension of the *Habeas Corpus*)
appears to me of a much deeper malignity.[1] During its progress through the House of Commons it has been amended,
so as to express, more distinctly than at first it did, the avowed
sentiments of those who framed it; and the main ground of
my exception to it is because it does express, and does carry
into execution, purposes which appear to me so contradictory to all the principles, not only of the constitutional policy
of Great Britain, but even of that species of hostile justice
which no asperity of war wholly extinguishes in the minds of
a civilized people.

It seems to have in view two capital objects—the first
to enable administration to confine, as long as it shall think
proper, those whom that Act is pleased to qualify by the
name of pirates. Those so qualified I understand to be the
commanders and mariners of such privateers and ships of
war belonging to the colonies as in the course of this unhappy contest may fall into the hands of the crown. They
are therefore to be detained in prison, under the criminal
description of piracy, to a future trial and ignominious punishment, whenever circumstances shall make it convenient

---

1. The suspension applied to North America and the high seas.

to execute vengeance on them under the color of that odious and infamous offense.

To this first purpose of the law I have no small dislike, because the Act does not (as all laws and all equitable transactions ought to do) fairly describe its object. The persons who make a naval war upon us in consequence of the present troubles may be rebels, but to call and treat them as pirates is confounding not only the natural distinction of things, but the order of crimes, which, whether by putting them from a higher part of the scale to the lower, or from the lower to the higher, is never done without dangerously disordering the whole frame of jurisprudence. Though piracy may be, in the eye of the law, a *less* offense than treason, yet as both are in effect punished with the same death, the same forfeiture, and the same corruption of blood, I never would take from any fellow creature whatever any sort of advantage which he may derive to his safety from the pity of mankind, or to his reputation from their general feelings, by degrading his offense when I cannot soften his punishment. The general sense of mankind tells me that those offenses which may possibly arise from mistaken virtue are not in the class of infamous actions. Lord Coke, the oracle of the English law, conforms to that general sense where he says that "those things which are of the highest criminality may be of the least disgrace." The Act prepares a sort of masked proceeding, not honorable to the justice of the kingdom, and by no means necessary for its safety. I cannot enter into it. If Lord Balmerino[2] in the last rebellion had driven off the cattle of twenty clans, I should have thought it

---

2.   Arthur Elphinstone, 6th Lord Balmerino, 1688–1746, Jacobite, beheaded for treason.

would have been a scandalous and low juggle, utterly unworthy of the manliness of an English judicature, to have tried him for felony as a stealer of cows.

Besides, I must honestly tell you that I could not vote for, or countenance in any way, a statute which stigmatizes with the crime of piracy these men whom an Act of Parliament had previously put out of the protection of the law. When the legislature of this Kingdom had ordered all their ships and goods, for the mere new-created offense of exercising trade, to be divided as a spoil among the seamen of the navy, to consider the necessary reprisal of an unhappy, proscribed, interdicted people as the crime of piracy would have appeared, in any other legislature than ours, a strain of the most insulting and most unnatural cruelty and injustice. I assure you I never remember to have heard of anything like it in any time or country.

The second professed purpose of the Act is to detain in England for trial those who shall commit high treason in America.

That you may be enabled to enter into the true spirit of the present law, it is necessary, gentlemen, to apprise you that there is an Act, made so long ago as in the reign of Henry the Eighth, before the existence or thought of any English colonies in America, for the trial in this kingdom of treasons committed out of the realm. In the year 1769, Parliament thought proper to acquaint the crown with their construction of that Act in a formal address, wherein they entreated his Majesty to cause persons charged with high treason in America to be brought into this kingdom for trial. By this Act of Henry the Eighth, *so construed and so applied*, almost all that is substantial and beneficial in a trial by jury is taken away from the subject in the colonies. This is, however, saying too little, for to try a man under that Act is, in effect, to condemn him unheard. A person is brought hither in the dungeon of a ship's hold, thence he is vomited into a dungeon on land, loaded with irons, unfurnished with money, unsupported by friends, three thousand miles from all means of calling upon or confronting evidence, where no one local circumstance that tends to detect perjury can possibly be judged of—such a person may be executed according to form, but he can never be tried according to justice.

I therefore could never reconcile myself to the bill I send you, which is expressly provided to remove all inconveniences from the establishment of a mode of trial which has ever appeared to me most unjust and most unconstitutional. Far from removing the difficulties which impede the execution of so mischievous a project, I would heap new difficulties upon it if it were in my power. All the ancient, honest, juridical principles and institutions of England are so many clogs to check and retard the headlong course of violence and oppression. They were invented for this one good purpose, that what was not just should not be convenient. Convinced of this I would leave things as I found them. The old, cool-headed, general law is as good as any deviation dictated by present heat.

I could see no fair, justifiable expedience pleaded to favor this new suspension of the liberty of the subject. If the English in the colonies can support the independency to which they have been unfortunately driven, I suppose nobody has such a fanatical zeal for the criminal justice of Henry the Eighth that he will contend for executions which must be retaliated tenfold on his own friends, or who has conceived so strange an idea of English dignity as to think the defeats in America compensated by the triumphs at Tyburn. If, on the contrary, the colonies are reduced to the obedience of the crown, there must be, under that authority, tribunals in the country itself fully competent to administer justice on all offenders. But if there are not, and that we must suppose a thing so humiliating to our Government as that all this vast continent should unanimously concur in thinking that no ill fortune can convert resistance to the royal authority into a criminal act, we may call the effect of our victory peace, or obedience, or what we will; but the war is not ended, the hostile mind continues in full vigor, and it continues under a worse form. If your peace be nothing more than a sullen pause from arms, if their quiet be nothing but the meditation of revenge, where smitten pride smarting from its wounds festers into new rancor, neither the Act of Henry the Eighth, nor its handmaid of this reign, will answer any wise end of policy or justice. For if the bloody fields which they saw and felt are not sufficient to subdue the reason of America (to use the expressive phrase of a great lord in office), it is not the judicial slaughter which is made in another hemisphere against their universal sense of justice that will ever reconcile them to the British Government.

I take it for granted, gentlemen, that we sympathize in a proper horror of all punishment further than as it serves for an example. To whom then does the example of an execution in England for this American rebellion apply? Remember, you are told every day, that the present is a contest between the two countries, and that we in England are at war for *our own* dignity against our rebellious children. Is this true? If it be, it is surely among such rebellious children that examples for disobedience should be made, to be in any degree instructive; for whoever thought of teaching parents their duty by an example from the punishment of an undutiful son? As well might the execution of a fugitive negro in the plantations be considered as a lesson to teach masters humanity to their slaves. Such executions may indeed satiate our revenge, they may harden our hearts, and puff us up with pride and arrogance. Alas, this is not instruction!

If anything can be drawn from such examples by a parity of the case, it is to show how deep their crime and how heavy their punishment will be who shall at any time dare to resist a distant power actually disposing of their property, without their voice or consent to the disposition, and overturning their franchises without charge or hearing. God forbid that England should ever read this lesson written in the blood of *any* of her offspring!

War is at present carried on between the king's natural and foreign troops on one side and the English in America on the other, upon the usual footing of other wars and accordingly an exchange of prisoners has been regularly made from the beginning. If notwithstanding this hitherto equal procedure, upon some prospect of ending the war with success (which, however, may be delusive), administration prepares to act against those as *traitors* who remain in their hands at the end of the troubles, in my opinion we shall exhibit to the world as indecent a piece of injustice as ever civil fury has produced. If the prisoners, who have been exchanged, have not by that exchange been *virtually pardoned*, the cartel (whether avowed or understood) is a cruel fraud; for you have received the life of a man, and you ought to return a life for it, or there is no parity of fairness in the transaction.

If, on the other hand, we admit that they who are actually exchanged are pardoned, but contend that you may justly reserve for vengeance those who remain unexchanged,
then this unpleasant and unhandsome consequence will
follow: that you judge of the delinquency of men merely
by the time of their guilt, and not by the heinousness of
it, and you make fortune and accidents, and not the moral
qualities of human action, the rule of your justice.

These strange incongruities must ever perplex those
who confound the unhappiness of civil dissensions with the
crime of treason. Whenever a rebellion really and truly exists, which is as easily known in fact as it is difficult to define
in words, government has not entered into such military
conventions, but has ever declined all intermediate treaty
which should put rebels in possession of the law of nations
with regard to war. Commanders would receive no benefits at their hands, because they could make no return for
them. Who has ever heard of capitulation, and parole of
honor, and exchange of prisoners, in the late rebellions in
this kingdom? The answer to all demands of that sort was,
"We can engage for nothing; you are at the king's pleasure."
We ought to remember, that if our present enemies be, in
reality and truth, rebels, the king's generals have no right to
release them upon any conditions whatsoever; and they are
themselves answerable to the law and as much in want of a
pardon for doing so as the rebels whom they release.

Lawyers, I know, cannot make the distinction for which
I contend, because they have their strict rule to go by. But
legislators ought to do what lawyers cannot; for they have
no other rules to bind them but the great principles of reason and equity, and the general sense of mankind. These
they are bound to obey and follow; and rather to enlarge and

enlighten law by the liberality of legislative reason than to fetter and bind their higher capacity by the narrow constructions of subordinate, artificial justice. If we had adverted to this, we never could consider the convulsions of a great empire, not disturbed by a little disseminated faction, but divided by whole communities and provinces, and entire legal representatives of a people, as fit matter of discussion under a commission of Oyer and Terminer. It is as opposite to reason and prudence as it is to humanity and justice.

This Act, proceeding on these principles, that is, preparing to end the present troubles by a trial of one sort of hostility under the name of piracy, and of another by the name of treason, and executing the Act of Henry the Eighth according to a new and unconstitutional interpretation, I have thought evil and dangerous, even though the instruments of effecting such purposes had been merely of a neutral quality.

But it really appears to me that the means which this Act employs are, at least, as exceptionable as the end. Permit me to open myself a little upon this subject, because it is of importance to me, when I am obliged to submit to the power without acquiescing in the reason of an Act, that I should justify my dissent by such arguments as may be supposed to have weight with a sober man.

The main operative regulation of the Act is to suspend the common law, and the statute *Habeas Corpus* (the sole securities either for liberty or justice), with regard to all those who have been out of the realm, or on the high seas, within a given time. The rest of the people, as I understand, are to continue as they stood before.

I confess, gentlemen, that this appears to me as bad in the principle, and far worse in the consequence, than

a universal suspension of the *Habeas Corpus* Act; and the
limiting qualification, instead of taking out the sting, does
in my humble opinion sharpen and envenom it to a greater
degree. Liberty, if I understand it at all, is a general principle, and the clear right of all the subjects within the realm
or of none. Partial freedom seems to me a most invidious
mode of slavery. But, unfortunately, it is the kind of slavery the most easily admitted in times of civil discord; for
parties are but too apt to forget their own future safety in
their desire of sacrificing their enemies. People without
too much difficulty admit the entrance of that injustice of
which they are not to be the immediate victims. In times
of high proceeding it is never the faction of the predominant power that is in danger; for no tyranny chastises its
own instruments. It is the obnoxious and the suspected
who want the protection of law; and there is nothing to
bridle the partial violence of state factions but this: "that
whenever an Act is made for a cessation of law and justice, the whole people should be universally subjected to the
same suspension of their franchises." The alarm of such a
proceeding would then be universal. It would operate as
a sort of call to the nation. It would become every man's
immediate and instant concern to be made very sensible
of *the absolute necessity* of this total eclipse of liberty. They
would more carefully advert to every renewal, and more
powerfully resist it. These great determined measures are
not commonly so dangerous to freedom. They are marked
with too strong lines to slide into use. No plea, nor pretense,
of *inconvenience or evil example* (which must in their nature be
daily and ordinary incidents) can be admitted as a reason
for such mighty operations. But the true danger is, when
liberty is nibbled away, for expedients, and by parts. The

Habeas Corpus Act supposes, contrary, to the genius of most
other laws, that the lawful magistrate may see particular
men with a malignant eye, and it provides for that identical
case. But when men, in particular descriptions, marked out
by the magistrate himself, are delivered over by Parliament
to this possible malignity, it is not the *Habeas Corpus* that is
occasionally suspended, but its spirit that is mistaken and its
principle that is subverted. Indeed nothing is security to any
individual but the common interest of all.

This Act, therefore, has this distinguished evil in it, that
it is the first partial suspension of the *Habeas Corpus* that has
been made. The precedent, which is always of very great
importance, is now established. For the first time a distinction is made among the people within this realm. Before this
Act, every man putting his foot on English ground, every
stranger owing only a local and temporary allegiance, even
negro slaves who had been sold in the colonies and under
an Act of Parliament, became as free as every other man
who breathed the same air with them. Now a line is drawn,
which may be advanced farther and farther at pleasure on
the same argument of mere expedience on which it was
first described. There is no equality among us; we are not
fellow-citizens, if the mariner who lands on the quay does
not rest on as firm legal ground as the merchant who sits in
his counting-house. Other laws may injure the community;
this dissolves it. As things now stand, every man in the West
Indies, every one inhabitant of three unoffending provinces
on the continent, every person coming from the East Indies, every gentleman who has travelled for his health or
education, every mariner who has navigated the seas, is,
for no other offense, under a temporary proscription. Let
any of these facts (now become presumptions of guilt) be

proved against him, and the bare suspicion of the crown puts him out of the law. It is even by no means clear to me whether the negative proof does not lie upon the person apprehended on suspicion to the subversion of all justice.

I have not debated against this bill in its progress through the House, because it would have been vain to oppose and impossible to correct it. It is some time since I have been clearly convinced that in the present state of things all opposition to any measures proposed by ministers, where the name of America appears, is vain and frivolous. You may be sure that I do not speak of my opposition, which in all circumstances must be so, but that of men of the greatest wisdom and authority in the nation. Everything proposed against America is supposed of course to be in favor of Great Britain. Good and ill success are equally admitted as reasons for persevering in the present methods. Several very prudent and very well-intentioned persons were of opinion that during the prevalence of such dispositions, all struggle rather inflamed than lessened the distemper of the public councils. Finding such resistance to be considered as factious by most within doors, and by very many without, I cannot conscientiously support what is against my opinion, nor prudently contend with what I know is irresistible. Preserving my principles unshaken, I reserve my activity for rational endeavors; and I hope that my past conduct has given sufficient evidence that if I am a single day from my place, it is not owing to indolence or love of dissipation. The slightest hope of doing good is sufficient to recall me to what I quitted with regret. In declining for some time my usual strict attendance, I do not in the least condemn the spirit of those gentlemen who, with a just confidence in their abilities (in which I claim a sort of share from my love

and admiration of them), were of opinion that their exertions in this desperate case might be of some service. They
thought that by contracting the sphere of its application
they might lessen the malignity of an evil principle. Perhaps
they were in the right. But when my opinion was so very
clearly to the contrary, for the reasons I have just stated, I
am sure *my* attendance would have been ridiculous.

I must add in further explanation of my conduct that,
far from softening the features of such a principle, and
thereby removing any part of the popular odium or natural terrors attending it, I should be sorry that anything
framed in contradiction to the spirit of our constitution
did not instantly produce, in fact, the grossest of the evils
with which it was pregnant in its nature. It is by lying dor-
mant a long time, or being at first very rarely exercised,
that arbitrary power steals upon a people. On the next unconstitutional Act, all the fashionable world will be ready
to say—Your prophecies are ridiculous, your fears are
vain, you see how little of the mischiefs which you formerly
foreboded are come to pass. Thus, by degrees, that artful
softening of all arbitrary power, the alleged infrequency or
narrow extent of its operation, will be received as a sort
of aphorism—and Mr. *Hume* will not be singular in telling
us that the felicity of mankind is no more disturbed by it
than by earthquakes or thunder or the other more unusual
accidents of nature.

The Act of which I speak is among the fruits of the
American war; a war in my humble opinion productive
of many mischiefs of a kind which distinguish it from all
others. Not only our policy is deranged, and our empire
distracted, but our laws and our legislative spirit appear to
have been totally perverted by it. We have made war on our

colonies, not by arms only, but by laws. As hostility and law are not very concordant ideas, every step we have taken in this business has been made by trampling on some maxim of justice, or some capital principle of wise government. What precedents were established, and what principles overturned (I will not say of English privilege, but of general justice), in the Boston Port, the Massachusetts Charter, the Military Bill, and all that long array of hostile Acts of Parliament by which the war with America has been begun and supported! Had the principles of any of these Acts been first exerted on English ground they would probably have expired as soon as they touched it. But by being removed from our persons they have rooted in our laws, and the latest posterity will taste the fruits of them.

Nor is it the worst effect of this unnatural contention that our *laws* are corrupted. While *manners* remain entire, they will correct the vices of law, and soften it at length to their own temper. But we have to lament that in most of the late proceedings we see very few traces of that generosity, humanity, and dignity of mind which formerly characterized this nation. War suspends the rules of moral obligation, and what is long suspended is in danger of being totally abrogated. Civil wars strike deepest of all into the manners of the people. They vitiate their politics, they corrupt their morals, they pervert even the natural taste and relish of equity and justice. By teaching us to consider our fellow-citizens in a hostile light, the whole body of our nation becomes gradually less dear to us. The very names of affection and kindred, which were the bond of charity while we agreed, become new incentives to hatred and rage, when the communion of our country is dissolved. We may flatter ourselves that we shall not fall into this misfortune. But we have no charter of exemption that I know of from the ordinary frailties of our nature.

What but that blindness of heart which arises from the frenzy of civil contention could have made any persons conceive the present situation of the British affairs as an object of triumph to themselves, or of congratulation to their sovereign? Nothing surely could be more lamentable to those who remember the flourishing days of this kingdom than to see the insane joy of several unhappy people, amidst the sad spectacle which our affairs and conduct exhibit to the scorn of Europe. We behold (and it seems some people rejoice in beholding) our native land, which used to sit the envied arbiter of all her neighbors, reduced to a servile dependence on their mercy, acquiescing in assurances of friendship which she does not trust, complaining of hostilities which she dares not resent, deficient to her allies, lofty to her subjects, and submissive to her enemies; while the liberal Government of this free nation is supported by the hireling sword of German boors and vassals; and three million of the subjects of Great Britain are seeking for protection to English privileges in the arms of France?[3]

These circumstances appear to me more like shocking prodigies than natural changes in human affairs. Men of firmer minds may see them without staggering or astonishment. Some may think them matters of congratulation and complimentary addresses; but I trust your candor will be so indulgent to my weakness, as not to have the worse opinion of me for my declining to participate in this joy, and my rejecting all share whatsoever in such a triumph. I am too old, too stiff in my inveterate partialities, to be ready

---

3.   The alliance between America and France was signed 4th February, 1778.

at all the fashionable evolutions of opinion. I scarcely know how to adapt my mind to the feelings with which the court gazettes mean to impress the people. It is not instantly that I can be brought to rejoice, when I hear of the slaughter and captivity of long lists of those names which have been familiar to my ears from my infancy, and to rejoice that they have fallen under the sword of strangers, whose barbarous appellations I scarcely know how to pronounce. The glory acquired at the White Plains by Colonel Raille has no charms for me; and I fairly acknowledge that I have not yet learned to delight in finding Fort Kniphausen in the heart of the British dominions.

It might be some consolation for the loss of our old regards if our reason were enlightened in proportion as our honest prejudices are removed. Wanting feelings for the honor of our country, we might then in cold blood be brought to think a little of our interests as individual citizens, and our private conscience as moral agents.

Indeed our affairs are in a bad condition. I do assure, those gentlemen who have prayed for war, and have obtained the blessing they have sought, that they are at this instant in very great straits. The abused wealth of this country continues a little longer to feel its distemper. As yet they, and their German allies of twenty hireling states, have contended only with the unprepared strength of our own infant colonies. But America is not subdued. Not one unattached village which was originally adverse throughout that vast continent has yet submitted from love or terror. You have the ground you encamp on, and you have no more. The cantonments of your troops and your dominions are exactly of the same extent. You spread devastation, but you do not enlarge the sphere of authority.

The events of this war are of so much greater magnitude than those who either wished or feared it ever looked for, that this alone ought to fill every considerate mind with anxiety and diffidence. Wise men often tremble at the very things which fill the thoughtless with security. For many reasons I do not choose to expose to public view all the particulars of the state in which you stood with regard to foreign powers during the whole course of the last year. Whether you are yet wholly out of danger from them is more than I know or than your rulers can divine. But even if I were certain of my safety, I could not easily forgive those who had brought me into the most dreadful perils, because by accidents, unforeseen by them or me, I have escaped.

Believe me, gentlemen, the way still before you is intricate, dark, and full of perplexed and treacherous mazes. Those who think they have the clue may lead us out of this labyrinth. We may trust them as amply as we think proper; but as they have most certainly a call for all the reason which their stock can furnish, why should we think it proper to disturb its operation by inflaming their passions? I may be unable to lend a helping band to those who direct the state, but I should be ashamed to make myself one of a noisy multitude to halloo and hearten them into doubtful and dangerous courses. A conscientious man would be cautious how he dealt in blood. He would feel some apprehension at being called to a tremendous account for engaging in so deep a play without any sort of knowledge of the game. It is no excuse for presumptuous ignorance that it is directed by insolent passion. The poorest being that crawls on earth, contending to save itself from injustice and oppression, is an object respectable in the eyes of God and man. But I cannot conceive any existence under heaven (which, in the depths of its wisdom, tolerates all sorts of things), that is more truly odious and disgusting than an impotent, help-less creature, without civil wisdom or military skill, without a consciousness of any other qualification for power but his servility to it, bloated with pride and arrogance, calling for battles which he is not to fight, contending for a violent dominion which he can never exercise, and satisfied to be himself mean and miserable in order to render others con-temptible and wretched.

If you and I find our talents not of the great and ruling kind, our conduct, at least, is conformable to our faculties. No man's life pays the forfeit of our rashness. No desolate widow weeps tears of blood over our ignorance. Scrupu-lous and sober in our well-grounded distrust of ourselves, we would keep in the port of peace and security; and per-haps, in recommending to others something of the same diffidence, we should show ourselves more charitable in their welfare than injurious to their abilities.

There are many circumstances in the zeal shown for civ-il war which seem to discover but little of real magnanimity. The addressers offer their own persons, and they are satisfied with hiring Germans. They promise their private fortunes, and they mortgage their country. They have all the merit of volunteers, without risk of person or charge of contribution; and when the unfeeling arm of a foreign soldiery pours out their kindred blood like water, they exult and triumph as if they themselves had performed some notable exploit. I am really ashamed of the fashionable language which has been held for some time past, which, to say the best of it, is full of levity. You know that I allude to the general cry against the cowardice of the Americans, as if we despised them for not making the king's soldiery purchase the advantage they have obtained at a dearer rate. It is not, gentlemen, it is not to respect the dispensations of Providence, nor to provide any decent retreat in the mutability of human affairs. It leaves no medium between insolent victory and infamous defeat. It tends to alienate our minds farther and farther from our natural regards, and to make an eternal rent and schism in the British nation. Those who do not wish for such a separation would not dissolve that cement of reciprocal esteem and regard which can alone bind together the parts of this great fabric. It ought to be our wish, as it is our duty, not only to forbear this style of outrage ourselves, but to make every one as sensible as we can of the impropriety and unworthiness of the tempers which give rise to it, and which designing men are laboring with such malignant industry to diffuse among us. It is our business to counteract them if possible, if possible to awake our natural regards, and to revive the old partiality to the English name. Without something of this kind I do not see how it is ever practicable really to reconcile with those whose affection, after all, must be the surest hold of our government, and which is a thousand times more worth to us than the mercenary zeal of all the circles of Germany.

I can well conceive a country completely overrun, and miserably wasted, without approaching in the least to settlement. In my apprehension, as long as English government is attempted to be supported over Englishmen by the sword alone, things will thus continue. I anticipate in my mind the moment of the final triumph of foreign military force. When that hour arrives (for it may arrive), then it is that all this mass of weakness and violence will appear in its full light. If we should be expelled from America, the delusion

of the partisans of military government might still continue. They might still feed their imaginations with the possible good consequences which might have attended success.
Nobody could prove the contrary by facts. But in case the
sword should do all that the sword can do, the success of
their arms and the defeat of their policy will be one and the
same thing. You will never see any revenue from America.
Some increase of the means of corruption, without ease of
the public burdens, is the very best that can happen. Is it for
this that we are at war—and in such a war?

As to the difficulties of laying once more the foundations of that government which, for the sake of conquer-
ing what was our own, has been voluntarily and wantonly
pulled down by a court faction here, I tremble to look at
them. Has any of these gentlemen, who are so eager to
govern all mankind, showed himself possessed of the first
qualification towards government, some knowledge of the
object and of the difficulties which occur in the task they
have undertaken?

I assure you that, on the most prosperous issue of your
arms, you will not be where you stood, when you called in
war to supply the defects of your political establishment.
Nor would any disorder or disobedience to government
which could arise from the most abject concession on our
part ever equal those which will be felt after the most tri-
umphant violence. You have got all the intermediate evils
of war into the bargain.

I think I know America. If I do not, my ignorance is
incurable, for I have spared no pains to understand it; and I
do most solemnly assure those of my constituents who put
any sort of confidence in my industry and integrity, that
everything that has been done there has arisen from a total

misconception of the object; that our means of originally holding America, that our means of reconciling with it
after quarrel, of recovering it after separation, of keeping
it after victory, did depend and must depend in their several stages and periods, upon a total renunciation of that
unconditional submission, which has taken such possession
of the minds of violent men. The whole of those maxims
upon which we have made and continued this war must be
abandoned. Nothing indeed (for I would not deceive you)
can place us in our former situation. That hope must be
laid aside. But there is a difference between bad and the
worst of all. Terms relative to the cause of the war ought
to be offered by the authority of Parliament. An arrangement at home promising some security for them ought to
be made. By doing this, without the least impairing of our
strength, we add to the credit of our moderation, which in
itself is always strength more of less.

I know many have been taught to think that moderation in a case like this is a sort of treason, and that all arguments for it are sufficiently answered by railing at rebels
and rebellion and by charging all the present or future mis-
eries which we may suffer on the resistance of our brethren.
But I would wish them in this grave matter, and if peace is
not wholly removed from their hearts, to consider seriously,
first, that to criminate and recriminate never yet was the
road to reconciliation in any difference among men. In the
next place, it would be right to reflect that the American
English (whom they may abuse if they think it honorable
to revile the absent) can, as things now stand, neither be
provoked at our railing nor bettered by our instruction. All
communication is cut off between us, but this we know with
certainty that, though we cannot reclaim them, we may

reform ourselves. If measures of peace are necessary, they must begin somewhere, and a conciliatory temper must precede and prepare every plan of reconciliation. Nor do I conceive that we suffer anything by thus regulating our own minds. We are not disarmed by being disencumbered of our passions. Declaiming on rebellion never added a bayonet or a charge of powder to your military force, but I am afraid that it has been the means of taking up many muskets against you.

This outrageous language, which has been encouraged and kept alive by every art, has already done incredible mischief. For a long time, even amidst the desolations of war and the insults of hostile laws daily accumulated on one another, the American leaders seem to have had the greatest difficulty in bringing up their people to a declaration of total independence. But the court gazette accomplished what the abettors of independence had attempted in vain. When that disingenuous compilation and strange medley of railing and flattery was adduced as a proof of the united sentiments of the people of Great Britain, there was a great change throughout all America. The tide of popular affection, which had still set towards the parent country, began immediately to turn, and to flow with great rapidity in a contrary course. Far from concealing these wild declarations of enmity, the author of the celebrated pamphlet,[4] which prepared the minds of the people for independence, insists largely on the

---

4. Paine's *Common Sense.* "O ye that love mankind, ye that dare oppose, not only the tyranny but the tyrant, stand forth: every spot of the Old World is overcome with oppression. Freedom, hath been hunted round the globe.... England hath given her warning to depart. O receive the fugitive, and provide in time an asylum for mankind." Thomas Paine, 1737–1809, author of *The Rights of Man.*

multitude and the spirit of these addresses; and he draws an argument from them which (if the fact was as he supposes) must be irresistible. For I never knew a writer on the theory of government so partial to authority as not to allow that the hostile mind of the rulers to their people did fully justify a change of government; nor can any reason whatever be given why one people should voluntarily yield any degree of preeminence to another but on a supposition of great affection and benevolence towards them. Unfortunately your rulers, trusting to other things, took no notice of this great principle of connection. From the beginning of this affair they have done all they could to alienate your minds from your own kindred; and if they could excite hatred enough in one of the parties towards the other, they seemed to be of opinion that they had gone half the way towards reconciling the quarrel.

I know it is said that your kindness is only alienated on account of their resistance, and therefore, if the colonies surrender at discretion, all sorts of regard and even much indulgence is meant towards them in future. But can those who are partisans for continuing a war to enforce such a surrender be responsible (after all that has passed) for such a future use of a power that is hound by no compacts and restrained by no terror? Will they tell us what they call indulgences? Do they not at this instant call the present war and all its horrors a lenient and merciful proceeding?

No conqueror that I ever heard of has *professed* to make a cruel, harsh, and insolent use of his conquest. No! The man of the most declared pride scarcely dares to trust his own heart with this dreadful secret of ambition. But it will appear in its time; and no man who professes to reduce another to the insolent mercy of a foreign arm ever had any

sort of goodwill towards him. The profession of kindness
with that sword in his hand and that demand of surrender
is one of the most provoking acts of his hostility. I shall be
told that all this is lenient as against rebellious adversaries.
But are the leaders of their faction more lenient to those
who submit? Lord Howe and General Howe have powers
under an Act of Parliament to restore to the king's peace
and to free trade any men or district which shall submit.
Is this done? We have been over and over informed by the
authorized gazette that the city of New York and the countries of Staten and Long Island have submitted voluntarily and cheerfully, and that many are very full of zeal to
the cause of administration. Were they instantly restored
to trade? Are they yet restored to it? Is not the benignity
of two commissioners, naturally most humane and generous men, some way fettered by instructions equally against
their dispositions and spirit of Parliamentary faith, when
Mr. Tryon, vaunting of the fidelity of the city in which he
is governor, is obliged to apply to Ministry for leave to protect the king's loyal subjects, and to grant to them (not the
disputed rights and privileges of freedom) but the common
rights of men by the name of *graces*? Why do not the commissioners restore them on the spot? Were they not named
as commissioners for that express purpose? But we see well
enough to what the whole leads. The trade of America is to
be dealt out in *private indulgences and graces*; that is, in jobs to
recompense the incendiaries of war. They will be informed
of the proper time in which to send out their merchandise.
From a national the American trade is to be turned into
a personal monopoly; and one set of merchants are to be
rewarded for the pretended zeal of which another set are
the dupes, and thus between craft and credulity the voice of

reason is stifled, and all the misconduct, all the calamities of the war are covered and continued.

If I had not lived long enough to be little surprised at anything, I should have been in some degree astonished at the continued rage of several gentlemen who, not satisfied with carrying fire and sword into America, are animated nearly with the same fury against those neighbors of theirs whose only crime it is that they have charitably and humanely wished them to entertain more reasonable sentiments, and not always to sacrifice their interest to their passion. All this rage against unresisting dissent convinces me that at bottom they are far from satisfied they are in the right. For what is it they would have? A war? They certainly have at this moment the blessing of something that is very like one, and if the war they enjoy at present be not sufficiently hot and extensive, they may shortly have it as warm and as spreading as their hearts can desire. Is it the force of the kingdom they call for? They have it already; and if they choose to fight their battles in their own person, nobody prevents their setting sail to America in the next transports. Do they think that the service is stinted for want of liberal supplies? Indeed they complain without reason. The table of the House of Commons will glut them let their appetite for expense be never so keen. And I assure them further that those who think with them in the House of Commons are full as easy in the control as they are liberal in the vote of these expenses. If this be not supply or confidence sufficient, let them open their own private purse-strings and give from what is left to them as largely and with as little care as they think proper.

Tolerated in their passions, let them learn not to persecute the moderation of their fellow-citizens. If all the world joined them in a full cry against rebellion, and were as hotly inflamed against the whole theory and enjoyment of freedom as those who are the most factious for servitude, it could not in my opinion answer any one end whatsoever in this contest. The leaders of this war could not hire (to gratify their friends) one German more than they do, or inspire him with less feeling for the persons or less value for the privileges of their revolted brethren. If we all adopted their sentiments to a man, their allies, the savage Indians, could not be more ferocious than they are; they could not murder one more helpless woman or child, or with more exquisite refinements of cruelty torment to death one more of their English flesh and blood than they do already. The public money is given to purchase this alliance—and they have their bargain.

They are continually boasting of unanimity, or calling for it. But before this unanimity can be matter either of wish or congratulation we ought to be pretty sure that we are engaged in a rational pursuit. Frenzy does not become a slighter distemper on account of the number of those who may be infected with it. Delusion and weakness produce not one mischief the less because they are universal. I declare that I cannot discern the least advantage which could accrue to us if we were able to persuade our colonies that they had not a single friend in Great Britain. On the contrary, if the affections and opinions of mankind be not exploded as principles of connection, I conceive it would be happy for us if they were taught to believe that there was even a formed American party in England to whom they could always look for support! Happy would it be for us if, in all tempers, they might turn their eyes to the parent state, so that their very turbulence and sedition should find vent in no other place than this. I believe there is not a man (except those who prefer the interest of some paltry faction to the very being of their country) who would not wish that the Americans should from time to time carry many points, and even some of them not quite reasonable, by the aid of any denomination of men here rather than they should be driven to seek for protection against the fury of foreign mercenaries and the waste of savages in the arms of France.

When any community is subordinately connected with another, the great danger of the connection is the extreme pride and self-complacency of the superior, which in all matters of controversy will probably decide in its own favor. It is a powerful corrective to such a very rational cause of fear if the inferior body can be made to believe that the party inclination, or political views, of several in the principal state will induce them in some degree to counteract this blind and tyrannical partiality. There is no danger that any one acquiring consideration or power in the presiding state should carry this leaning to the inferior too far. The fault of human nature is not of that sort. Power, in whatever hands, is rarely guilty of too strict limitations on itself. But one great advantage to the support of authority attends such an amicable and protecting connection, that those who have conferred favors obtain influence, and from the foresight of future events can persuade men who have received obligations sometimes to return them. Thus, by the mediation of those healing principles (call them good or evil), troublesome discussions are brought to some sort of adjustment, and every hot controversy is not a civil war.

But if the colonies (to bring the general matter home to us) could see that, in Great Britain, the mass of the people are melted into its Government, and that every dispute with the Ministry must of necessity be always a quarrel with the nation, they can stand no longer in the equal and friendly relations of fellow citizens to the subjects of this kingdom. Humble as this relation may appear to some, when it is once broken a strong tie is dissolved. Other sort of connections will be sought. For there are very few in the world who will not prefer a useful ally to an insolent master.

Such discord has been the effect of the unanimity into which so many have of late been seduced or bullied, or into the appearance of which they have sunk through mere despair. They have been told that their dissent from violent measures is an encouragement to rebellion. Men of great presumption and little knowledge will hold a language which is contradicted by the whole course of history. *General* rebellions and revolts of a whole people never *were encouraged*, now or at any time. They are always *provoked*. But if this unheard-of doctrine of the encouragement of rebellion were true, if it were true that an assurance of the friendship of numbers in this country towards the colonies could become an encouragement to them to break off all connection with it, what is the inference? Does anybody seriously maintain that, charged with my share of the public councils, I am obliged not to resist projects which I think mischievous lest men who suffer should be encouraged to resist? The very tendency of such projects to produce rebellion is one of the chief reasons against them. Shall that reason not be given? Is it then a rule that no man in this nation shall open his mouth in favor of the colonies, shall defend their rights, or complain of their sufferings? Or, when war finally breaks out, no man shall express his desires of peace? Has this been the law of our past, or is it to be the terms of our future connection? Even looking no further than ourselves, can it be true loyalty to any government, or true patriotism towards any country, to degrade their solemn councils into servile drawing rooms, to flatter their pride and passions, rather than to enlighten their reason, and to prevent them from being cautioned against violence lest others should be encouraged to resistance? By such acquiescence great kings and mighty nations have been undone; and if any are at this day in a perilous situation from resisting truth and listening to flattery, it would rather become them to reform the errors under which they suffer than to reproach those who forewarned them of their danger.

But the rebels looked for assistance from this country. They did so in the beginning of this controversy most certainly, and they sought it by earnest supplications to Government, which dignity rejected, and by a suspension of commerce, which the wealth of this nation enabled you to despise. When they found that neither prayers nor menaces had any sort of weight, but that a firm resolution was taken to reduce them to unconditional obedience by a military force, they came to the last extremity. Despairing of us, they trusted in themselves. Not strong enough themselves, they sought succor in France. In proportion as all encouragement here lessened, their distance from this country increased. The encouragement is over; the alienation is complete.

In order to produce this favorite unanimity in delusion, and to prevent all possibility of a return to our ancient happy concord, arguments for our continuance in this course are drawn from the wretched situation itself into which we have been betrayed. It is said that, being at war with the colonies, whatever our sentiments might have been before all ties between us are now dissolved, and all the policy we have left is to strengthen the hands of Government to reduce them. On the principle of this argument, the more mischiefs we suffer from any administration, the more our trust in it is to be confirmed. Let them but once get us into a war, and then their power is safe, and an Act of oblivion passed for all their misconduct.

But is it really true, that Government is always to be strengthened with the instruments of war, but never furnished with the means of peace? In former times ministers, I allow, have been sometimes driven by the popular voice to assert by arms the national honor against foreign powers. But the wisdom of the nation has been far more clear when those ministers have been compelled to consult its interests by treaty. We all know that the sense of the nation obliged the court of King Charles the Second to abandon the *Dutch war*—a war, next to the present, the most impolitic which we ever carried on. The good people of England considered Holland as a sort of dependency on this kingdom; they dreaded to drive it to the protection, or subject it to the power of France, by their own inconsiderate hostility. They paid but little respect to the court jargon of that day; nor were they inflamed by the pretended rivalship of the Dutch in trade, by their massacre at Amboyna, acted on the stage to provoke the public vengeance, nor by declamations against the ingratitude of the United Provinces for the benefits England had conferred upon them in their infant state. They were not moved from their evident interest by all these arts, nor was it enough to tell them they were at war, that they must go through with it, and that the cause of the dispute was lost in the consequences. The people of England were then, as they are now, called upon to make Government strong. They thought it a great deal better to make it wise and honest.

When I was among my constituents at the last summer assizes, I remember that men of all descriptions did then express a very strong desire for peace, and no slight hopes of attaining it from the commission sent out by my Lord Howe. And it is not a little remarkable that, in proportion as every person showed a zeal for the court measures, he was then earnest in circulating an opinion of the extent of the supposed powers of that commission. When I told them that Lord Howe had no powers to treat, or to promise satisfaction on any point whatsoever of the controversy, I was hardly credited, so strong and general was the desire of terminating this war by the method of accommodation. As far as I could discover, this was the temper then prevalent through the kingdom. The king's forces, it must be observed, had at that time been obliged to evacuate Boston. The superiority of the former campaign rested wholly with the colonists. If such powers of treaty were to be wished while success was very doubtful, how came they to be less so since his Majesty's arms have been crowned with many considerable advantages? Have these successes induced us to alter our mind, as thinking the season of victory not the time for treating with honor or advantage? Whatever changes have happened in the national character, it can scarcely be our wish that terms of accommodation never should be proposed to our enemy, except when they must be attributed solely to our fears. It has happened, let me say unfortunately, that we read of his Majesty's commission for making peace and his troops evacuating his last town in the thirteen colonies at the same hour and in the same gazette. It was still more unfortunate that no commission went to America to settle the troubles there until several months after an Act had been passed to put the colonies out of the protection of this Government, and to divide their trading property, without a possibility of restitution, as spoil among the seamen of the navy. The most abject submission on the part of the colonies could not redeem them. There was no man on that whole continent, or within three thousand miles of it, qualified by law to follow allegiance with protection or submission with pardon. A proceeding of this kind has no example in history. Independency, and independency with an enmity (which, putting ourselves out of the question, would be called natural and much provoked), was the inevitable consequence. How this came to pass the nation may be one day in a humor to inquire.

All the attempts made this session to give fuller powers of peace to the commanders in America were stifled by the fatal confidence of victory and the wild hopes of unconditional submission. There was a moment favorable to the king's arms, when if any powers of concession had existed on the other side of the Atlantic, even after all our errors, peace in all probability might have been restored. But calamity is unhappily the usual season of reflection, and the pride of men will not often suffer reason to have any scope until it can be no longer of service.

I have always wished that, as the dispute had its apparent origin from things done in Parliament, and as the Acts passed there had provoked the war, that the foundations of peace should be laid in Parliament also. I have been astonished to find that those whose zeal for the dignity of our body was so hot as to light up the flames of civil war should even publicly declare that these delicate points ought to be wholly left to the crown. Poorly as I may be thought affected to the authority of Parliament, I shall never admit that our constitutional rights can ever become a matter of ministerial negotiation.

I am charged with being an American. If warm affection towards those over whom I claim any share of authority be a crime, I am guilty of this charge. But I do assure you (and they who know me publicly and privately will bear witness to me), that if ever one man lived more zealous than another for the supremacy of Parliament and the rights of this imperial crown, it was myself. Many others, indeed, might be more knowing in the extent of the foundation of these rights. I do not pretend to be an antiquary, a lawyer, or qualified for the chair of professor in metaphysics. I never ventured to put your solid interests upon speculative grounds. My having constantly declined to do so has been attributed to my incapacity for such disquisitions; and I am inclined to believe it is partly the cause. I never shall be ashamed to confess that where I am ignorant I am diffident. I am indeed not very solicitous to clear myself of this imputed incapacity, because men, even less conversant than I am in this kind of subtleties, and placed in stations to which I ought not to aspire, have, by the mere force of civil discretion, often conducted the affairs of great nations with distinguished felicity and glory.

When I first came into a public trust, I found your Parliament in possession of an unlimited legislative power over the colonies. I could not open the statute book without seeing the actual exercise of it, more or less, in all cases whatsoever. This possession passed with me for a title. It does so in all human affairs. No man examines into the defects of his title to his paternal estate, or to his established Government. Indeed common sense taught me that a legislative authority, not actually limited by the express terms of its foundation, or by its own subsequent acts, cannot have its powers parceled out by argumentative distinctions, so as to enable us to say that here they can, and there they cannot, bind. Nobody was so obliging as to produce to me any record of such distinctions, by compact or otherwise, either at the successive formation of the several colonies, or during the existence of any of them. If any gentlemen[5] were able to see how one power could be given up (merely on abstract reasoning) without giving up the rest, I can only say that they saw farther than I could; nor did I ever presume to condemn any one for being clear-sighted when I was blind. I praise the penetration and learning, and hope that their practice has been correspondent to their theory.

I had indeed very earnest wishes to keep the whole body of this authority perfect and entire as I found it; and to keep it so, not for our advantage solely, but principally for the sake of those on whose account all just authority exists—I mean the people to be governed. For I thought I saw that many cases might well happen in which the exercise of every power comprehended in the broadest idea of legislature might become, in its time and circumstances, not a little expedient for the peace and union of the colonies among themselves, as well as for their perfect harmony with Great Britain. Thinking so (perhaps erroneously), but being honestly of that opinion, I was at the same time very sure that the authority, of which I was so jealous, could not under the actual circumstances of our plantations be at all preserved in any of its members but by the greatest reserve in its application, particularly in those delicate points in which the feelings of mankind are the most irritable. They who thought otherwise have found a few more difficulties in their work than, I hope, they were thoroughly aware of when they undertook the present business. I must beg leave to observe that it is not only the invidious branch of taxation that will be resisted, but that no other given part of legislative rights can be exercised without regard to the general opinion of those who are to be governed. That general opinion is the vehicle and organ of legislative omnipotence. Without this it may be a theory to entertain the mind, but it is nothing in the direction of affairs. The completeness of the legislative authority of Parliament *over this kingdom* is not questioned, and yet many things indubitably included in the abstract idea of that power, and which carry no absolute injustice in themselves, yet being contrary to the opinions and feelings of the people, can as little be exercised as if Parliament in that case had been possessed of no right at all. I see no abstract reason which can be given why the same power which made and repealed the high commission court and the star-chamber might not revive them again; and these courts, warned by their former fate, might possibly exercise their powers with some degree of justice. But the madness would be as unquestionable as the competence of that Parliament which should attempt such things. If anything can be supposed out of the power of human legislature it is religion: I admit, however, that the established religion of this country has been three or four times altered by Act of Parliament, and therefore that a statute binds even in that case. But we may very safely affirm that, notwithstanding this apparent omnipotence, it would be now found as impossible for king and Parliament to alter the established religion of this country as it was to King James alone, when he attempted to make such an alteration without a Parliament. In effect, to follow not to force the public inclination, to give a direction, a form, a

technical dress, and a specific sanction to the general sense
of the community, is the true end of legislature.

It is so with regard to the exercise of all the powers
which our constitution knows in any of its parts, and indeed
to the substantial existence of any of the parts themselves.
The king's negative to bills is one of the most indisputed of
the royal prerogatives, and it extends to all cases whatsoever. I am far from certain that if several laws which I know
had fallen under the stroke of that scepter that the public
would have had a very heavy loss. But it is not the *propriety* of the exercise which is in question. The exercise itself
is wisely forborne. Its repose may be the preservation of
its existence, and its existence may be the means of saving
the constitution itself, on an occasion worthy of bringing
it forth. As the disputants, whose accurate and logical reasonings have brought us into our present condition, think it
absurd that powers or members of any constitution should
exist rarely or never to be exercised, I hope I shall be excused in mentioning another instance that is material. We
know that the convocation of the clergy had formerly been
called, and sat with nearly as much regularity to business
as Parliament itself. It is now called for form only. It sits for
the purpose of mankind some polite ecclesiastical compliments to the king, and, when that grace is said, retires and
is heard of no more. It is, however, *a part of the constitution*,
and may be called out into act and energy whenever there
is occasion, and whenever those who conjure up that spirit
will choose to abide the consequences. It is wise to permit
its legal existence; it is much wiser to continue it a legal existence only. So truly has prudence (constituted as the god
of this lower world) the entire dominion over every exercise
of power committed into its hands; and yet I have lived to

see prudence and conformity to circumstances wholly set at nought in our late controversies, and treated as if they were the most contemptible and irrational of all things. I have heard it a hundred times very gravely alleged that, in order to keep power in mind, it was necessary, by preference, to exert it in those very points in which it was most likely to be resisted and the least likely to be productive of any advantage.

These were the considerations, gentlemen, which led me early to think that, in the comprehensive dominion which the Divine Providence had put into our hands, instead of troubling our understandings with speculations concerning the unity of empire, and the identity or distinction of legislative powers, and inflaming our passions with the heat and pride of controversy, it was our duty, in all soberness, to conform our government to the character and circumstances of the several people who composed this mighty and strangely diversified mass. I never was wild enough to conceive that one method would serve for the whole; that the natives of Hindustan and those of Virginia could be ordered in the same manner, or that the Cutchery court and the grand jury of Salem could be regulated on a similar plan. I was persuaded that government was a practical thing, made for the happiness of mankind, and not to furnish out a spectacle of uniformity to gratify the schemes of visionary politicians. Our business was to rule, not to wrangle; and it would have been a poor compensation that we had triumphed in a dispute, while we lost an empire.

If there be one fact in the world perfectly clear it is this: "That the disposition of the people of America is wholly averse to any other than a free government," and this is indication enough to any honest statesman how he ought to adapt whatever power he finds in his hands to their case. If any ask me what a free government is, I answer that, for any practical purpose, it is what the people think so; and that they, and not I, are the natural, lawful, and competent judges of this matter. If they practically allow me a greater degree of authority over them than is consistent with any correct ideas of perfect freedom, I ought to thank them for so great a trust and not to endeavor to prove from thence that they have reasoned amiss, and that, having gone so far, by analogy, they must hereafter have no enjoyment but by my pleasure.

If we had seen this done by any others, we should have concluded them far gone in madness. It is melancholy as well as ridiculous to observe the kind of reasoning with which the public has been amused, in order to divert our minds from the common sense of our American policy. There are people who have split and anatomized the doctrine of free government as if it were an abstract question concerning metaphysical liberty and necessity, and not a matter of moral prudence and natural feeling. They have disputed whether liberty be a positive or a negative idea; whether it does not consist in being governed by laws without considering what are the laws or who are the makers; whether man has any rights by nature; and whether all the property he enjoys be not the alms of his government, and his life itself their favor and indulgence. Others, corrupting religion as these have perverted philosophy, contend that Christians are redeemed into captivity, and the blood of the Savior of mankind has been shed to make them the slaves of a few proud and insolent sinners. These shocking extremes provoking to extremes of another kind, speculations are let loose as destructive to all authority as the former are to all freedom; and every government is called tyranny and usurpation which is not formed on their fancies. In this manner the stirrers-up of this contention, not satisfied with distracting our dependencies and filling them with blood and slaughter, are corrupting our understandings; they are endeavoring to tear up, along with practical liberty, all the foundations of human society, all equity and justice, religion, and order.

Civil freedom, gentlemen, is not, as many have endeavored to persuade you, a thing that lies hid in the depth of abstruse science. It is a blessing and a benefit, not an abstract speculation; and all the just reasoning that can be upon it is of so coarse a texture as perfectly to suit the ordinary capacities of those who are to enjoy, and of those who are to defend it. Far from any resemblance to those propositions in geometry and metaphysics, which admit no medium, but must be true or false in all their latitude, social and civil freedom, like all other things in common life, are variously mixed and modified, enjoyed in very different degrees, and shaped into an infinite diversity of forms, according to the temper and circumstances of every community. The *extreme* of liberty (which is its abstract perfection, but its real fault) obtains nowhere, nor ought to obtain anywhere. Because extremes, as we all know, in every point which relates either to our duties or satisfactions in life, are destructive both to virtue and enjoyment. Liberty too must be limited in order to be possessed. The degree of restraint it is impossible in any case to settle precisely. But it ought to be the constant aim of every wise public council to find out, by cautious experiments and rational, cool endeavors, with how little, not how much, of this restraint the community can subsist. For liberty is a good to be improved, and not an evil to be lessened. It is not only a private blessing of the first order, but the vital spring and energy of the state itself, which has just so much life and vigor as there is liberty in it. But whether liberty be advantageous or not (for I know it is a fashion to decry the very principle), none will dispute that peace is a blessing; and peace must in the course of human affairs be frequently bought by some indulgence and toleration at least to liberty. For as the Sabbath (though of Divine institution) was made for man, not man for the Sabbath, government, which can claim no higher origin or authority, in its exercise at least, ought to conform to the exigencies of the time and the temper and character of the people with whom it is concerned, and not always to attempt violently to bend the people to their theories of subjection. The bulk of mankind on their part are not excessively curious concerning any theories, while they are really happy, and one sure symptom of an ill-conducted state is the propensity of the people to resort to them.

But when subjects, by a long course of such ill conduct, are once thoroughly inflamed, and the state itself violently distempered, the people must have some satisfaction to their feelings more solid than a sophistical speculation on law and government. Such was our situation, and such a satisfaction was necessary to prevent recourse to arms; it was necessary towards laying them down: it will be necessary to prevent the taking them up again and again. Of what nature this satisfaction ought to be I wish it had been the disposition of Parliament seriously to consider. It was certainly a deliberation that called for the exertion of all their wisdom.

I am, and ever have been, deeply sensible of the difficulty of reconciling the strong presiding power, that is so useful towards the conservation of a vast, disconnected, infinitely diversified empire, with that liberty and safety of the provinces, which they must enjoy (in opinion and practice at least) or they will not be provinces at all. I know, and have long felt, the difficulty of reconciling the unwieldy haughtiness of a great ruling nation, habituated to command, pampered by enormous wealth, and confident from a long course of prosperity and victory, to the high spirit of free dependencies, animated with the first glow and activity of juvenile heat, and assuming to themselves, as their birthright some part of that very pride which oppresses them. They who perceive no difficulty in reconciling these tempers (which however to make peace must some way or other be reconciled), are much above my capacity or much below the magnitude of the business. Of one thing I am perfectly clear, that it is not by deciding the suit, but by compromising the difference that peace can be restored or kept. They who would put an end to such quarrels, by declaring roundly in favor of the whole demands of either party, have mistaken, in my humble opinion, the office of a mediator.

The war is now of full two years' standing; the controversy, of many more. In different periods of the dispute, different methods of reconciliation were to be pursued. I mean to trouble you with a short state of things at the most important of these periods, in order to give you a more distinct idea of our policy with regard to this most delicate of all objects. The colonies were from the beginning subject to the legislature of Great Britain, on principles which they never examined; and we permitted to them many local privileges, without asking how they agreed with that legislative authority. Modes of administration were formed in an insensible and very unsystematic manner. But they gradually adapted themselves to the varying condition of things: what was first a single kingdom, stretched into an empire; and an imperial superintendency, of some kind or other, became necessary. Parliament, from a mere representative of the people, and a guardian of popular privileges for its own immediate constituents, grew into a mighty sovereign. Instead of being a control on the crown on its own behalf, it communicated a sort of strength to the royal authority, which was wanted for the conservation of a new object, but which could not be safely trusted to the crown alone. On the other hand, the colonies, advancing by equal steps and governed by the same necessity, had formed within themselves, either by royal instruction or royal charter, assemblies so exceedingly resembling a Parliament in all their forms, functions, and powers, that it was impossible they should not imbibe some opinion of a similar authority.

At the first designation of these assemblies they were probably not intended for anything more (nor perhaps did they think themselves much higher) than the municipal corporations within this island, to which some at present love to compare them. But nothing in progression can rest on its original plan. We may as well think of rocking a grown man in the cradle of an infant. Therefore, as the colonies prospered and increased to a numerous and mighty people, spreading over a very great tract of the globe, it was natural that they should attribute to assemblies, so respectable in their formal constitution, some part of the dignity of the great nations which they represented. No longer tied to bye-laws, these assemblies made Acts of all sorts and in all cases whatsoever. They levied money, not for parochial purposes, but upon regular grants to the crown, following all the rules and principles of a Parliament, to which they approached every day more and more nearly. Those who think themselves wiser than Providence and stronger than the course of nature may complain of all this variation on the one side or the other, as their several humors and prejudices may lead them. But things could not be otherwise, and English colonies must be had on these terms or not had at all. In the meantime neither party felt any inconvenience from this double legislature, to which they had been formed by imperceptible habits and old custom, the great support of all the governments in the world. Though these two legislatures were sometimes found perhaps performing the very same functions, they did not very grossly or systematically clash. In all likelihood this arose from mere neglect, possibly from the natural operation, of things which, left to themselves, generally fall into their proper order. But whatever was the cause, it is certain that a regular revenue, by the authority of Parliament, for the support of civil and military establishments, seems not to have been thought of until the colonies were too proud to submit, too strong to be forced, too enlightened not to see all the consequences which must arise from such a system.

If ever this scheme of taxation was to be pushed against the inclinations of the people, it was evident that discussions must arise which would let loose all the elements that composed this double constitution, would show how much each of their members had departed from its original principles, and would discover contradictions in each legislature, as well to its own first principles as to its relation to the other, very difficult, if not absolutely impossible, to be reconciled.

Therefore at the first fatal opening of this contest, the wisest course seemed to be to put an end as soon as possible to the immediate causes of the dispute, and to quiet a discussion, not easily settled upon clear principles, and arising from claims which pride would permit neither party to abandon, by resorting as nearly as possible to the old, successful course. A mere repeal of the obnoxious tax, with a declaration of the legislative authority of this kingdom, was then fully sufficient to procure peace to *both sides*. Man is a creature of habit, and the first breach being of very short continuance, the colonies fell back exactly into their ancient state. The congress has used an expression with regard to this pacification which appears to me truly significant. After the repeal of the Stamp Act, "the colonies fell," says this assembly, "into their ancient state of *unsuspecting confidence in the mother-country*." This *unsuspecting confidence* is the true center of gravity among mankind, about which all the parts are at rest. It is this unsuspecting confidence that removes all difficulties and reconciles all the contradictions which occur in the complexity of all ancient, puzzled, political establishments. Happy are the rulers which have the secret of preserving it!

The whole empire has reason to remember with eternal gratitude, the wisdom and temper of that man and his excellent associates, who, to recover this confidence, formed a plan of pacification in 1766. That plan, being built upon the nature of man and the circumstances and habits of the two countries, and not on any visionary speculations, perfectly answered its end as long as it was thought proper to adhere to it. Without giving a rude shock to the dignity (well or ill understood) of this Parliament, they gave perfect content to our dependencies. Had it not been for the mediatorial spirit and talents of that great man, between such clashing pretensions and passions, we should then have rushed headlong (I know what I say) into the calamities of that civil war in which, by departing from his system, we are at length involved; and we should have been precipitated into that war at a time when circumstances both at home and abroad were far, very far, more unfavorable unto us than they were at the breaking out of the present troubles.

I had the happiness of giving my first votes[6] in Parliament for their pacification. I was one of those almost unanimous members who, in the necessary concessions of Parliament, would as much as possible have preserved its authority and respected its honor. I could not at once tear from my heart prejudices which were dear to me, and which bore a resemblance to virtue. I had then and I have still my partialities. What Parliament gave up I wished to be given as of grace and favor and affection, and not as a restitution of stolen goods. High dignity relented as it was soothed, and a benignity from old acknowledged greatness had its full effect on out dependencies. Our unlimited declaration of legislative authority produced not a single murmur. If this undefined power has become odious since that time and full of horror to the colonies, it is because the *unsuspicious confidence* is lost, and the parental affection, in the bosom of whose boundless authority they reposed their privileges, is become estranged and hostile.

It will be asked, if such was then my opinion of the mode of pacification, how I came to be the very person who moved, not only for a repeal of all the late coercive statutes, but for mutilating by a positive law, the entireness of the legislative power of Parliament, and cutting off from it the whole right of taxation?[7] I answer, because a different

6.   Compare Speech on Taxation, p. 122.

7.   See p. 52, and p. 79, *Note*.

state of things requires a different conduct. When the dispute had gone to these last extremities (which no man labored more to prevent than I did), the concessions which had satisfied in the beginning could satisfy no longer, because the violation of tacit faith required explicit security. The same cause which has introduced all formal compacts and covenants among men made it necessary. I mean habits of soreness, jealousy, and distrust. I parted with it as with a limb, but as a limb to save the body, and I would have parted with more if more had been necessary, anything rather than a fruitless, hopeless, unnatural civil war. This mode of yielding would, it is said, give way to independency without a war. I am persuaded from the nature of things and from every information that it would have had a directly contrary effect. But if it had this effect I confess that I should prefer independency without war to independency with it, and I have so much trust in the inclinations and prejudices of mankind and so little in anything else that I should expect ten times more benefit to this kingdom from the affection of America, though under a separate establishment, than from her perfect submission to the crown and Parliament, accompanied with her terror, disgust, and abhorrence. Bodies tied together by so unnatural a bond of union as mutual hatred are only connected to their ruin.

One hundred and ten respectable members of Parliament voted for that concession. Many not present when the motion was made were of the sentiments of those who voted. I knew it would then have made peace. I am not without hopes that it would do so at present if it were adopted. No benefit, no revenue could be lost by it; something might possibly be gained by its consequences. For be fully assured: that of all the phantoms that ever deluded the fond hopes

of a credulous world, a Parliamentary revenue in the colonies is the most perfectly chimerical. Your breaking them to
any subjection, far from relieving your burdens (the pretext
for this war) will never pay that military force which will be
kept up to the destruction of their liberties and yours. I risk
nothing in this prophecy.

Gentlemen, you have my opinion on the present state
of public affairs. Mean as they may be in themselves, your
partiality has made them of some importance. Without
troubling myself to inquire whether I am under a formal
obligation to it, I have a pleasure in accounting for my conduct to my constituents. I feel warmly on this subject, and
I express myself as I feel. If I presume to blame any public
proceeding I cannot be supposed to be personal. Would to
God I could be suspected of it. My fault might be greater, but the public calamity would be less extensive. If my
conduct has not been able to make any impression on the
warm part of that ancient and powerful party, with whose
support I was not honored at my election, on my side my
respect, regard, and duty to them is not at all lessened. I owe
the gentlemen who compose it my most humble service in
everything. I hope that whenever any of them were pleased
to command me that they found me perfectly equal in my
obedience. But flattery and friendship are very different
things, and to mislead is not to serve them. I cannot purchase the favor of any man by concealing from him what I
think his ruin. By the favor of my fellow-citizens I am the
representative of an honest, well-ordered, virtuous city—of
a people who preserve more of the original English simplicity and purity of manners than perhaps any other. You
possess among you several men and magistrates of large
and cultivated understandings, fit for any employment in

any sphere. I do, to the best of my power, act so as to make myself worthy of so honorable a choice. If I were ready on any call of my own vanity or interest, or to answer any election purpose to forsake principles (whatever they are) which I had formed at a mature age on full reflection, and which had been confirmed by long experience, I should forfeit the only thing which makes you pardon so many errors and imperfections in me. Not that I think it fit for any one to rely too much on his own understanding, or to be filled with a presumption not becoming a Christian man in his own personal stability and rectitude. I hope I am far from that vain confidence which almost always fails in trial. I know my weakness in all respects, as much at least as any enemy I have, and I attempt to take security against it. The only method which has ever been found effectual to preserve any man against the corruption of nature and example is a habit of life and communication of counsels with the most virtuous and public-spirited men of the age you live in. Such a society cannot be kept without advantage, or deserted without shame. For this rule of conduct I may be called in reproach a *party man*, but I am little affected with such aspersions. In the way which they call party I worship the constitution of your fathers, and I shall never blush for my political company. All reverence to honor, all idea of what it is will be lost out of the world before it can be imputed as a fault to any man that he has been closely connected with those incomparable persons, living and dead, with whom for eleven years I have constantly thought and acted. If I have wandered out of the paths of rectitude into those of interested faction it was in company with the Saviles, the Dowdeswells, the Wentworths, the Bentincks, with the Lenoxes, the Manchesters, the Keppels, the Saunderses, with the temperate, permanent, hereditary virtue of the whole house of Cavendish—names among which some have extended your fame and empire in arms, and all have fought the battle of your liberties in fields not less glorious. These, and many more like these, grafting public principles on private honor, have redeemed the present age, and would have adorned the most splendid period in your history. Where could any man, conscious of his own inability to act alone, and willing to act as he ought to do, have arranged himself better? If anyone thinks this kind of society to be taken up as the best method of gratifying low, personal pride or ambitious interest he is mistaken, and he knows nothing of the world.

Preferring this connection, I do not mean to detract in the slightest degree from others. There are some of those whom I admire at something of a greater distance, with whom I have had the happiness also perfectly to agree in almost all the particulars in which I have differed with some successive administrations, and they are such as it never can be reputable to any Government to reckon among its enemies. I hope there are none of you corrupted with the doctrine taught by wicked men for the worst purposes, and received by the malignant credulity of envy and ignorance, which is that the men who act upon the public stage are all alike, all equally corrupt, all influenced by no other views than the sordid lure of salary and pension. The thing I know by experience to be false. Never expecting to find perfection in men, and not looking for divine attributes in created beings, in my commerce with my contemporaries I have found much human virtue. I have seen not a little public spirit, a real subordination of interest to duty, and a decent and regulated sensibility to honest fame and reputation. The age unquestionably produces (whether in a greater or less number than former times I know not) daring profligates and insidious hypocrites. What then? Am I not to avail myself of whatever good is to be found in the world because of the mixture of evil that will always be in it? The smallness of the quantity in currency only heightens the value. They who raise suspicions on the good on account of the behavior of ill men are of the party of the latter. The common cant is no justification for taking this party. I have been deceived, say they, by *Titius* and *Mævius*, I have been the dupe of this pretender or of that mountebank, and I can trust appearances no longer. But my credulity and want of discernment cannot, as I conceive, amount to a fair presumption against any man's integrity. A conscientious person would rather doubt his own judgment than condemn his species. He would say, I have observed without attention, or judged upon erroneous maxims; I trusted to profession when I ought to have attended to conduct. Such a man will grow wise, not malignant, by his acquaintance with the world. But he that accuses all mankind of corruption ought to remember that he is sure to convict only one. In truth I should much rather admit those whom at any time I have disrelished the most to be patterns of perfection than seek a consolation to my own unworthiness in a general communion of depravity with all about me.

That this ill-natured doctrine should be preached by the missionaries of a court I do not wonder. It answers their purpose. But that it should be heard among those who pretend to be strong assertors of liberty, is not only surprising but hardly natural. This moral levelling is a *servile principle*. It leads to practical passive obedience far better than all the doctrines which the pliant accommodation of theology to power has ever produced. It cuts up by the roots, not only all idea of forcible resistance, but even of civil opposition. It disposes men to an abject submission, not by opinion, which may be shaken by argument or altered by passion, but by the strong ties of public and private interest. For if all men who act in a public situation are equally selfish, corrupt, and venal, what reason can be given for desiring any sort of change, which, besides the evils which must attend all changes, can be productive of no possible advantage? The active men in the state are true samples of the mass. If they are universally depraved the commonwealth itself is not sound. We may amuse ourselves with talking as much as we please of the virtue of middle or humble life; that is, we may place our confidence in the virtue of those who have never been tried. But if the persons who are continually emerging out of that sphere be no better than those whom birth has placed above it, what hopes are there in the remainder of the body, which is to furnish the perpetual succession of the state? All who have ever written on government are unanimous that among a people generally corrupt, liberty cannot long exist. And indeed, how is it possible, when those who are to make the laws, to guard, to enforce, or to obey them, are by a tacit confederacy of manners indisposed to the spirit of all generous and noble institutions?

I am aware that the age is not what we all wish. But I am sure that the only means of checking its precipitate degeneracy is heartily to concur with whatever is the best in our time: and to have some more correct standard of judging what that best is than the transient and uncertain favor of a court. If once we are able to find and can prevail on ourselves to strengthen a union of such men, whatever accidentally becomes indisposed to ill-exercised power, even by the ordinary operation of human passions, must join with that society, and cannot long be joined without in some degree assimilating to it. Virtue will catch as well as vice by contact, and the public stock of honest manly principle will daily accumulate. We are not too nicely to scrutinize motives as long as action is irreproachable. It is enough (and for a worthy man perhaps too much) to deal out its infamy to convicted guilt and declared apostasy.

This, gentlemen, has been from the beginning the rule of my conduct, and I mean to continue it as long as such a body as I have described can by any possibility be kept together, for I should think it the most dreadful of all offenses, not only towards the present generation but to all the future, if I were to do anything which could make the minutest breach in this great conservatory of free principles. Those who perhaps have the same intentions but are separated by some little political animosities will I hope discern at last how little conducive it is to any rational purpose to lower its reputation. For my part, gentlemen, from much experience, from no little thinking, and from comparing a great variety of things, I am thoroughly persuaded that the last hope of preserving the spirit of the English constitution, or of reuniting the dissipated members of the English race upon a common plan of tranquility and liberty, does entirely depend on their firm and lasting union, and above all on their keeping themselves from that despair which is so very apt to fall on those whom a violence of character and a mixture of ambitious views do not support through a long, painful, and unsuccessful struggle.

There never, gentlemen, was a period in which the steadfastness of some men has been put to so sore a trial. It

is not very difficult for well-formed minds to abandon their
interest, but the separation of fame and virtue is a harsh
divorce. Liberty is in danger of being made unpopular to
Englishmen. Contending for an imaginary power we begin
to acquire the spirit of domination and to lose the relish of
honest equality. The principles of our forefathers become
suspected to us, because we see them animating the present
opposition of our children. The faults which grow out of
the luxuriance of freedom appear much more shocking to
us than the base vices which are generated from the rank-
ness of servitude. Accordingly, the least resistance to power appears more inexcusable in our eyes than the greatest
abuses of authority. All dread of a standing military force is
looked upon as a superstitious panic. All shame of calling
in foreigners and savages in a civil contest is worn off. We
grow indifferent to the consequences inevitable to ourselves
from the plan of ruling half the empire by a mercenary
sword. We are taught to believe that a desire of domineer-
ing over our countrymen is love to our country, that those
who hate civil war abate rebellion, and that the amiable
and conciliatory virtues of leniency, moderation, and tenderness to the privileges of those who depend on this kingdom are a sort of treason to the state.

It is impossible that we should remain long in a situation which breeds such notions and dispositions without
some great alteration in the national character. Those ingenuous and feeling minds who are so fortified against all
other things, and so unarmed to whatever approaches, in
the shape of disgrace, finding these principles, which they
considered as sure means of honor, to be grown into dis-
repute, will retire disheartened and disgusted. Those of a
more robust make, the bold, able, ambitious men who pay

some of their court to power through the people, and substitute the voice of transient opinion in the place of true
glory, will give in to the general mode; and those superior
understandings which ought to correct vulgar prejudice will
confirm and aggravate its errors. Many things have been
long operating towards a gradual change in our principles.
But this American war has done more in a very few years
than all the other causes could have effected in a century. It
is therefore not on its own separate account, but because of
its attendant circumstances that I consider its continuance
or its ending in any way but that of all honorable and liberal accommodation as the greatest evils which can befall
us. For that reason I have troubled you with this long letter.
For that reason I entreat you again and again neither to
be persuaded, shamed, or frightened out of the principles
that have hitherto led so many of you to abhor the war, its
cause, and its consequences. Let us not be among the first
who renounce the maxims of our forefathers.

I have the honor to be, gentlemen, your most obedient and faithful humble servant,

EDMUND BURKE.

Beaconsfield, April 3, 1777.

P.S. You may communicate this letter in any manner
you think proper to my constituents.

Letter to Dr. Benjamin Franklin
August, 1781

Dear Sir,—

I feel, as an honest man and as a good citizen ought to feel, the calamities of the present unhappy war. The only part, however, of those calamities which personally affects myself is that I have been obliged to discontinue my intercourse with you; but that one misfortune I must consider as equivalent to many. I may, indeed, with great truth, assure you that your friendship has always been an object of my ambition, and that, if a high and very sincere esteem for your talents and virtues could give me a title to it, I am not wholly unworthy of that honor. I flatter myself that your belief in the reality of these sentiments will excuse the liberty I take, in laying before you a matter in which I have no small concern. The application I make originates wholly from myself, and has not been suggested to me by any person whatsoever.

I have lately been informed with great certainty, and with no less surprise, that the congress have made an application for the return of my friend General Burgoyne to captivity in America, at a time when the exchange of almost all the rest of the convention officers has been completed. It is true that this requisition has been for the present withdrawn; but then, it may be renewed at every instant, and no arrangement has been made or proposed, which may prevent a thing on all accounts so very disagreeable, as to see the most opposite interests conspiring in the persecution of a man, formed, by the unparalleled candor and moderation of his mind, to unite the most discordant parties in his favor.

I own this proceeding of the congress fills me with astonishment. I am persuaded that some unusually artful management, or very unexampled delusion, has operated to produce an effect which cannot be accounted for on any of the ordinary principles of nature or of policy.

I shall not enter into the particulars of the convention under which this claim is made, nor into the construction of it, nor the execution. I am not, perhaps, capable of doing justice to the merits of the cause; and if I were, I am not disposed to put them upon any ground of argument, because (whatever others might and possibly ought to do) I am not pleading a point of strict right, but appealing to your known principles of honor and generosity, with the freedom and privileges of an old friendship. And as I suppose you perfectly acquainted with the whole history of the extraordinary treatment General Burgoyne has met with, I am resolved not to show so much distrust in so sound a memory and so good a judgment as yours, as to attempt to refresh the one or to lead the other.

I am ready to admit that General Burgoyne has been and (as far as what is left him will suffer) is a very affectionate and a very jealous servant of the crown, and that in America he acted as an officer of the king (so long as fortune favored him) with great abilities, and distinguished fidelity, activity, and spirit. You, my dear sir, who have made such astonishing exertions in the cause which you espouse, and are so deeply read in human nature and in human morals, know better than anybody that men will and that sometimes are bound to take very different views and measures of their duty from local and from professional situation, and that we may all have equal merit in extremely different lines of conduct. You know that others may deserve the whole of your admiration in a cause, in which your judgment leads you to oppose them. But whatever may be our opinions on the origin of this fatal war, I assure you, General Burgoyne has the merit of never having driven it on with violence, or fostered or kept it alive by any evil arts, or aggravated its natural mischiefs by unnecessary rigor; but has behaved on all occasions with that temper which becomes a great military character, which loves nothing so well in the profession as the means it so frequently furnishes of splendid acts of generosity and humanity.

You have heard of the sacrifices he has made to his nice sense of honor on this side of the water—sacrifices far beyond the just demands of the principle to which they were made. This has been no advantage to the country where he was piqued to it. Shall America, too, call for sacrifices that are still more severe, and of full as little advantage to those who demand them? I know the rigor of political necessity, but I see here as little of necessity, or even expedience, as of propriety. I know the respect that is due to all public bodies, but none of them are exempt from mistake; and the most disrespectful thing that can be done towards them is to suppose them incapable of correcting an error.

If I were not fully persuaded of your liberal and manly way of thinking, I should not presume, in the hostile situation in which I stand, to make an application to you. But in this piece of experimental philosophy I run no risk of offending you. I apply not to the ambassador of America, but to Dr. Franklin, the philosopher—the friend and the lover of his species. In that light, whatever color politics may take, I shall ever have the honor to be, dear sir, etc., etc.,

EDM. BURKE.

Letter from Benjamin Franklin to Edmund Burke
Passy, October 15, 1781

Sir,—

I received but a few days ago your very friendly letter of August last, on the subject of General Burgoyne.

Since the foolish part of mankind will make wars from time to time with each other, not having sense enough otherwise to settle their differences, it certainly becomes the wiser part, who cannot prevent these wars, to alleviate as much as possible the calamities attending them.

Mr. Burke always stood high in my esteem. His affectionate concern for his friend renders him still more amiable, and makes the honor he does me in admitting me of the number still more precious.

I do not think the congress have any wish to persecute General Burgoyne. I never heard till I received your letter that they had recalled him. If they have made such a resolution, it must be, I suppose, a conditional one—to take place in case their offer of exchanging him for Mr. Laurens should not be accepted—a resolution intended to enforce that offer.

I have just received an authentic copy of the resolve containing that offer, and authorizing me to make it. As I have no communication with your ministers, I send it enclosed to you. If you can find any means of negotiating this business, I am sure the restoring another worthy man to his family and friends will be an addition to your pleasure.

With great and invariable respect and affection, I am, sir, your most humble and most obedient servant,

B. FRANKLIN.

APPENDIX

Short Account of a Late Short Administration (1766)

The late administration came into employment, under the mediation of the Duke of Cumberland, on the tenth day of July, 1765, and was removed, upon a plan settled by the Earl of Chatham, on the thirtieth day of July, 1766, having lasted just one year and twenty days.

In that space of time, the distractions of the British empire were composed, by *the repeal of the American Stamp Act*, but the constitutional superiority of Great Britain was preserved, by *the Act for securing the dependence of the colonies*.

Private houses were relieved from the jurisdiction of the excise, by *the repeal of the cider-tax*. The personal liberty of the subject was confirmed, by *the resolution against general warrants*.

The lawful secrets of business and friendship were rendered inviolable, by *the resolution for condemning the seizure of papers*.

The trade of America was set free from injudicious and ruinous impositions—its revenue was improved, and settled upon a rational foundation—its commerce extended with foreign countries, while all the advantages were secured to Great Britain, by *the Act for repealing certain duties, and encouraging, regulating, and securing the trade of this kingdom, and the British dominions in America.*

Materials were provided and insured to our manufactures, the sale of these manufactures was increased, the African trade preserved and extended, the principles of the Act of Navigation pursued, and the plan improved—and the trade for bullion rendered free, secure, and permanent by *the Act for opening certain ports in Dominica and Jamaica.*

That administration was the first which proposed and encouraged public meetings, and free consultations of merchants from all parts of the kingdom, by which means the truest lights have been received; great benefits have been already derived to manufactures and commerce; and the most extensive prospects are opened for further improvement.

Under them, the interests of our northern and southern colonies, before that time jarring and dissonant, were understood, compared, adjusted, and perfectly reconciled. The passions and animosities of the colonies, by judicious and lenient measures, were allayed and composed, and the foundation laid for a lasting agreement among them.

While that administration provided for the liberty and commerce of their country, as the true basis of its power, they consulted its interests, they asserted its honor abroad, with temper and with firmness, by making an advantageous treaty of commerce with Russia; by obtaining a liquidation of the Canada bills, to the satisfaction of the proprietors; by reviving and raising from its ashes the negotiation for the Manilla ransom, which had been extinguished and abandoned by their predecessors.

They treated their sovereign with decency, with rever-

ence. They discountenanced, and, it is hoped, forever abol-
ished, the dangerous and unconstitutional practice of removing military officers for their votes in Parliament. They
firmly adhered to those friends of liberty, who had run all
hazards in its cause, and provided for them in preference to
every other claim.

With the Earl of Bute they had no personal connection,
no correspondence of councils. They neither courted him
nor persecuted him. They practiced no corruption; nor
were they even suspected of it. They sold no offices. They
obtained no reversions or pensions, either coming in or going out, for themselves, their families, or their dependents.

In the prosecution of their measures they were traversed by an opposition of a new and singular character,
an opposition of placemen and pensioners. They were supported by the confidence of the nation. And having held
their offices under many difficulties and discouragements,
they left them at the express command, as they had accepted them at the earnest request, of their royal master.

These are plain facts of a clear and public nature,
neither extended by elaborate reasoning, nor heightened
by the coloring of eloquence. They are the services of a
single year.

The removal of that administration from power is not
to them premature; since they were in office long enough to
accomplish many plans of public utility, and, by their perseverance and resolution, rendered the way smooth and easy
to their successors, having left their king and their country
in a much better condition than they found them. By the
temper they manifest, they seem to have now no other wish
than that their successors may do the public as real and as
faithful service as they have done.

Observations on a
Late Publication, Entitled
"The Present State Of The Nation"
(1769)
(Three Extracts relating to America)

"O Tite, si quid ego adjuvero curamve revasso,
Quae nunc te coquit, et versat sub pectore fixa,
Ecquid erit pretii?" Cicero, *De Senectute*

Party divisions, whether on the whole operating for
good or evil, are things inseparable from free government.
This is a truth which, I believe, admits little dispute, having
been established by the uniform experience of all ages. The
part a good citizen ought to take in these divisions has been
a matter of much deeper controversy. But God forbid that
any controversy relating to our essential morals should admit of no decision. It appears to me that this question, like
most of the others which regard our duties in life, is to be
determined by our station in it. Private men may be wholly neutral, and entirely innocent; but they who are legally
invested with public trust, or stand on the high ground of
rank and dignity, which is trust implied, can hardly in any
case remain indifferent, without the certainty of sinking

into insignificance; and thereby in effect deserting that post in which, with the fullest authority, and for the wisest purposes, the laws and institutions of their country have fixed them. However, if it be the office of those who are thus circumstanced, to take a decided part, it is no less their duty that it should be a sober one. It ought to be circumscribed by the same laws of decorum, and balanced by the same temper which bound and regulate all the virtues. In a word, we ought to act in party with all the moderation which does not absolutely enervate that vigor, and quench that fervency of spirit, without which the best wishes for the public good must evaporate in empty speculation.

It is probably from some such motives that the friends of a very respectable party in this kingdom have been hitherto silent. For these two years past, from one and the same quarter of politics, a continual fire has been kept upon them; sometimes from the unwieldy column of quartos and octavos; sometimes from the light squadrons of occasional pamphlets and flying sheets. Every month has brought on its periodical calumny. The abuse has taken every shape which the ability of the writers could give it: plain invective, clumsy raillery, misrepresented anecdote (*History of the Minority*; *History of the Repeal of the Stamp Act*; *Considerations on Trade and Finance*; *Political Register*, etc., etc.). No method of vilifying the measures, the abilities, the intentions, or the persons which compose that body, has been omitted.

On their part nothing was opposed but patience and character. It was a matter of the most serious and indignant affliction to persons who thought themselves in conscience bound to oppose a ministry dangerous from its very constitution, as well as its measures, to find themselves, whenever they faced their adversaries, continually attacked on the rear by a set of men who pretended to be actuated by motives similar to theirs. They saw that the plan long pursued, with but too fatal a success, was to break the strength of this kingdom by frittering down the bodies which compose it, by fomenting bitter and sanguinary animosities, and by dissolving every tie of social affection and public trust. These virtuous men, such I am warranted by public opinion to call them, were resolved rather to endure everything than cooperate in that design. A diversity of opinion upon almost every principle of politics had indeed drawn a strong line of separation between them and some others. However, they were desirous not to extend the misfortune by unnecessary bitterness; they wished to prevent a difference of opinion on the commonwealth from festering into rancorous and incurable hostility. Accordingly, they endeavored that all past controversies should be forgotten, and that enough for the day should be the evil thereof. There is, however, a limit at which forbearance ceases to be a virtue. Men may tolerate injuries while they are only personal to themselves. But it is not the first of virtues to bear with moderation the indignities that are offered to our country. A piece has at length appeared, from the quarter of all the former attacks, which upon every public consideration demands an answer. While persons more equal to this business may be engaged in affairs of greater moment, I hope I shall be excused, if, in a few hours of a time not very important, and from such materials as I have by me (more than enough however for this purpose), I undertake to set the facts and arguments of this wonderful performance in a proper light. I will endeavor to state what this piece is; the purpose for which I take it to have been written; and the effects (supposing it should have any effect at all) it must necessarily produce.

This piece is called *The Present State of the Nation*. It may be considered as a sort of digest of the avowed maxims of a certain political school, the effects of whose doctrines and practices this country will feel long and severely. It is made up of a farrago of almost every topic which has been agitated in Parliamentary debate, or private conversation, on national affairs for these last seven years. The oldest controversies are hauled out of the dust with which time and neglect had covered them. Arguments ten times repeated, a thousand times answered before, are here repeated again. Public accounts formerly printed and reprinted revolve once more, and find their old station in this sober meridian. All the commonplace lamentations upon the decay of trade, the increase of taxes, and the high price of labor and provisions, are here retailed again and again in the same tone with which they have drawled through columns of Gazetteers and Advertisers for a century together. Paradoxes which affront common sense, and uninteresting barren truths which generate no conclusion, are thrown in to augment unwieldy bulk, without adding anything to weight. Because two accusations are better than one, contradictions are set staring one another in the face, without even an attempt to reconcile them. And, to give the whole a sort of portentous air of labor and information, the table of the House of Commons is swept into this grand reservoir of politics.

The purpose of this pamphlet, at which it aims directly or obliquely in every page, is to persuade the public of three or four of the most difficult points in the world—that all the advantages of the late war were on the part of the Bourbon alliance; that the peace of Paris perfectly consulted the dignity and interest of this country; and that the American

Stamp Act was a masterpiece of policy and finance; that the only good minister this nation has enjoyed since his Majesty's accession is the Earl of Bute; and the only good Managers of revenue we have seen are Lord Despenser and Mr. George Grenville; and, under the description of men of virtue and ability, he holds them out to us as the only persons fit to put our affairs in order. Let not the reader mistake me: he does not actually name these persons, but, having highly applauded their conduct in all its parts, and heavily censured every other set of men in the kingdom, he then recommends us to his men of virtue and ability.

Such is the author's scheme. Whether it will answer his purpose I know not. But surely that purpose ought to be a wonderfully good one, to warrant the methods he has taken to compass it. If the facts and reasonings in this piece are admitted, it is all over with us. The continuance of our tranquility depends upon the compassion of our rivals. Unable to secure to ourselves the advantages of peace, we are at the same time utterly unfit for war. It is impossible, if this state of things be credited abroad, that we can have any alliance; all nations will fly from so dangerous a connection, lest, instead of being partakers of our strength, they should only become sharers in our ruin. If it is believed at home, all that firmness of mind and dignified national courage, which used to be the great support of this isle against the powers of the world, must melt away, and fail within us.

In such a state of things, can it be amiss if I aim at holding out some comfort to the nation; another sort of comfort, indeed, than that which this writer provides for it; a comfort, not from its physician, but from its constitution? If I attempt to show that all the arguments upon which he founds the decay of that constitution, and the necessity of that physician, are vain and frivolous? I will follow the author closely in his own long career, through the war, the peace, the finances, our trade, and our foreign politics—not for the sake of the particular measures which he discusses (that can be of no use: they are all decided; their good is all enjoyed, or their evil incurred)—but for the sake of the principles of war, peace, trade, and finances. These principles are of infinite moment. They must come again and again under consideration; and it imports the public, of all things, that those of its ministers be enlarged, and just, and well-confirmed, upon all these subjects. What notions this author entertains we shall see presently: notions in my opinion very irrational, and extremely dangerous, and which, if they should crawl from pamphlets into counsels, and be realized from private speculation into national measures, cannot fail of hastening and completing our ruin.

It is surely a little unfortunate for us that he has picked out the *Navy* as the very first object of his economical experiments. Of all the public services, that of the navy is the one in which tampering may be of the greatest danger, which can worst be supplied upon an emergency, and of which any failure draws after it the longest and heaviest train of consequences. I am far from saying that this or any service ought not to be conducted with economy. But I will never suffer the sacred name of economy to be bestowed upon arbitrary defalcation of charge. The author tells us himself, "that to suffer the navy to rot in harbor for want of repairs and marines, would be to invite destruction." It would be so. When the author talks therefore of savings on the navy estimate, it is incumbent on him to let us know, not what sums he will cut off, but what branch of that service he deems superfluous. Instead of putting us off with unmeaning generalities, he ought to have stated what naval force, what naval works, and what naval stores, with the lowest estimated expense, are necessary to keep our marine in a condition commensurate to its great ends. And this too not for the contracted and deceitful space of a single year, but for some reasonable term. Everybody knows that many charges cannot be in their nature regular or annual. In the year 1767 a stock of hemp, etc., was to be laid in; that charge intermits, but it does not end. Other charges of other kinds take their place. Great works are now carrying on at Portsmouth, but not of greater magnitude than utility, and they must be provided for. A year's estimate is therefore no just idea at all of a permanent peace establishment. Had the author opened this matter upon these plain principles, a judgment might have been formed, how far he had contrived to reconcile national defense with public economy. Till he has done it, those who had rather depend on any man's reason than the greatest man's authority will not give him credit on this head, for the saving of a single shilling. As to those savings which are already made, or in course of being made, whether right or wrong, he has nothing at all to do with them; they can be no part of his project, considered as a plan of reformation. I greatly fear that the error has not lately been on the side of profusion.

Another head is the saving on the army and ordnance extraordinaries, particularly in the American branch. What or how much reduction may be made, none of us, I believe, can with any fairness pretend to say; very little, I am convinced. The state of America is extremely unsettled; more troops have been sent thither; new dispositions have been made; and this augmentation of number, and change of disposition, has rarely, I believe, the effect of lessening the

bill for extraordinaries, which, if not this year, yet in the
next we must certainly feel. Care has not been wanting to
introduce economy into that part of the service. The author's great friend has made, I admit, some regulations; his
immediate successors have made more and better. This part
will be handled more ably and more minutely at another
time; but no one can cut down this bill of extraordinaries
at his pleasure. The author has given us nothing but his
word, for any certain or considerable reduction, and this we
ought to be the more cautious in taking, as he has promised
great savings in his *Considerations*, which he has not chosen
to abide by in his *State of the Nation*.

On this head also of the American extraordinaries, he
can take credit for nothing. As to his next, the lessening of
the deficiency of the land and malt tax, particularly of the
malt tax, any person the least conversant in that subject
cannot avoid a smile. This deficiency arises from charge of
collection, from anticipation, and from defective produce.
What has the author said on the reduction of any head
of this deficiency upon the land tax? On these points he
is absolutely silent. As to the deficiency on the malt tax,
which is chiefly owing to a defective produce, he has, and
can have, nothing to propose. If this deficiency should be
lessened by the increase of malting in any years more than
in others (as it is a greatly fluctuating object), how much of
this obligation shall we owe to this author's ministry? Will
it not be the case under any administration? Must it not
go to the general service of the year, in some way or other,
let the finances be in whose hands they will? But why take
credit for so extremely reduced a deficiency at all? I can tell
him he has no rational ground for it in the produce of the
year 1767, and I suspect will have full as little reason from

the produce of the year 1768. That produce may indeed become greater, and the deficiency of course will be less. It may too be far otherwise. A fair and judicious financier will not, as this writer has done, for the sake of making out a specious account, select a favorable year or two, at remote periods, and ground his calculations on those. In 1768 he will not take the deficiencies of 1753 and 1754 for his standard. Sober men have hitherto (and must continue this course, to preserve this character) taken indifferently the mediums of the years immediately preceding. But a person who has a scheme from which he promises much to the public ought to be still more cautious; he should ground his speculation rather on the lowest mediums, because all new schemes are known to be subject to some defect or failure not foreseen, and which therefore every prudent proposer will be ready to allow for, in order to lay his foundation as low and as solid as possible. Quite contrary is the practice of some politicians. They first propose savings, which they well know cannot be made, in order to get a reputation for economy. In due time they assume another, but a different method, by providing for the service they had before cut off or straitened, and which they can then very easily prove to be necessary. In the same spirit they raise magnificent ideas of revenue on funds which they know to be insufficient. Afterwards, who can blame them, if they do not satisfy the public desires? They are great artificers, but they cannot work without materials.

These are some of the little arts of great statesmen. To such we leave them, and follow where the author leads us, to his next resource, the Foundling Hospital. Whatever particular virtue there is in the mode of this saving, there seems to be nothing at all new, and indeed nothing wonderfully

important in it. The sum annually voted for the support of
the Foundling Hospital has been in a former Parliament
limited to the establishment of the children then in the hospital. When they are apprenticed, this provision will cease.
It will therefore fall in more or less at different times, and
will at length cease entirely. But, until it does, we cannot
reckon upon it as the saving on the establishment of any
given year nor can anyone conceive how the author comes
to mention this, any more than some other articles, as a part
of a *new* plan of economy which is to retrieve our affairs.
This charge will indeed cease in its own time. But will no
other succeed to it? Has he ever known the public free from
some contingent charge, either for the just support of royal
dignity, or for national magnificence, or for public charity,
or for public service? Does he choose to flatter his readers
that no such will ever return? Or does he in good earnest
declare, that let the reason, or necessity, be what they will,
he is resolved not to provide for such services?

Another resource of economy yet remains, for he gleans
the field very closely: £1800 for the American Surveys. Why,
what signifies a dispute about trifles? He shall have it. But
while he is carrying it off, I shall just whisper in his ear, that
neither the saving that is allowed, nor that which is doubted
of, can at all belong to that future proposed administration,
whose touch is to cure all our evils. Both the one and the
other belong equally (as indeed all the rest do) to the present
administration, to any administration; because they are the
gift of time, and not the bounty of the exchequer.

I have now done with all the minor, preparatory parts
of the author's scheme, the several articles of saving which
he proposes. At length comes the capital operation, his new
resources. Three hundred thousand pounds a year from

America and Ireland—alas, alas, if that too should fail us, what will become of this poor undone nation? The author, in a tone of great humility, *hopes* they may be induced to pay it. Well, if that be all, we may hope so too, and for any light he is pleased to give us into the ground of this hope, and the ways and means of this inducement, here is a speedy end both of the question and the revenue.

It is the constant custom of this author, in all his writings, to take it for granted, that he has given you a revenue, whenever he can point out to you where you may have money, if you can contrive how to get it, and this seems to be the masterpiece of his financial ability. I think however, in his way of proceeding, he has behaved rather like a harsh step-dame, than a kind nursing-mother to his country. Why stop at £300,000? If his state of things be at all founded, America and Ireland are much better able to pay £600,000 than we are to satisfy ourselves with half that sum. However, let us forgive him this one instance of tenderness towards Ireland and the colonies.

He spends a vast deal of time (p. 35) in an endeavor to prove that Ireland is able to bear greater impositions. He is of opinion that the poverty of the lower class of people there is, in a great measure, owing to a *want* of judicious taxes; that a land tax will enrich her tenants; that taxes are paid in England which are not paid there; that the colony trade is increased above £100,000 since the peace; that she *ought* to have further indulgence in that trade; and ought to have further privileges in the woolen manufacture. From these premises, of what she has, what she has not, and what she ought to have, he infers that Ireland will contribute £100,000 towards the extraordinaries of the American establishment.

I shall make no objections whatsoever, logical or financial, to this reasoning. Many occur; but they would lead me from my purpose, from which I do not intend to be diverted, because it seems to me of no small importance. It will be just enough to hint, what I dare say many readers have before observed, that when any man proposes new taxes in a country with which he is not personally conversant by residence or office, he ought to lay open its situation much more minutely and critically than this author has done, or than perhaps he is able to do. He ought not to content himself with saying that a single article of her trade is increased £100,000 a year; he ought, if he argues from the increase of trade to the increase of taxes, to state the whole trade, and not one branch of trade only! He ought to enter fully into the state of its remittances, and the course of its exchange; he ought likewise to examine whether all its establishments are increased or diminished, and whether it incurs or discharges debts annually. But I pass over all this and am content to ask a few plain questions.

Does the author then seriously mean to propose in Parliament a land tax, or any tax, for £100,000 a year upon Ireland? If he does, and if fatally, by his temerity and our weakness, he should succeed, then I say he will throw the whole empire from one end of it to the other into mortal convulsions. What is it that can satisfy the furious and perturbed mind of this man? Is it not enough for him that such projects have alienated our colonies from the mother country, and not to propose violently to tear our sister kingdom also from our side, and to convince every dependent part of the empire, that when a little money is to be raised, we have no sort of regard to their ancient customs, their opinions, their circumstances, or their affections? He has, however, a *douceur* for Ireland in his pocket: benefits in trade, by opening the woolen manufacture to that nation. A very right idea in my opinion, but not more strong in reason, than likely to be opposed by the most powerful and most violent of all local prejudices and popular passions. First, a fire is already kindled by his schemes of taxation in America; he then proposes one which will set all Ireland in a blaze; and his way of quenching both is by a plan which may kindle perhaps ten times a greater flame in Britain.

Will the author pledge himself previously to his proposal of such a tax, to carry this enlargement of the Irish trade? If he does not, then the tax will be certain; the benefit will be less than problematical. In this view his compensation to Ireland vanishes into smoke; the tax to their prejudices will appear stark naked in the light of an act of arbitrary power and oppression. But if he should propose the benefit and tax together, then the people of Ireland, a very high and spirited people, would think it the worst bargain in the world. They would look upon the one as wholly vitiated and poisoned by the other, and, if they could not be separated, would infallibly resist them both together. Here would be taxes indeed, amounting to a handsome sum: £100,000 very effectually voted, and passed through the best and most authentic forms—but how to be collected? This is his perpetual manner. One of his projects depends for success upon another project, and this upon a third, all of them equally visionary. His finance is like the Indian philosophy: his earth is poised on the horns of a bull, his bull stands upon an elephant, his elephant is supported by a tortoise; and so on forever.

As to his American £200,000 a year, he is satisfied to repeat gravely, as he has done a hundred times before, that

the Americans are able to pay it. Well, and what then? Does
he lay open any part of his plan how they may be compelled to pay it, without plunging ourselves into calamities
that outweigh tenfold the proposed benefit? Or does he
show how they may be induced to submit to it quietly? Or
does he give any satisfaction concerning the mode of levying it (in commercial colonies, one of the most important
and difficult of all considerations)? Nothing like it. To the
Stamp Act, whatever its excellences may be, I think he will
not in reality recur, or even choose to assert that he means
to do so, in case his minister should come again into power. If he does, I will predict that some of the fastest friends
of that minister will desert him upon this point. As to port
duties, he has damned them all in the lump, by declaring
them "contrary to the first principles of colonization, and
not less prejudicial to the interests of Great Britain than to
those of the colonies" (p. 37). Surely this single observation
of his ought to have taught him a little caution; he ought
to have begun to doubt, whether there is not something in
the nature of commercial colonies, which renders them an
unfit object of taxation, when port duties, so large a fund
of revenue in all countries, are by himself found, in this
case, not only improper, but destructive. However, he has
here pretty well narrowed the field of taxation. Stamp Act,
hardly to be resumed. Port duties, mischievous. Excises, I
believe, he will scarcely think worth the collection (if any
revenue should be so) in America. Land tax (notwithstanding his opinion of its immense use to agriculture) he will
not directly propose, before he has thought again and again
on the subject. Indeed, he very readily recommends it for
Ireland, and seems to think it not improper for America,
because, he observes, they already raise most of their taxes

internally, including this tax. A most curious reason, truly! Because their lands are already heavily burdened, he thinks it right to burden them still further. But he will recollect, for surely he cannot be ignorant of it, that the lands of America are not, as in England, let at a rent certain in money, and therefore cannot, as here, be taxed at a certain pound rate. They value them in gross among themselves, and none but themselves in their several districts can value them. Without their hearty concurrence and cooperation, it is evident, we cannot advance a step in the assessing or collecting any land tax. As to the taxes which in some places the Americans pay by the acre, they are merely duties of regulation: they are small; and to increase them, notwithstanding the secret virtues of a land tax, would be the most effectual means of preventing that cultivation they are intended to promote. Besides, the whole country is heavily in arrear already for land taxes and quit rents. They have different methods of taxation in the different provinces, agreeable to their several local circumstances. In New England by far the greatest part of their revenue is raised by *faculty taxes and capitations.* Such is the method in many others. It is obvious that Parliament, unassisted by the colonies themselves, cannot take so much as a single step in this mode of taxation. Then what tax is it he will impose? Why, after all the boasting speeches and writings of his faction for these four years, after all the vain expectations which they have held out to a deluded public, this their great advocate, after twisting the subject every way, after writhing himself in every posture, after knocking at every door, is obliged fairly to abandon every mode of taxation whatsoever in America. He thinks it the best method for Parliament to impose the sum (pp. 37–38), and reserve the account to itself, leaving the mode of taxation to the colonies. But how and in what proportion? What does the author say? Oh, not a single syllable on this the most material part of the whole question. Will he, in Parliament, undertake to settle the proportions of such payments from Nova Scotia to Nevis, in no fewer than six and twenty different countries, varying in almost every possible circumstance one from another? If he does, I tell him, he adjourns his revenue to a very long day. If he leaves it to themselves to settle these proportions, he adjourns it to doomsday.

Then what does he get by this method on the side of acquiescence? Will the people of America relish this course, of giving and granting and applying their money, the better because their assemblies are made commissioners of the taxes? This is far worse than all his former projects. For here, if the assemblies shall refuse, or delay, or be negligent, or fraudulent, in this new-imposed duty, we are wholly without remedy, and neither our custom-house officers, nor our troops, nor our armed ships, can be of the least use in the collection. No idea can be more contemptible (I will not call it an oppressive one, the harshness is lost in the folly) than that of proposing to get any revenue from the Americans but by their freest and most cheerful consent. Most monied men know their own interest right well, and are as able as any financier in the valuation of risks. Yet I think this financier will scarcely find that adventurer hardy enough, at any premium, to advance a shilling upon a vote of such taxes. Let him name the man, or set of men, that would do it. This is the only proof of the value of revenues. What would an interested man rate them at? His subscription would be at ninety-nine *per cent*, discount the very first day of its opening. Here is our only national security from ruin, a security upon which no man in his senses would

venture a shilling of his fortune. Yet he puts down those
articles as gravely in his supply for the peace establishment,
as if the money had been all fairly lodged in the exchequer.

American revenue: £200,000
Ireland: £100,000

Very handsome indeed! But if supply is to be got in such
a manner, farewell the lucrative mystery of finance! If you
are to be credited for savings, without showing how, why,
or with what safety, they are to be made; and for revenues,
without specifying on what articles, or by what means, or at
what expense, they are to be collected; there is not a clerk in
a public office who may not outbid this author, or his friend,
for the department of chancellor of the exchequer; not an
apprentice in the city, that will not strike out, with the same
advantages, the same, or a much larger, plan of supply.

Here is the whole of what belongs to the author's
scheme for saving us from impending destruction. Take it
even in its most favorable point of view, as a thing within
possibility, and imagine what must be the wisdom of this
gentleman, or his opinion of ours, who could first think
of representing this nation in such a state, as no friend can
look upon but with horror, and scarcely an enemy without compassion, and afterwards of diverting himself with
such inadequate, impracticable, puerile methods for our
relief? If these had been the dreams of some unknown,
unnamed, and nameless writer, they would excite no alarm;
their weakness had been an antidote to their malignity. But
as they are universally believed to be written by the hand,
or, what amounts to the same thing, under the immediate
direction, of a person who has been in the management of

the highest affairs, and may soon be in the same situation, I think it is not to be reckoned among our greatest consolations, that the yet remaining power of this kingdom is to be employed in an attempt to realize notions that are at once so frivolous, and so full of danger. That consideration will justify me in dwelling a little longer on the difficulties of the nation, and the solutions of our author.

I am then persuaded that he cannot be in the least alarmed about our situation, let his outcry be what he pleases. I will give him a reason for my opinion, which, I think, he cannot dispute. All that he bestows upon the nation, which it does not possess without him, and supposing it all sure money, amounts to no more than a sum of £300,000 a year. This, he thinks, will do the business completely, and render us flourishing at home and respectable abroad. If the option between glory and shame, if our salvation or destruction, depended on this sum, it is impossible that he should have been active, and made a merit of that activity, in taking off a shilling in the pound of the land tax, which came up to his grand desideratum, and upwards of £100,000 more. By this maneuver, he left our trade, navigation, and manufactures on the verge of destruction, our finances in ruin, our credit expiring, Ireland on the point of being ceded to France, the colonies of being torn to pieces, the succession of the crown at the mercy of our great rival, and the kingdom itself on the very point of becoming tributary to that haughty power. All this for want of £300,000; for I defy the reader to point out any other revenue, or any other precise and defined scheme of politics which he assigns for our redemption.

I know that two things may be said in his defense, as bad reasons are always at hand in an indifferent cause: that

he was not sure the money would be applied as he thinks it
ought to be, by the present ministers. I think as ill of them
as he does to the full. They have done very near as much
mischief as they can do, to a constitution so robust as this is.
Nothing can make them more dangerous, but that, as they
are already in general composed of his disciples and instruments, they may add to the public calamity of their own
measures the adoption of his projects. But be the ministers
what they may, the author knows that they could not avoid
applying this £450,000 to the service of the establishment,
as faithfully as he, or any other minister, could do. I say they
could not avoid it, and have no merit at all for the application. But supposing that they should greatly mismanage this
revenue. Here is a good deal of room for mistake and prod-
igality before you come to the edge of ruin. The difference
between the amount of that real and his imaginary revenue
is, £150,000 a year, at least. A tolerable sum for them to play
with, this might compensate the difference between the author's economy and their profusion; and still, notwithstanding their vices and ignorance, the nation might he saved.
The author ought also to recollect that a good man would
hardly deny, even to the worst of ministers, the means of
doing their duty, especially in a crisis when our being depended on supplying them with some means or other. In
such a case their penury of mind, in discovering resources,
would make it rather the more necessary not to strip such
poor providers of the little stock they had in hand.

Besides, here is another subject of distress, and a very
serious one, which puts us again to a stand. The author
may possibly not come into power (I only state the possibility); he may not always continue in it; and if the contrary to
all this should fortunately for us happen, what insurance on

his life can be made for a sum adequate to his loss? Then
we are thus unluckily situated that the *chance* of an American and Irish revenue of £300,000 to be managed by him,
is to save us from ruin two or three years hence at best, to
make us happy at home and glorious abroad, and the actual possession of £400,000 English taxes cannot so much
as protract our ruin without him. So we are staked on four
chances: his power, its permanence, the success of his projects, and the duration of his life. Any one of these failing,
we are gone. *Propria haec si dona fuissent!* This is no unfair
representation; ultimately all hangs on his life, because, in
his account of every set of men that have held or supported administration, he finds neither virtue nor ability in any
but himself. Indeed he pays (through their measures) some
compliments to Lord Bute and Lord Despenser. But to the
latter, this is, I suppose, but a civility to old acquaintance;
to the former, a little stroke of politics. We may therefore
fairly say, that our only hope is his life; and he has, to make
it the more so, taken care to cut off any resource which we
possessed independent of him.

　　In the next place it may be said, to excuse any appearance of inconsistency between the author's actions and his
declarations, that he thought it right to relieve the landed
interest, and lay the burden where it ought to lie, on the
colonies. What! To take off a revenue so necessary to our
being, before anything whatsoever was acquired in the place
of it? In prudence, he ought to have waited at least for the
first quarter's receipt of the new anonymous American revenue and Irish land tax. Is there something so specific for
our disorders in American, and something so poisonous in
English money, that one is to heal, the other to destroy us?
To say that the landed interest *could* not continue to pay it

for a year or two longer is more than the author will attempt
to prove. To say that they *would* pay it no longer is to treat
the landed interest, in my opinion, very scurvily. To suppose
that the gentry, clergy, and freeholders of England do not
rate the commerce, the credit, the religion, the liberty, the
independency of their country, and the succession of their
crown, at a shilling in the pound land tax. They never gave
him reason to think so meanly of them. And, if I am rightly
informed, when that measure was debated in Parliament,
a very different reason was assigned by the author's great
friend, as well as by others, for that reduction—one very
different from the critical and almost desperate state of our
finances. Some people then endeavored to prove that the
reduction might be made without detriment to the national
credit, or the due support of a proper peace establishment;
otherwise it is obvious that the reduction could not be defended in argument. So that this author cannot despair so
much of the commonwealth, without this American and
Irish revenue, as he pretends to do. If he does, the reader
sees how handsomely he has provided for us, by voting away
one revenue, and by giving us a pamphlet on the other.

Now comes his American representation. Here too, as
usual, he takes no notice of any difficulty, nor says anything
to obviate those objections that must naturally arise in the
minds of his readers. He throws you his politics as he does
his revenue: do you make something of them if you can.
Is not the reader a little astonished at the proposal of an
American representation from that quarter? It is proposed
merely as a project (pp. 39–40) of speculative improvement;
not from the necessity in the case, not to add anything to the
authority of Parliament, but that we may afford a greater
attention to the concerns of the Americans, and give them

a better opportunity of stating their grievances, and of obtaining redress. I am glad to find the author has at length discovered that we have not given a sufficient attention to their concerns, or a proper redress to their grievances. His great friend would once have been exceedingly displeased with any person, who should tell him that he did not attend sufficiently to those concerns. He thought he did so, when he regulated the colonies over and over again; he thought he did so, when he formed two general systems of revenue, one of port-duties, and the other of internal taxation. These systems supposed, or ought to suppose, the greatest attention to, and the most detailed information of, all their affairs. However, by contending for the American representation, he seems at last driven virtually to admit that great caution ought to be used in the exercise of *all* our legislative rights over an object so remote from our eye, and so little connected with our immediate feelings; that in prudence we ought not to be quite so ready with our taxes, until we can secure the desired representation in Parliament. Perhaps it may be some time before this hopeful scheme can be brought to perfect maturity, although the author seems to be no wise aware of any obstructions that lie in the way of it. He talks of his union, just as he does of his taxes and his savings, with as much *sang froid* and ease as if his wish and the enjoyment were exactly the same thing. He appears not to have troubled his head with the infinite difficulty of settling that representation on a fair balance of wealth and numbers throughout the several provinces of America and the West Indies, under such an infinite variety of circumstances. It costs him nothing to fight with nature, and to conquer the order of Providence, which manifestly opposes itself to the possibility of such a Parliamentary union.

But let us, to indulge his passion for projects and power, suppose the happy time arrived, when the author comes into the ministry, and is to realize his speculations. The writs are issued for electing members for America and the West Indies. Some provinces receive them in six weeks, some in ten, some in twenty. A vessel may be lost, and then some provinces may not receive them at all. But let it be that they all receive them at once, and in the shortest time. A proper space must be given for proclamation and for the election, some weeks at least. But the members are chosen; and, if ships are ready to sail, in about six more they arrive in London. In the meantime, the Parliament has sat and business far advanced, without American representatives. Nay, by this time it may happen, that the Parliament is dissolved, and then the members ship themselves again, to be again elected. The writs may arrive in America, before the poor members of a Parliament in which they never sat can arrive at their several provinces. A new interest is formed, and they find other members are chosen while they are on the high seas. But, if the writs and members arrive together, here is at best a new trial of skill among the candidates, after one set of them have well aired themselves with their two voyages of 6000 miles.

However, in order to facilitate everything to the author, we will suppose them all once more elected, and steering again to Old England, with a good heart, and a fair westerly wind in their stern. On their arrival, they find all in a hurry and bustle; in and out; condolence and congratulation; the crown is demised. Another Parliament is to be called. Away back to America again on a fourth voyage, and to a third election. Does the author mean to make our kings as immortal in their personal as in their politic character? Or, while he bountifully adds to their life, will he take from them their prerogative of dissolving Parliaments, in favor of the American union? Or are the American representatives to be perpetual, and to feel neither demises of the crown, nor dissolutions of Parliament.

But these things may be granted to him, without bringing him much nearer to his point. What does he think of re-election? Is the American member the only one who is not to take a place, or the only one to be exempted from the ceremony of re-election? How will this great politician preserve the rights of electors, the fairness of returns, and the privilege of the House of Commons, as the sole judge of such contests? It would undoubtedly be a glorious sight to have eight or ten petitions, or double returns, from Boston and Barbados, from Philadelphia and Jamaica, the members returned, and the petitioners, with all their train of attorneys, solicitors, mayors, select men, provost-marshals, and about five hundred or a thousand witnesses, come to the bar of the House of Commons. Possibly we might be interrupted in the enjoyment of this pleasing spectacle, if a war should break out, and our constitutional fleet, loaded with members of Parliament, returning officers, petitions, and witnesses, the electors and elected, should become a prize to the French or Spaniards, and be conveyed to Cartagena, or to La Vera Cruz, and from thence perhaps to Mexico, or Lima, there to remain until a cartel for members of Parliament can be settled, or until the war is ended.

In truth, the author has little studied this business, or he might have known that some of the most considerable provinces of America, such, for instance, as Connecticut and Massachusetts Bay, have not in each of them two men who can afford, at a distance from their estates, to spend a thousand pounds a year. How can these provinces be represented at Westminster? If their province pays them, they are American agents, with salaries, and not independent members of Parliament. It is true, that formerly in England members had salaries from their constituents; but they all had salaries, and were all, in this way, upon a par. If these American representatives have no salaries, then they must add to the list of our pensioners and dependents at court, or they must starve. There is no alternative.

Enough of this visionary union, in which much extravagance appears without any fancy, and the judgment is shocked without anything to refresh the imagination. It looks as if the author had dropped down from the moon, without any knowledge of the general nature of this globe, of the general nature of its inhabitants, without the least acquaintance with the affairs of this country. Governor Pownal has handled the same subject. To do him justice, he treats it upon far more rational principles of speculation and much more like a man of business. He thinks (erroneously, I conceive, but he does think) that our legislative rights are incomplete without such a representation. It is no wonder, therefore, that he endeavors by every means to obtain it. Not like our author, who is always on velvet, he is aware of some difficulties and he proposes some solutions. But nature is too hard for both these authors, and America is, and ever will be, without actual representation in the House of Commons; nor will any minister be wild enough even to propose such a representation in Parliament; however, he may choose to throw out that project, together with others equally far from his real opinions, and remote from his designs, merely to fall in with the different views, and captivate the affections, of different sorts of men. Whether these projects arise from the author's real political principles, or are only brought out in subservience to his political views, they compose the whole of anything that is like precise and definite, which the author has given us to expect from that administration which is so much the subject of his praises and prayers. As to his general propositions, that "there is a deal of difference between impossibilities and great difficulties"; that "a great scheme cannot be carried, unless made the business of successive administrations"; that "virtuous and able men are the fittest to serve their country"; all this I look on as no more than so much rubble to fill up the spaces between the regular masonry. Pretty much in the same light I cannot forbear considering his detached observations on commerce, such as that "the system for colony regulations would be very simple, and mutually beneficial to Great Britain and her colonies, if the old navigation laws were adhered to" (p. 39). That "the transportation should be in all cases in ships belonging to British subjects." That "even British ships should not be *generally* received into the colonies from any part of Europe, except the dominions of Great Britain." That "it is unreasonable that corn and such like products should be restrained to come first to a British port." What do all these fine observations signify? Some of them condemn, as ill practices, things that were never practiced at all. Some recommend to be done things that always have been done.

Others indeed convey, though obliquely and loosely, some insinuations highly dangerous to our commerce. If I could prevail on myself to think the author meant to ground any practice upon these general propositions, I should think it very necessary to ask a few questions about some of them. For instance, what does he mean by talking of an adherence to the old navigation laws? Does he mean, that the particular law, 12 Car. II. c. 19, commonly called "The Act of Navigation," is to be adhered to, and that the several subsequent additions, amendments, and exceptions, ought to be all repealed? If so, he will make a strange havoc in the whole system of our trade laws, which have been universally acknowledged to be full as well founded in the alterations and exceptions, as the Act of Charles the Second in the original provisions; and to pursue full as wisely the great end of that very politic law, the increase of the British navigation. I fancy the writer could hardly propose anything more alarming to those immediately interested in that navigation than such a repeal. If he does not mean this, he has got no farther than a nugatory proposition, which nobody can contradict and for which no man is the wiser.

That "the regulations for the colony trade would be few and simple if the old navigation laws were adhered to," I utterly deny as a fact. That they ought to be so sounds well enough, but this proposition is of the same nugatory nature with some of the former. The regulations for the colony trade ought not to be more nor fewer, nor more nor less complex, than the occasion requires. And, as that trade is in a great measure a system of art and restriction, they can neither be few nor simple. It is true, that the very principle may be destroyed, by multiplying to excess the means of securing it. Never did a minister depart more from the author's ideas of simplicity, or more embarrass the trade of America with the multiplicity and intricacy of regulations and ordinances, than his boasted minister of 1764. That minister seemed to be possessed with something hardly short of a rage for regulation and restriction. He had so multiplied bonds, certificates, affidavits, warrants,

sufferances, and cockets; had supported them with such severe penalties, and extended them without the least consideration of circumstances to so many objects, that, had they
all continued in their original force, commerce must speed-
ily have expired under them. Some of them the ministry
which gave them birth was obliged to destroy. With their
own hand they signed the condemnation of their own regulations, confessing in so many words, in the preamble of
their act of the 5th Geo. III., that some of these regulations
had *laid an unnecessary restraint on the trade and correspondence of
his Majesty's American subjects.* This, in that ministry, was a
candid confession of a mistake: but every alteration made
in those regulations by their successors is to be the effect
of envy, and American misrepresentation. So much for the
author's simplicity in regulation.

I have now gone through all which I think immediately
essential in the author's ideas of war, of peace, of the comparative states of England and France, of our actual situation; in his projects of economy, of finance, of commerce,
and of constitutional improvement. There remains nothing
now to be considered, except his heavy censures upon the
administration which was formed in 1765, which is commonly known by the name of the Marquis of Rockingham's
administration, as the administration which preceded it is
by that of Mr. Grenville. These censures relate chiefly to
three heads: (1) To the repeal of the American Stamp Act;
(2) To the commercial regulations then made; and (3) To the
course of foreign negotiations during that short period.

A person who knew nothing of public affairs but from
the writings of this author would be led to conclude that,
at the time of the change in June 1765, some well-digest-
ed system of administration, founded in national strength,

and in the affections of the people, proceeding in all points
with the most reverential and tender regard to the laws,
and pursuing with equal wisdom and success everything
which could tend to the internal prosperity, and to the external honor and dignity, of this country, had been all at
once subverted, by an irruption of a sort of wild, licentious,
unprincipled invaders, who wantonly, and with a barbarous rage, had defaced a thousand fair monuments of the
constitutional and political skill of their predecessors. It is
natural indeed that this author should have some dislike of
the administration which was formed in 1765. Its views,
in most things, were different from those of his friends;
in some, altogether opposite to them. It is impossible that
both of these administrations should be the objects of public esteem. Their different principles compose some of the
strongest political lines which discriminate the parties even
now subsisting among us. The ministers of 1764 are not indeed followed by very many in their opposition; yet a large
part of the people now in office entertain, or pretend to
entertain, sentiments entirely conformable to theirs; while
some of the former colleagues of the ministry which was
formed in 1765, however they may have abandoned the
connection, and contradicted by their conduct the principles, of their former friends, pretend, on their parts, still to
adhere to the same maxims. All the lesser divisions, which
are indeed rather names of personal attachment than of
party distinction, fall in with the one or the other of these
leading parties.

I intend to state, as shortly as I am able, the general
condition of public affairs, and the disposition of the minds
of men, at the time of the remarkable change of system in
1765. The reader will have thereby a more distinct view of

the comparative merits of these several plans, and will receive more satisfaction concerning the ground and reason of the measures which were then pursued, than, I believe, can be derived from the perusal of those partial representations contained in the *State of the Nation*, and the other writings of those who have continued, for now near three years, in the undisturbed possession of the press. This will, I hope, be some apology for my dwelling a little on this part of the subject.

On the resignation of the Earl of Bute in 1763, our affairs had been delivered into the hands of three ministers of his recommendation: Mr. Grenville, the Earl of Egremont, and the Earl of Halifax. This arrangement, notwithstanding the retirement of Lord Bute, announced to the public a continuance of the same measures; nor was there more reason to expect a change from the death of the Earl of Egremont. The Earl of Sandwich supplied his place. The Duke of Bedford, and the gentlemen who act in that connection, and whose general character and politics were sufficiently understood, added to the strength of the ministry without making any alteration in their plan of conduct. Such was the constitution of the ministry which was changed in 1765.

As to their politics, the principles of the peace of Paris governed in foreign affairs. In domestic, the same scheme prevailed, of contradicting the opinions and disgracing most of the persons who had been countenanced and employed in the late reign. The inclinations of the people were little attended to and a disposition to the use of forcible methods ran through the whole tenor of administration. The nation in general was uneasy and dissatisfied. Sober men saw causes for it in the constitution of the ministry and the conduct of the ministers. The ministers, who have usually a short method on such occasions, attributed their unpopularity wholly to the efforts of faction. However this might be, the licentiousness and tumults of the common people, and the contempt of government, of which our author so often and so bitterly complains as owing to the mismanagement of the subsequent administrations, had at no time risen to a greater or more dangerous height. The measures taken to suppress that spirit were as violent and licentious as the spirit itself: injudicious, precipitate, and some of them illegal. Instead of allaying, they tended infinitely to inflame the distemper; and whoever will be at the least pains to examine, will find those measures not only the causes of the tumults which then prevailed, but the real sources of almost all the disorders which have arisen since that time. More intent on making a victim to party than an example of justice, they blundered in the method of pursuing their vengeance. By this means a discovery was made of many practices, common indeed in the office of secretary of state, but wholly repugnant to our laws, and to the genius of the English constitution. One of the worst of these was the wanton and indiscriminate seizure of papers, even in cases where the safety of the state was not pretended in justification of so harsh a proceeding. The temper of the ministry had excited a jealousy, which made the people more than commonly vigilant concerning every power which was exercised by government. The abuse, however sanctioned by custom, was evident; but the ministry, instead of resting in a prudent inactivity, or (what would have been still more prudent) taking the lead, in quieting the minds of the people, and ascertaining the law upon those delicate points, made use of the whole influence of government to prevent a Parliamentary resolution against these practices of office. And lest the colorable reasons, offered in argument against this Parliamentary procedure, should be mistaken for the real motives of their conduct, all the advantage of privilege, all the arts and finesses of pleading, and great sums of public money were lavished, to prevent any decision upon those practices in the courts of justice. In the meantime, in order to weaken, since they could not immediately destroy the liberty of the press, the privilege of Parliament was voted away in all accusations for a seditious libel. The freedom of debate in Parliament itself was no less menaced. Officers of the army, of long and meritorious service, and of small fortunes, were chosen as victims for a single vote by an exertion of ministerial power, which had been very rarely used, and which is extremely unjust, as depriving men not only of a place, but a profession, and is indeed of the most pernicious example both in a civil and a military light.

While all things were managed at home with such a spirit of disorderly despotism, abroad there was a proportionable abatement of all spirit. Some of our most just and valuable claims were in a manner abandoned. This indeed seemed not very inconsistent conduct in the ministers who had made the treaty of Paris. With regard to our domestic affairs, there was no want of industry, but there was a great deficiency of temper and judgment, and manly comprehension of the public interest. The nation certainly wanted relief, and government attempted to administer it. Two ways were principally chosen for this great purpose. The first by regulations; the second by new funds of revenue. Agreeably to this plan, a new naval establishment was formed at a good deal of expense, and to little effect, to aid in the collection of the customs. Regulation was added to regulation, and the strictest and most unreserved orders were given, for a prevention of all contraband trade here, and in every part of America. A teasing custom-house, and a multiplicity of perplexing regulations, ever have, and ever will appear, the masterpiece of finance to people of narrow views; as a paper against smuggling, and the importation of French finery, never fails of furnishing a very popular column in a newspaper.

The greatest part of these regulations were made for America; and they fell so indiscriminately on all sorts of contraband, or supposed contraband, that some of the most valuable branches of trade were driven violently from our ports, which caused a universal consternation through-out the colonies. Every part of the trade was infinite-ly distressed by them. Men of war now for the first time, armed with regular commissions of custom-house officers, invested the coasts, and gave to the collection of revenue the air of hostile contribution. About the same time that these regulations seemed to threaten the destruction of the only trade from whence the plantations derived any spe-cie, an act was made, putting a stop to the future emission of paper currency, which used to supply its place among them. Hand in hand with this went another act for obliging the colonies to provide quarters for soldiers. Instantly fol-lowed another law, for levying throughout all America new port duties, upon a vast variety of commodities of their consumption, and some of which lay heavy upon objects necessary for their trade and fishery. Immediately upon the heels of these, and amidst the uneasiness and confusion produced by a crowd of new impositions and regulations, some good, some evil, some doubtful, all crude and ill-con-sidered, came another act, for imposing a universal stamp duty on the colonies, and this was declared to be little more than an experiment, and a foundation of future revenue. To render these proceedings the more irritating to the colonies, the principal argument used in favor of their ability to pay such duties was the liberality of the grants of their assemblies during the late war. Never could any argument be more insulting and mortifying to a people habituated to the granting of their own money.

Taxes for the purpose of raising revenue had hitherto been sparingly attempted in America. Without ever doubting the extent of its lawful power, Parliament always doubted the propriety of such impositions. And the Americans on their part never thought of contesting a right by which they were so little affected. Their assemblies in the main answered all the purposes necessary to the internal economy of a free people, and provided for all the exigencies of government which arose among themselves. In the midst of that happy enjoyment, they never thought of critically settling the exact limits of a power, which was necessary to their union, their safety, their equality, and even their liberty. Thus the two very difficult points, superiority in the presiding state, and freedom in the subordinate, were on the whole sufficiently, that is, practically, reconciled; without agitating those vexatious questions, which in truth rather belong to metaphysics than politics, and which can never be moved without shaking the foundations of the best governments that have ever been constituted by human wisdom. By this measure was let loose that dangerous spirit of disquisition, not in the coolness of philosophical inquiry, but inflamed with all the passions of a haughty, resentful people, who thought themselves deeply injured, and that they were contending for everything that was valuable in the world.

In England our ministers went on without the least attention to these alarming dispositions, just as if they were
doing the most common things in the most usual way, and
among a people not only passive but pleased. They took no
one step to divert the dangerous spirit which began even
then to appear in the colonies, to compromise with it, to
mollify it, or to subdue it. No new arrangements were made
in civil government; no new powers or instructions were
given to governors; no augmentation was made, or new dispositions, of force. Never was so critical a measure pursued
with so little provision against its necessary consequences.
As if all common prudence had abandoned the ministers,
and as if they meant to plunge themselves and us headlong
into that gulf which stood gaping before them, by giving
a year's notice of the project of their Stamp Act, they allowed time for all the discontents of that country to fester
and come to a head, and for all the arrangements which
factious men could make towards an opposition to the law.
At the same time they carefully concealed from the eye of
Parliament those remonstrances which they had actually
received; and which in the strongest manner indicated the
discontent of some of the colonies, and the consequences
which might be expected. They concealed them, even in
defiance of an order of council that they should be laid
before Parliament. Thus, by concealing the true state of the
case, they rendered the wisdom of the nation as improvi-
dent as their own temerity, either in preventing or guarding
against the mischief. It has indeed, from the beginning to
this hour, been the uniform policy of this set of men, in
order at any hazard to obtain a present credit, to propose
whatever might be pleasing, as attended with no difficulty,
and afterwards to throw all the disappointment of the wild

expectations they had raised, upon those who have the hard task of freeing the public from the consequences of their pernicious projects.

While the commerce and tranquility of the whole empire were shaken in this manner, our affairs grew still more distracted by the internal dissensions of our ministers; treachery and ingratitude were charged from one side; despotism and tyranny from the other; the vertigo of the regency bill; the awkward reception of the silk bill in the House of Commons, and the inconsiderate and abrupt rejection of it in the House of Lords; the strange and violent tumults which arose in consequence, and which were rendered more serious by being charged by the ministers upon one another; the report of a gross and brutal treatment of the ——, by a minister at the same time odious to the people; all conspired to leave the public, at the close of the session of 1765, in as critical and perilous a situation, as ever the nation was, or could be, in a time when she was not immediately threatened by her neighbors.

It was at this time, and in these circumstances, that a new administration was formed. Professing even industriously, in this public matter, to avoid anecdotes, I say nothing of those famous reconciliations and quarrels, which weakened the body that should have been the natural support of this administration. I run no risk in affirming, that, surrounded as they were with difficulties of every species, nothing but the strongest and most uncorrupt sense of their duty to the public could have prevailed upon some of the persons who composed it to undertake the king's business at such a time. Their preceding character, their measures while in power, and the subsequent conduct of many of them, I think, leave no room to charge this assertion to flattery. Having undertaken the commonwealth, what remained for them to do? To piece their conduct upon the broken chain of former measures? If they had been so inclined, the ruinous nature of those measures, which began instantly to appear, would not have permitted it. Scarcely had they entered into office, when letters arrived from all parts of America, making loud complaints, backed by strong reasons, against several of the principal regulations of the late ministry, as threatening destruction to many valuable branches of commerce. These were attended with representations from many merchants and capital manufacturers at home, who had all their interests involved in the support of lawful trade, and in the suppression of every sort of contraband. While these things were under consideration, that conflagration blazed out at once in North America a universal disobedience and open resistance to the Stamp Act and, in consequence, a universal stop to the course of justice, and to trade and navigation, throughout that great important country, an interval during which the trading interest of England lay under the most dreadful anxiety which it ever felt.

The repeal of that act was proposed. It was much too serious a measure, and attended with too many difficulties upon every side, for the then-ministry to have undertaken it, as some paltry writers have asserted, from envy and dislike to their predecessors in office. As little could it be owing to personal cowardice, and dread of consequences to themselves. Ministers, timorous from their attachment to place and power, will fear more from the consequences of one court intrigue, than from a thousand difficulties to the commerce and credit of their country by disturbances at three thousand miles distance. From which of these the

ministers had most to apprehend at that time is known, I
presume, universally. Nor did they take that resolution from
a want of the fullest sense of the inconveniences which
must necessarily attend a measure of concession from the
sovereign to the subject. That it must increase the insolence
of the mutinous spirits in America was but too obvious. No
great measure indeed, at a very difficult crisis, can be pursued, which is not attended with some mischief; none but
conceited pretenders in public business will bold any other
language; and none but weak and unexperienced men will
believe them, if they should. If we were found in such a
crisis, let those whose bold designs, and whose defective arrangements, brought us into it, answer for the consequences. The business of the then-ministry evidently was, to take
such steps, not as the wishes of our author, or as their own
wishes, dictated, but as the bad situation in which their predecessors had left them absolutely required.

The disobedience to this act was universal throughout
America; nothing, it was evident, but the sending of a very
strong military, backed by a very strong naval force, would
reduce the seditious to obedience. To send it to one town
would not be sufficient; every province of America must be
traversed, and must be subdued. I do not entertain the least
doubt but this could be done. We might, I think, without
much difficulty, have destroyed our colonies. This destruction might be effected, probably in a year, or in two at the
utmost. If the question was upon a foreign nation, where
every successful stroke adds to your own power, and takes
from that of a rival, a just war with such a certain superiority would be undoubtedly an advisable measure. But
four million of debt due to our merchants, the total cessation
of a trade annually worth *four million* more, a large foreign

traffic, much home manufacture, a very capital immediate revenue arising from colony imports, indeed the produce of every one of our revenues greatly depending on this trade, all these were very weighty accumulated consider-ations, at least well to be weighed, before that sword was drawn, which even by its victories must produce all the evil effects of the greatest national defeat. How public credit must have suffered, I need not say. If the condition of the nation, at the close of our foreign war, was what this author represents it, such a civil war would have been a bad couch on which to repose our wearied virtue. Far from being able to have entered into new plans of economy, we must have launched into a new sea, I fear a boundless sea, of expense. Such an addition of debt, with such a diminution of reve-nue and trade, would have left us in no want of a *State of the Nation* to aggravate the picture of our distresses.

Our trade felt this to its vitals; and our then-ministers were not ashamed to say that they sympathized with the feelings of our merchants. The universal alarm of the whole trading body of England will never be laughed at by them as an ill-grounded or a pretended panic. The univer-sal desire of that body will always have great weight with them in every consideration connected with commerce; neither ought the opinion of that body to be slighted (not-withstanding the contemptuous and indecent language of this author and his associates) in any consideration what-soever of revenue. Nothing among us is more quickly or deeply affected by taxes of any kind than trade; and if an American tax was a real relief to England, no part of the community would be sooner, or more materially, relieved by it than our merchants. But they well know that the trade of England must be more burdened by one penny raised in

America, than by three in England; and if that penny be raised with the uneasiness, the discontent, and the confusion of America, more than by ten.

If the opinion and wish of the landed interest is a motive, and it is a fair and just one, for taking away a real and large revenue, the desire of the trading interest of England ought to be a just ground for taking away a tax, of little better than speculation, which was to be collected by a war, which was to be kept up with the perpetual discontent of those who were to be affected by it, and the value of whose produce, even after the *ordinary* charges of collection, was very uncertain[1]; after the *extraordinary*, the dearest purchased revenue that ever was made by any nation.

These were some of the motives drawn from principles of convenience for that repeal. When the object came to be more narrowly inspected, every motive concurred. These colonies were evidently founded in subservience to the commerce of Great Britain. From this principle, the whole system of our laws concerning them became a system of restriction. A double monopoly was established on the part of the parent country: (1) A monopoly of their whole import, which is to be altogether from Great Britain; (2) A monopoly of all their export, which is to be nowhere but to Great Britain, as far as it can serve any purpose here. On the same idea it was contrived that they should send all their products to us raw, and in their first state; and that they should take everything from us in the last stage of manufacture.

---

1.   It is observable that the partisans of American taxation, when they have a mind to represent this tax as wonderfully beneficial to England, state it as worth £100,000 a year; when they are to represent it as very light on the Americans, it dwindles to £60,000. Indeed it is very difficult to compute what its produce might have been.

Were ever a people under such circumstances—that is, a people who were to export raw, and to receive manufactured, and this, not a few luxurious articles, but all articles, even to those of the grossest, most vulgar, and necessary consumption, a people who were in the hands of a general monopolist, were ever such a people suspected of a possibility of becoming a just object of revenue? All the ends of their foundation must be supposed utterly contradicted before they could become such an object. Every trade law we have made must have been eluded, and become useless, before they could be in such a condition.

The partisans of the new system, who, on most occasions, take credit for full as much knowledge as they possess, think proper on this occasion to counterfeit an extraordinary degree of ignorance, and in consequence of it to assert, "that the balance (between the colonies and Great Britain) is unknown, and that no important conclusion can be drawn from premises so very uncertain" (*Considerations*, p. 74). Now to what can this ignorance be owing? Were the navigation laws made that this balance should be unknown? Is it from the course of exchange that it is unknown, which all the world knows to be greatly and perpetually against the colonies? Is it from the doubtful nature of the trade we carry on with the colonies? Are not these schemists well apprised, that the colonists, particularly those of the northern provinces, import more from Great Britain, ten times more than they send in return to us? That a great part of their foreign balance is, and must be, remitted to London? I shall be ready to admit that the colonies ought to be taxed to the revenues of this country, when I know that they are out of debt to its commerce. This author will furnish some ground to his theories, and communicate a discovery to the public, if he can show this by any medium. But he tells us that "their seas are covered with ships, and their rivers floating with commerce" (ibid., p. 79). This is true. But it is with *our* ships that the seas are covered and their rivers float with British commerce. The American merchants are our factors; all in reality, most even in name. The Americans trade, navigate, cultivate, with English capitals, to their own advantage, to be sure; for without these capitals their ploughs would be stopped, and their ships wind-bound. But he who furnishes the capital must, on the whole, be the person principally benefited; the person who works upon it profits on his part too, but he profits in a subordinate way, as our colonies do; that is, as the servant of a wise and indulgent master, and no otherwise. We have all, except the *peculium*, without which even slaves will not labor.

If the author's principles, which are the common notions, be right, that the price of our manufactures is so greatly enhanced by our taxes, then the Americans already pay in that way a share of our impositions. He is not ashamed to assert, that "France and China may be said, on the same principle, to bear a part of our charges, for they consume our commodities" (*Considerations*, p. 74). Was ever such a method of reasoning heard of? Do not the laws absolutely confine the colonies to buy from us, whether foreign nations sell cheaper or not? On what other idea are all our prohibitions, regulations, guards, penalties, and forfeitures framed? To secure to us, not a commercial preference, which stands in need of no penalties to enforce it, it finds its own way; but to secure to us a trade, which is a creature of law and institution. What has this to do with the principles of a foreign trade, which is under no monopoly, and in which we cannot raise the

price of our goods, without hazarding the demand for
them? None but the authors of such measures could ever
think of making use of such arguments.

Whoever goes about to reason on any part of the policy
of this country with regard to America, upon the mere abstract principles of government, or even upon those of our
own ancient constitution, will be often misled. Those who
resort for arguments to the most respectable authorities, ancient or modern, or rest upon the clearest maxims, drawn
from the experience of other states and empires, will be liable to the greatest errors imaginable. The object is wholly
new in the world. It is singular; it is grown up to this magnitude and importance within the memory of man; nothing
in history is parallel to it. All the reasonings about it, that
are likely to be at all solid, must be drawn from its actual
circumstances. In this new system a principle of commerce,
of artificial commerce, must predominate. This commerce
must be secured by a multitude of restraints very alien from
the spirit of liberty, and a powerful authority must reside in
the principal state, in order to enforce them. But the people
who are to be the subjects of these restraints are descendants
of Englishmen; and of a high and free spirit. To hold over
them a government made up of nothing but restraints and
penalties, and taxes in the granting of which they can have
no share, will neither be wise, nor long practicable. People
must be governed in a manner agreeable to their temper and
disposition, and men of free character and spirit must be
ruled with, at least, some condescension to this spirit and this
character. The British colonist must see something which will
distinguish him from the colonists of other nations.

Those reasonings, which infer from the many restraints
under which we have already laid America, to our right to

lay it under still more, and indeed under all manner of restraints, are conclusive; conclusive as to right, but the very reverse as to policy and practice. We ought rather to infer from our having laid the colonies under many restraints, that it is reasonable to compensate them by every indulgence that can by any means be reconciled to our interest. We have a great empire to rule, composed of a vast mass of heterogeneous governments, all more or less free and popular in their forms, all to be kept in peace, and kept out of conspiracy, with one another, all to he held in subordination to this country; while the spirit of an extensive, and intricate, and trading interest pervades the whole, always qualifying, and often controlling, every general idea of constitution and government. It is a great and difficult object; and I wish we may possess wisdom and temper enough to manage it as we ought. Its importance is infinite. I believe the reader will be struck, as I have been, with one singular fact. In the year 1704, but sixty-five years ago, the whole trade with our plantations was but a few thousand pounds more in the export article, and a third less in the import, than that which we now carry on with the single island of Jamaica:

Total English plantations in 1704:
Exports:	£483,265
Imports.	£814,491

Jamaica in 1767:
Exports:	£467,681
Imports:	£1,243,742

From the same information I find that our dealing with most of the European nations is but little increased; these nations have been pretty much at a stand since that time, and we have rivals in their trade. This colony intercourse is a new world of commerce in a manner created; it stands upon principles of its own, principles hardly worth endangering for any little consideration of extorted revenue.

The reader sees that I do not enter so fully into this matter as obviously I might. I have already been led into greater lengths than I intended. It is enough to say, that before the ministers of 1765 had determined to propose the repeal of the Stamp Act in Parliament, they had the whole of the American constitution and commerce very fully before them. They considered maturely; they decided with wisdom and, let me add, with firmness. For they resolved, as a preliminary to that repeal, to assert in the fullest and least equivocal terms the unlimited legislative right of this country over its colonies; and, having done this, to propose the repeal, on principles, not of constitutional right, but on those of expediency, of equity, of leniency, and of the true interests present and future of that great object for which alone the colonies were founded, navigation and commerce. This plan, I say, required an uncommon degree of firmness, when we consider that some of those persons who might be of the greatest use in promoting the repeal, violently withstood the declaratory act; and they who agreed with administration in the principles of that law, equally made, as well the reasons on which the declaratory act itself stood, as those on which it was opposed, grounds for an opposition to the repeal.

If the then-ministry resolved first to declare the right, it was not from any opinion they entertained of its future use in regular taxation. Their opinions were full and declared against the ordinary use of such a power. But it was plain, that the general reasonings which were employed against that power went directly to our whole legislative right, and one part of it could not be yielded to such arguments, without a virtual surrender of all the rest. Besides, if that very specific power of levying money in the colonies were not retained as a sacred trust in the hands of Great Britain (to be used, not in the first instance for supply, but in the last exigence for control), it is obvious that the presiding authority of Great Britain, as the head, the arbiter, and director of the whole empire, would vanish into an empty name, without operation or energy. With the habitual exercise of such a power in the ordinary course of supply, no trace of freedom could remain in America.[2] If Great Britain were stripped of this right, every principle of unity and subordination in the empire was gone forever. Whether all this can be reconciled in legal speculation is a matter of no consequence. It is reconciled in policy, and politics ought to be adjusted, not to human reasonings, but to human nature, of which the reason is but a part, and by no means the greatest part.

Founding the repeal on this basis, it was judged proper to lay before Parliament the whole detail of the American affairs, as fully as it had been laid before the ministry themselves. Ignorance of those affairs had misled Parliament.

---

2.   I do not here enter into the unsatisfactory disquisition concerning representation real or presumed. I only say, that a great people, who have their property, without any reserve, in all cases, disposed of by another people at an immense distance from them, will not think themselves in the enjoyment of freedom. It will be hard to show to those who are in such a state, which of the usual parts of the definition or description of a free people are applicable to them; and it is neither pleasant nor wise to attempt to prove that they have no right to be comprehended in such a description.

Knowledge alone could bring it into the right road. Every paper of office was laid upon the table of the two Houses; every denomination of men, either of America, or connected with it by office, by residence, by commerce, by interest, even by injury; men of civil and military capacity, officers of the revenue, merchants, manufacturers of every species, and from every town in England, attended at the bar. Such evidence never was laid before Parliament. If an emulation arose among the ministers and members of Parliament, as the author rightly observes (p. 21), for the repeal of this act as well as for the other regulations, it was not on the confident assertions, the airy speculations, or the vain promises of ministers, that it arose. It was the sense of Parliament on the evidence before them. No one so much as suspects that ministerial allurements or terrors had any share in it.

Our author is very much displeased that so much credit was given to the testimony of merchants. He has a habit of railing at them, and he may, if he pleases, indulge himself in it. It will not do great mischief to that respectable set of men. The substance of their testimony was that their debts in America were very great: that the Americans declined to pay them, or to renew their orders, while this act continued; that, under these circumstances, they despaired of the recovery of their debts, or the renewal of their trade in that country; that they apprehended a general failure of mercantile credit. The manufacturers deposed to the same general purpose, with this addition, that many of them had discharged several of their artificers; and, if the law and the resistance to it should continue, must dismiss them all.

This testimony is treated with great contempt by our author. It must be, I suppose, because it was contradicted by the plain nature of things. Suppose then that the

merchants had, to gratify this author, given a contrary evidence, and had deposed, that while America remained in
a state of resistance, while four million of debt remained
unpaid, while the course of justice was suspended for want
of stamped paper, so that no debt could be recovered, while
there was a total stop to trade, because every ship was subject to seizure for want of stamped clearances, and while
the colonies were to be declared in rebellion, and subdued
by armed force, that in these circumstances they would still
continue to trade cheerfully and fearlessly as before. Would
not such witnesses provoke universal indignation for their
folly or their wickedness, and be deservedly hooted from
the bar?[3] Would any human faith have given credit to such
assertions? The testimony of the merchants was necessary
for the detail, and to bring the matter home to the feeling
of the house; as to the general reasons, they spoke abundantly for themselves.

---

3.   Here the author has a note altogether in his usual strain of reason-
      ing; he finds out that somebody, in the course of this multifarious
      evidence, had said, "that a very considerable part of the orders of
      1765 transmitted from America had been afterwards suspended;
      but that in case the Stamp Act was repealed, those orders were to
      be executed in the present year 1766"; and that, on the repeal of
      the Stamp Act, "the exports to the colonies would be at least dou-
      ble the value of the exports of the past year." He then triumphs
      exceedingly on their having fallen short of it on the state of the
      custom-house entries. I do not well know what conclusion he draws
      applicable to his purpose, from these facts. He does not deny that
      all the orders which came from America subsequent to the distur-
      bances of the Stamp Act were on the condition of that act being re-
      pealed; and, he does not assert that, notwithstanding that act should
      be enforced by a strong hand, still the orders would be executed.
      Neither does he quite venture to say that this decline of the trade
      in 1766 was owing to the repeal. What does he therefore infer from
      it, favorable to the enforcement of that law? It only comes to this,

Upon these principles was the act repealed, and it produced all the good effect which was expected from it. Quiet was restored; trade generally returned to its ancient channels; time and means were furnished for the better strengthening of government there, as well as for recovering, by judicious measures, the affections of the people, had that ministry continued, or had a ministry succeeded with dispositions to improve that opportunity.

Such an administration did not succeed. Instead of profiting of that season of tranquility, in the very next year they chose to return to measures of the very same nature with those which had been so solemnly condemned, though

and no more, those merchants, who thought our trade would be doubled in the subsequent year, were mistaken in their speculations. So that the Stamp Act was not to be repealed unless this speculation of theirs was a probable event. But it was not repealed in order to double our trade in that year, as everybody knows (whatever some merchants might have said), but lest in that year we should have no trade at all. The fact is, that during the greatest part of the year 1765, that is, until about the month of October, when the accounts of the disturbances came thick upon us, the American trade went on as usual. Before this time, the Stamp Act could not affect it. Afterwards, the merchants fell into a great consternation, a general stagnation in trade ensued. But as soon as it was known that the ministry favored the repeal of the Stamp Act, several of the bolder merchants ventured to execute their orders; others more timid hung back. In this manner the trade continued in a state of dreadful fluctuation between the fears of those who had ventured for the event of their boldness, and the anxiety of those whose trade was suspended, until the royal assent was finally given to the bill of repeal. That the trade of 1766 was not equal to that of 1765, could not be owing to the repeal; it arose from quite different causes, of which, the author seems not to be aware: First, our conquests during the war had laid open the trade of the French and Spanish West Indies to our colonies much more largely than they had ever enjoyed it; this continued for some time after the peace; but at length it was ex-

upon a smaller scale. The effects have been correspondent. America is again in disorder, not indeed in the same degree as formerly, nor anything like it. Such good effects have attended the repeal of the Stamp Act, that the colonies have actually paid the taxes, and they have sought their redress (upon however improper principles) not in their own violence, as formerly,[4] but in the experienced benignity of Parliament. They are not easy indeed, nor ever will be so, under this author's schemes of taxation; but we see no longer the same general fury and confusion, which attended their resistance to the Stamp Act. The author may rail at the repeal, and those who proposed it, as he pleases. Those honest men

---

tremely contracted, and in some places reduced to nothing. Such in particular was the state of Jamaica. On the taking of Havana all the stores of that island were emptied into that place, which produced unusual orders for goods, for supplying their own consumption, as well as for further speculations of trade. These ceasing, the trade stood on its own bottom. This is one cause of the diminished export to Jamaica, and not the childish idea of the author, of an impossible contraband from the opening of the ports. Second, the war had brought a great influx of cash into America for the pay and provision of the troops, and this caused an unnatural increase of trade, which, as its cause failed, must in some degree return to its ancient and natural bounds. Third, when the merchants met from all parts, and compared their accounts, they were alarmed at the immensity of the debt due to them from America. They found that the Americans had overtraded their abilities. And, as they found too that several of them were capable of making the state of political events an excuse for their failure in commercial punctuality, many of our merchants in some degree contracted their trade from that moment. However, it is idle, in such an immense mass of trade, so liable to fluctuation, to infer anything from such a deficiency as one or even two hundred thousand pounds. In 1767, when the disturbances subsided, this deficiency was made up again.

4.   The disturbances have been in Boston only, and were not in consequence of the late duties.

suffer all his obloquy with pleasure, in the midst of the quiet which they have been the means of giving to their country, and would think his praises for their perseverance in a pernicious scheme a very bad compensation for the disturbance of our peace and the ruin of our commerce. Whether the return to the system of 1764, for raising a revenue in America, the discontents which have ensued in consequence of it, the general suspension of the assemblies in consequence of these discontents, the use of the military power, and the new and dangerous commissions which now hang over them, will produce equally good effects, is greatly to be doubted. Never, I fear, will this nation and the colonies fall back upon their true center of gravity, and natural point of repose, until the ideas of 1766 are resumed, and steadily pursued.

As to the regulations, a great subject of the author's accusation, they are of two sorts: one of a mixed nature, of revenue and trade; the other simply relative to trade. With regard to the former I shall observe, that, in all deliberations concerning America, the ideas of that administration were principally these: to take trade as the primary end, and revenue but as a very subordinate consideration. Where trade was likely to suffer, they did not hesitate for an instant to prefer it to taxes, whose produce at best was contemptible, in comparison of the object which they might endanger. The other of their principles was to suit the revenue to the object. Where the difficulty of collection, from the nature of the country, and of the revenue establishment, is so very notorious, it was their policy to hold out as few temptations to smuggling as possible, by keeping the duties as nearly as they could on a balance with the risk. On these principles they made many alterations in the port duties of 1764, both in the mode and in the quantity. The author has not attempted to prove them erroneous. He complains enough to show that he is in an ill humor, not that his adversaries have done amiss.

As to the regulations which were merely relative to commerce, many were then made, and they were all made upon this principle, that many of the colonies, and those some of the most abounding in people, were so situated as to have very few means of traffic with this country. It became therefore our interest to let them into as much foreign trade as could be given them without interfering with her own; and to secure by every method the returns to the mother country. Without some such scheme of enlargement, it was obvious that any benefit we could expect from these colonies must be extremely limited. Accordingly, many facilities were given to their trade with the foreign plantations, and with the southern parts of Europe. As to the confining of the returns to this country, administration saw the mischief and folly of a plan of indiscriminate restraint. They applied their remedy to that part where the disease existed, and to that only: on this idea they established regulations, far more likely to check the dangerous, clandestine trade with Hamburg and Holland, than this author's friends, or any of their predecessors, had ever done.

The friends of the author have a method surely a little whimsical in all this sort of discussions. They have made an innumerable multitude of commercial regulations, at which the trade of England exclaimed with one voice, and many of which have been altered on the unanimous opinion of that trade. Still they go on, just as before, in a sort of droning panegyric on themselves, talking of these regulations as prodigies of wisdom; and, instead of appealing to those who are most affected and the best judges, they turn round in a perpetual circle of their own reasonings and pretenses; they hand you over from one of their own pamphlets to another: "See," say they, "this demonstrated in *The Regulations of the Colonies*." "See this satisfactorily proved in *The Considerations*." By and by we shall have another. "See for this *The State of the Nation*." I wish to take another method in vindicating the opposite system. I refer to the petitions of merchants for these regulations; to their thanks when they were obtained; and to the strong and grateful sense they have ever since expressed of the benefits received under that administration.

All administrations have in their commercial regulations been generally aided by the opinion of some merchants; too frequently by that of a few, and those a sort of favorites. They have been directed by the opinion of one or two merchants, who were to merit in flatteries, and to be paid in contracts, who frequently advised, not for the general good of trade, but for their private advantage. During the administration of which this author complains, the meetings of merchants upon the business of trade were numerous and public; sometimes at the house of the Marquis of Rockingham, sometimes at Mr. Dowdeswell's, sometimes at Sir George Savile's—a house always open to every deliberation favorable to the liberty or the commerce of his country. Nor were these meetings confined to the merchants of London. Merchants and manufacturers were invited from all the considerable towns in England. They conferred with the ministers and active members of Parliament. No private views, no local interests prevailed. Never were points in trade settled upon a larger scale of information. They who attended these meetings well know what ministers they were who heard the most patiently, who comprehended the most clearly, and who provided the most wisely. Let then this author and his friends still continue in possession of the practice of exalting their own abilities, in their pamphlets and in the newspapers. They never will persuade the public that the merchants of England were in a general confederacy to sacrifice their own interests to those of North America, and to destroy the vent of their own goods in favor of the manufactures of France and Holland.

Had the friends of this author taken these means of information, his extreme terrors of contraband in the West India Islands would have been greatly quieted, and his objections to the opening of the ports would have ceased. He would have learned, from the most satisfactory analysis of the West India trade, that we have the advantage in every essential article of it, and that almost every restriction on our communication with our neighbors there is a restriction unfavorable to ourselves.

Such were the principles that guided, and the authority that sanctioned, these regulations. No man ever said, that in the multiplicity of regulations made in the administration of their predecessors, none were useful. Some certainly were so, and I defy the author to show a commercial regulation of that period, which he can prove, from any authority except his own, to have a tendency beneficial to commerce, that has been repealed. So far were that ministry from being guided by a spirit of contradiction or of innovation.

INDEX

INDEX

Salem, 259

Sandwich, Earl of, 318

Saunders family, 270

Savile family, 270

Savile, Sir George, 179, 341

Scotland, 11

Seven Years' War, 124, n. 15

Short Account of a Late
Short Administration, 286ff.

Slavery, 32–33, 35, 76, 110,
149–50, 191, 232

Slaves, 22, 30, 32–33, 66,
215, 229, 233

Slave-dealers, West African,
116, n. 11

Smith, Adam, 133, n. 19,
106, n. 8

Smuggling, 88, 92115–16, n.
11, 321, 339

Smuggling, in the Isle of
Man, 102

Smyrna, 25

Spain, 25, 43, 76, 153

Spaniards, 312

Spanish colonies, 115, n. 11

Spanish settlements, 105, n. 8

Spanish trade, with America,
121–22

Spanish West Indies, 337, n. 3

Speaker of the Commons,
12, 67–68, 87, 104, 142

Speech on Taxation, 226

Stamp Act. *See* Act, Stamp

State of the Nation, 266,
274, 285

Staten, 208

Stormont, Lord, 134

Made in the USA
San Bernardino, CA
22 April 2016